LEWIS

AMONG T

BOOKS BY PAUL SCHULLERY

1979   *Old Yellowstone Days* (editor)

1980   *The Bears of Yellowstone*

1981   *The Grand Canyon: Early Impressions* (editor)

1981   *The Orvis Story* (with Austin Hogan)

1983   *American Bears: Selections from the Writings of Theodore Roosevelt* (editor)

1983   *Freshwater Wilderness: Yellowstone Fishes and Their World* (with John D. Varley)

1984   *Mountain Time*

1986   *Theodore Roosevelt: Wilderness Writings* (editor)

1986   *The National Parks* (editor and coauthor)

1986   *Wildlife in Transition: Man and Nature on Yellowstone's Northern Range* (with Don Despain, Douglas B. Houston, and Mary Meagher)

1987   *Island in the Sky: Pioneering Accounts of Mount Rainier* (editor)

1987   *American Fly Fishing: A History*

1987   *Bud Lilly's Guide to Western Fly Fishing* (with Bud Lilly)

1988   *The Bear Hunter's Century: Profiles from the Golden Age of Bear Hunting*

1988   *A Trout's Best Friend* (with Bud Lilly)

1991   *Pregnant Bears and Crawdad Eyes: Excursions and Encounters in Animal Worlds*

1991   *Yellowstone Bear Tales* (editor)

1991   *The National Park Service: A Seventy-Fifth Anniversary Album* (with William Sontag and Linda Griffin)

1994   *Bears—Their Biology and Management* (editor, with James Claar)

1995   *Yellowstone's Ski Pioneers: Peril and Heroism on the Winter Trail*

1996   *Glacier Waterton: Land of Hanging Valleys*

1996   *Shupton's Fancy: A Tale of the Fly-Fishing Obsession*

1996   *Echoes from the Summit: Writings and Photographs* (editor)

1996   *Mark of the Bear: Legend and Lore of an American Icon* (editor)

1996   *The Yellowstone Wolf: A Guide and Sourcebook* (editor)

1997   *Yellowstone's Northern Range: Complexity and Change in a Wildland Ecosystem* (with Norman A. Bishop, Francis J. Singer, and John D. Varley)

1997   *Searching for Yellowstone: Ecology and Wonder in the Last Wilderness*

1999   *Royal Coachman: The Lore and Legends of Fly-Fishing*

2000   *Bud Lilly's Guide to Fly Fishing the New West* (with Bud Lilly)

2001   *Real Alaska: Finding Our Way in the Wild Country*

2001   *America's National Parks: The Spectacular Forces That Shaped Our Treasured Lands*

Lewis and Clark
AMONG THE GRIZZLIES

Legend and Legacy in the American West

PAUL SCHULLERY

FALCON®

GUILFORD, CONNECTICUT
HELENA, MONTANA

AN IMPRINT OF THE GLOBE PEQUOT PRESS

Cover art from a painting by Monte Dolack © 2001, www.dolack.com. *Lewis and Clark and the Corps of Discovery at the White Cliffs of the Missouri* was commissioned by the Lewis and Clark Interpretive Association of Great Falls, Montana (406–452–5661), and is available as a fine art poster.

Cover design by Libby Kingsbury
Text design by Nancy Freeborn

Library of Congress Cataloging-in-Publication Data is available.

ISBN 0-7627-2524-9   .

Manufactured in the United States of America
First Edition/First Printing

FOR MARSHA

TABLE OF CONTENTS

Introduction 1

1. First Bears, and Other Matters. 11

2. "tracks of white bear, verry large" 23

3. Red and Yellow, Black and White 31

4. "a turrible looking animal" 41

5. "I do not like the gentleman". 59

6. Seeking and Sorting Bears 71

7. Courage 85

8. The Great Falls Bear Crisis 103

9. Shy Bears 113

10. Rare Bears. 127

11. Pacific Slope Bears. 139

12. Variagated Bears 149

13. "a sertain fatality" 165

14. Yellowstone River Bears. 171

15. Big-Picture Bears. 175

16. Legacies 183

Sources and Editorial Procedures 203

Notes 211

Acknowledgments 237

Index 240

Missouri River trader Pierre Cruzatte had only one functioning eye, and he was nearsighted in it, at that. "Disabilities" of this magnitude would probably disqualify him for any risky position in a modern exploring party but seemed not to deter Meriwether Lewis and William Clark from giving the man important responsibilities throughout their famous expedition. Despite his limited vision, he was frequently sent out to hunt the large animals upon which the expedition was so dependent. And as the party ascended the river in 1804, Cruzatte served as bowman on the keelboat, to watch the tricky currents of the Missouri for trouble. He was fondly nicknamed "St. Peter" by the other men, and was also valued for his familiarity with the Omaha Indian tongue, his skills at sign language, and his indefatiguable fiddle playing.[1]

Yet as colorful and deserving of respect as he may have been, this short "wiry" man is probably most often remembered now for an August day in 1806 when, while hunting in heavy brush along the river, he mistook Meriwether Lewis for an elk and shot him in the left thigh. This is not the sort of mistake for which history is ever likely to completely forgive Cruzatte. For good or bad, he is now most often remembered as "the guy who shot Lewis in the butt." This achievement has certainly overshadowed some of his other distinctions, among them his peculiar place in the history of the grizzly bear.

As the Lewis and Clark Expedition ascended the Missouri River that fall of 1804, they saw evidence of grizzly bears long before they saw the bears themselves. They heard about the big bears from Indians, some of whom were wearing necklaces of bear claws much larger than any the white men, who were familiar only with black bears, had ever seen.

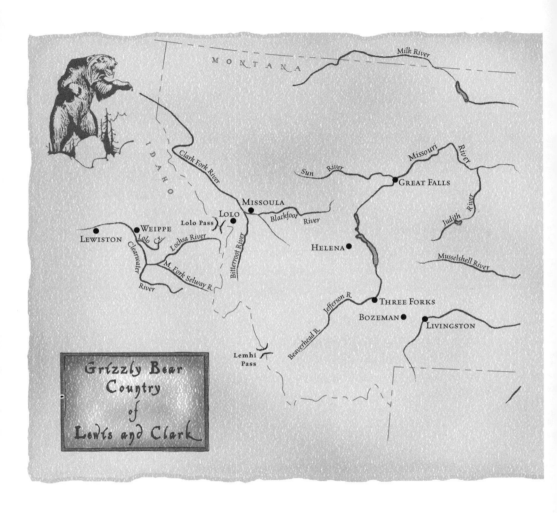

MONTANA

Milk River

IDAHO

Clark Fork River

Sun River

Missouri River

GREAT FALLS

MISSOULA

LOLO

Blackfoot River

Judith River

Lolo Pass

WEIPPE

Lolo Cr.

Lochsa River

Bitterroot River

HELENA

LEWISTON

Clearwater

M. Fork Selway R.

River

Musselshell River

Jefferson R.

THREE FORKS

BOZEMAN

LIVINGSTON

Beaverhead R.

Lemhi Pass

Grizzly Bear Country of Lewis and Clark

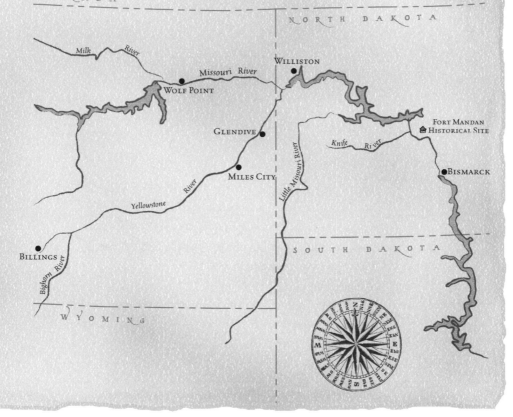

Then, on October 20, in what is now North Dakota, well inside the historic range of the grizzly bear, Clark said that "I saw Several fresh track of those animals which is 3 times as large as a mans track." This bear demanded a whole new sense of scale.

October 20 was also Cruzatte's big day in bear history—the day he opened negotiations between the U.S. government and this already legendary carnivore. Though we could wish for much more information, Lewis gave us the fullest description of what happened to Cruzatte that day:

> Peter Crusat this day shot at a white bear   he wounded him, but being alarmed at the formidable appearance of the bear he left his tomahalk and gun; but shortly after returned and found that the bear had taken the oposite rout.

Cruzatte researcher Dan Slosberg summed up the momentous occasion like this:

> Cruzatte himself was the first member of the expedition, and thus the first American, to get off a shot at a Grizzly bear. Within seconds, he became the first American to run away from what the explorers came to learn was a formidable adversary when hurt and angry.[2]

Today, when we drive along the Missouri River near Bismarck, North Dakota, we perceive the epic scale of long, arcing meanders, sprawling river bottoms thick with cottonwoods, and long hills that slope back from both shores. But in the reality of the river trip as experienced by the men of Lewis and Clark, this was, in the words of scholar Albert Furtwangler, "a land both grand and intricately surprising."[3] Cruzatte's somewhat slapstick pioneering encounter with the grizzly bear invites us to move from the vast sweep of the Lewis and Clark Expedition's route—the heroic transcontinental saga of their journey—to the urgent immediacy of very local, minute-to-minute concerns. The biggest surprises were usually not the pleasant ones.

To the nearsighted Cruzatte that day, the salient features of the landscape must have been much fewer, more specific, and a lot nearer at hand.

Maybe he had wandered up one of the small drainages into thick cover and limited visibility. He would have been looking for deer, elk, or bison, but he met the bear instead. Maybe he roused it from a daybed. Maybe it was resting by the remains of its own most recent kill.

We have no way of knowing now which of these two distinguished individuals was the more alarmed by the sudden encounter. Perhaps the bear left in as much of a panic as did Cruzatte—it often works that way in bear encounters, even today.[4]

Or perhaps the bear hung around long enough to sniff curiously at Cruzatte's abruptly abandoned weapons. If it had spent much time along the river, this bear probably wasn't a complete stranger to such devices, which both local Indians and other white traders would have been using for some years there.

For all we know, it may even have circled around to follow Cruzatte. We can imagine it trailing him for some distance, finally poking its huge head cautiously through the riverside brush to gaze at the extraordinary sight of a keelboat drawn up to shore, with strangely dressed men and their gear scattered around nearby—a historic moment that a cartoonist might memorialize by giving the bear a "thought balloon" over its head that said, "Well, there goes the neighborhood."

During the twenty-five or so years that I have been seriously reading and writing about bears, I have felt constantly in the presence of Lewis and Clark. They were by no means the first Euro-Americans to see (and kill) grizzly bears, but for the practical purposes of how we perceive the bear today they might as well have been. They haunt the literature and folklore of the grizzly bear as surely as the animal itself has haunted the collective imagination of every human society to encounter it.

The power of Lewis and Clark in shaping our idea of the grizzly bear first came home to me about twenty years ago. At the time I was reading the scientific bear literature voraciously, and I had noticed several popular misconceptions about bears. It was "common knowledge," for example, that bears couldn't run downhill. Some people believed that bears were easily driven away by the scent of mothballs. Others believed that grizzly bears did indeed kill people but wouldn't eat them. These and other examples of "barstool biology" seemed a little too common for the public good, so I wrote what I thought was a lively little essay on "bear myths" and sent it off to one of the big outdoor magazines. I soon received it back, with a nice rejection letter, telling me that what they really preferred was more like the enclosed article, which they had just published.

The enclosed article was, of course, a retelling of the Lewis and Clark adventures with grizzly bears. I recognized it immediately because I had seen dozens like it in generations of outdoor magazines and books. The article contained nothing new, nothing even freshly described—just the same wonderful old tales, retold for editors and readers who never tired of the story. It seemed to be the most important story that could be told about American bears. I suspect that it still is.

I immediately sold my bear-myth story to another magazine, but that was less important than what I learned.[5] I learned that the adventures of Lewis and Clark tower above almost all subsequent American bear stories and remain irresistible to us two hundred years later. They have a gospel-like value in the popular bear lore. As my collection of out-of-print books about bears grew to include all the essential volumes, this lesson was reinforced. Again and again, the writer of each new book felt compelled to start with Lewis and Clark, often devoting a whole chapter to them.

Likewise, books and articles about Lewis and Clark typically paid special homage to the grizzly bear. Of the many wonders and spectacles the explorers anticipated on their journey, the bear has always been seen as among the most frightening, as well as the most charismatic. The bears they met have helped us define the dangers of the journey, the element of the unknown in a hostile land, and, perhaps most simply, the heroism of the men. Whether viewed by students of the bear or by students of the expedition, the grizzly bear constituted one of the sternest tests faced by the expedition.

This positioning of the grizzly bear as a supreme contestant for the land the men were exploring was hardly fair to the bear, the land, or the men. The men could have been hurt by a hundred things, from treacherous rivers to exposure to rattlesnakes to hailstorms to the people they met all along the way. Those outdoor editors who remain eager to publish yet another carbon-copy rendition of the grizzly bear adventures of Lewis and Clark have never shown a similar interest in articles about hailstorms, slippery river rocks, cacti, or any of the other hazards that were as urgently real to the explorers.

The reason for this preference is simple. There is nothing else like a bear, and there are few things about the American wilderness—or any other northern circumpolar wilderness—that so enchant us as the knowledge that we share it with these animals.

Entire books and monographs have been devoted to what human culture has made of bears. Few, if any, other wildlife species have inspired an equal richness of belief, myth, legend, spirituality, and raw wonder. What the scholars Paul Shepard and Barry Sanders, in their popular book *The Sacred Paw: The Bear in Nature, Myth, and Literature* (1985), described as "that ursine quality" has engaged our imaginations for as long as we've had them.[6] The bear's similarities to us, such as its ability to stand com-

Wood engraving of European brown bear from Edward Topsell's The History of Four-Footed Beasts *(1607). By Topsell's time, the bear was firmly established as a nearly fantastic figure in natural history and lore. Parroting earlier "authorities," Topsell gave straight-faced reports of bears that kidnapped maidens, bears whose mere breath could putrefy the flesh of other animals, and bears that could gain weight while denning simply "by sucking their forefeet." Elements of the European heritage of beliefs about these animals were transported to the New World long before Lewis and Clark set out to meet the real grizzly bear of the American West.*

fortably on its hind legs (though wild bears rarely ever walk that way), strengthen the haunting familiarity, the near-recognition of self, we feel in its presence. And the bear's extraordinary differences from us, such as its ability to sleep for several months, intrigue us for its near-alien way of life. The familiarity and strangeness combine in a creature that inspires fear, admiration, humor, awe, and other conflicting, fleeting emotions that race through us when we see one. And once we've seen one, we quickly grow confident that we can imagine what it must have been like to be Lewis, Clark, Cruzatte, and the rest as they blundered, paddled, and hunted their way through the grizzly bears of the western wilderness. Perhaps that confidence is not justified, but our imaginations are already in gear and not likely to be dissuaded from pursuing, along with Lewis and Clark, our own personal ideas of these great lore-ridden creatures.

This book is about that pursuit—what the legendary "Corps of Discovery" saw and reported, and what we have made of it since.[7] One of the great joys of studying Lewis and Clark is that of a hearty, stimulating conversation. We read not only what the corps members said but also what so many after them said about the same things. Each new generation of Lewis and Clark students participates in that conversation, adding a new response here and there—perhaps doubting this impression of Lewis's, or applauding that interpretation by a previous scholar, or even proudly pointing out something no one seems to have noticed before—always knowing full well that later, someone else will enter the conversation and likewise put us in our place in the long, winding exchange of impressions and reactions. It is one of the historian's great prospects—both exhilarating and humbling—that we will all become part of such a dynamic and constructive process of discovery.

For upward of two hundred years now, students have been pondering what biologist Daniel Botkin has called the lessons of Lewis and Clark.[8] Some of these students were brilliant, some were reckless, some didn't have a clue. Many found only the lessons they wanted to find; many others didn't even realize the lessons were there. Here on the eve of the two hundredth anniversary of the expedition, we are more conscious than ever before of just how important those lessons might be. So besides letting you hear the voices of Lewis, Clark, Gass, Ordway, and the other journalists who described their harrowing, fascinating, comic experiences with grizzly bears, I hope to share with you some of the voices that they inspired.

Historian John Logan Allen concluded his great study of how Lewis and Clark reshaped the image of the American West by saying that they did much more than map the land and sort out erroneous geographical knowledge. Allen said that "out of that same experience there emerged newer editions of the ancient myths."[9] It is good to recognize that all exploration does this. Our vastly improved scientific knowledge of the grizzly bear today has in no way diminished the power of our myths about the bear; indeed, it has probably heightened them. Among the great gifts the Lewis and Clark Expedition gave us is that they started us on our own more modest explorations, following not merely in their footsteps but also in the meandering courses of their perceptions, their imaginations, and their dreams. I suspect that in no other sphere were their perceptions more astute, their imaginations more challenged, and their dreams more vividly fulfilled, than in their dealings with the grizzly bear.

First Bears, and Other Matters

The Lewis and Clark bear chronicles actually begin while the men were still in winter quarters at Camp DuBois, which the men built in early December 1803 on the Illinois side of the Mississippi River not far upstream from St. Louis. Two days after Christmas, Clark reported that he "Sent out Drewyer to hunt to day, early—he returned Late with a Buck, he Saw three Bar on the other Side of the Prarie." Thankfully, the expedition members, because of their official orders to report on so many aspects of the country they visited, felt considerable responsibility to record sightings of wildlife, whether they interacted with the animals or not. This means that there is a high probability that if any of the diarists saw a bear, we can count on them reporting it.

On January 5, 1804, Clark reported that "Two men whome I sent to hunt grouse returned with part of a hog which they found hung up in the woods & brought it in a[s] Bear meat." It might seem odd that they should mistake a hog for a bear (if that is indeed what Clark is suggesting, and it seems to be), but without a skin the two species are not all that dissimilar, especially if the limbs and head have been cut off. On the other hand, it seems even odder that Clark's men felt free simply to abscond with someone else's butchered meat, when it must have been obvious to them that it had been killed and hung to drain or dry—and that whoever owned the hog and did all that work on it would probably not take kindly to its disappearance. Historian Charles Clarke, in *The Men of the Lewis and Clark Expedition* (1970), suggested that Captain Clark once referred to John Collins as a "blackguard" because the latter killed a domestic pig, essentially stealing it and representing it as bear meat.[1]

As the corps worked their way west toward grizzly bear country, their journals made regular mention of black bears. These mentions provide a useful introduction to the more fulsome descriptions of their later encounters with grizzly bears. Bears were of course interesting animals to many people of the time, especially those who had to contend with bears raiding their crops or killing their domestic animals, or who worried about their personal safety in the presence of such a large if usually unthreatening carnivore. The human population of the United States was far more rural in 1804 than it is today, and a considerably higher percentage of the citizens would have had such immediate and practical reasons to know about bears.

It seems that, like most people, expedition members didn't regard black bears as especially dangerous. Their mentions of black bears are as brief and matter-of-fact as are their mentions of the deer and other animals they killed.

And they seem to have killed bears whenever they could. The corps was large (about forty-two people on this first leg of the journey up the Missouri River, then thirty-three from Fort Mandan on to the West Coast), and the men worked long, exhausting hours. Finding food was a constant and urgent matter on the minds of Lewis and Clark. The expedition's hunters were almost always out seeking game, and Lewis and Clark themselves also hunted opportunistically as they made their many forays on foot from the main party's line of travel.

Altogether, party members killed hundreds of large mammals along the way. For example, wildlife biologist Ken Walcheck has recently calculated that in the course of their round trip, the men killed a minimum of 396 elk and eighty-three pronghorn.[2] Far fewer bears were killed, of course, because they were less abundant than the herding animals.[3] But like many other earlier travelers, corps members probably welcomed a little variety in their diet.

For most people in modern North America, any kind of wild game meat is a novelty, and the extent to which a dead animal fulfilled other needs of the explorers may be a surprise. Bear meat, for example, was often fat, and seems to have been greeted with enthusiasm by corps members, but perhaps more important, bear grease, or "oil," was valued for cooking and other purposes. In early America, people living on the edge of settled country, where commercial products were perhaps less available and bears were still abundant, seem often to have regarded bear oil as a staple. Swedish traveler Peter Kalm, who roamed eastern North America in the mid-eighteenth century, left an excellent summary of the high regard many Americans had for bear oil and described a few of the uses that Euro-American colonists and Native Americans made of it:

> When one shoots a bear here, the meat is eaten and is considered almost as valuable as pork. The fat or suet is retained and melted; the oil made thereof is preserved. Not only the natives but also the French, especially on their journeys, use this oil in place of butter for stewing and preparing their food. Just recently when I was at Fort St. Jean, Madame La Croix had no oil with which to prepare the salad. She used bear oil therefore, and the salad tasted almost as good as with the usual cotton seed oil, though the flavor was a bit peculiar. . . . When the natives have lean and dried meat, they pour bear oil into a dish and dip strips of the meat before mentioned into it and eat it. The Indians, particularly the women, often oil their hair with it. It is said that the hair grows better because of it and that this oiling prevents the hair from becoming matted.[4]

As their trip continued, the corps would routinely demonstrate the many values they found in a dead bear. Among these values was the simple responsibility to report what was seen. For example, on May 31, 1804, near the mouth of the Osage River in western Missouri, Sergeant Charles Floyd reported seeing "one perogue Loaded with Bare Skins and Beav and Deer Skins from the osoge village." The observation reflects the journalist's awareness of the need to report on trade as well as on trade items.

The corps's early reports of black bears are a handy example of how the party's various diarists provided us with nearly—but not quite—identical information and observations. My goal in this book is to offer a

The North American black bear, the first bear species encountered by Lewis and Clark on their westward journey, was well known to the explorers. The black bear's western color variations contributed to confusion over species designation that would continue until well into the twentieth century. NATIONAL PARK SERVICE PHOTOGRAPH

reasonably full accounting, in the words of the explorers themselves, of their dealings with bears and then to add whatever interpretation and commentary seems helpful to place their words in a modern context. I don't intend to ask you to read every word every man wrote on every bear that was reported. But here at the start, it's worth seeing how the record-keeping process worked, and their reports of bears give us some fine opportunities to do just that.

On June 7, 1804, in the middle of the present state of Missouri (about where Interstate 70 crosses the Missouri River), Clark reported that "our Hunters brought in three *Bear* this evening." In his June 7 entry, John Ordway was more talkative about this episode, saying that "we Encamped at the mouth of good womans River on Right the hunters came in with 3 Bears this evening." Joseph Whitehouse, in his June 7 entry, said more, writing that "our daily hunters met us there with three Bears, One Old famel & her two Cubbs brought By G. Drewyer." Whitehouse followed up with a little more information in his June 8 entry, saying that "the white pierogue had hard Crossing the River to bring the Meat from the hunters."

In these brief entries we find several reasons why understanding the original journals requires a little undaunted courage itself. First, there are often peculiar words, usually but not always the result of the idiosyncratic and creative spelling styles of the writers. Whitehouse's "Old famel" might at casual glance seem an abbreviated form of "family," but the context makes it obvious he is referring to an old female. His mention of the "pierogue" is actually closer to the correct spelling of "pirogue," one of the watercraft the expedition used, than many others (elsewhere he referred to it as the "Pettiauger"). ("Drewyer" was a particularly popular, if mangled, variation on the surname of expedition member George Drouillard.)

Especially in difficult conditions, when the men were putting all their energies into travel and saving little time for reflection and writing, diaries could be neglected. And then, when opportunity allowed, they would sit down and catch up, often by copying from each other's diaries. Most of us very quickly lose track of exactly what day last week something happened, especially if we're busy and the days have been eventful.

But here is another shock for first-time readers of the journals: These men felt no compunction about simply copying each other's entries. Though this may look like "cheating" to us, and certainly would be in any school we might have attended when we were growing up, it must have seemed perfectly reasonable to them.[5] After all, the most important task they faced was to ensure the survival of at least one complete set of records of the trip, and what better way to do that than to make copies and spread them around among the men? And even though they routinely copied from one another, individual observations just as routinely crept into each man's description of some event, or place, or animal, so that each journal took on a personality of its own.

But that is sometimes small comfort if we're trying to pin down something as precise as the date on which an animal was killed. Expedition members might not have any reason to regard such precision as meaningful.

Pat's Encounter With The Bear, *from Anne Bowman's* The Bear-Hunters of the Rocky Mountains *(1862), is typical of the scenes of peril common in nineteenth-century bear books. Tree climbing is common among black bears and rare among grizzly bears, but early illustrators were not likely to be concerned about such details.*

For example, we might be hoping to determine when a specific animal was killed, but what we are told instead is when the hunters returned with the animal they had killed sometime during their most recent hunting trip. To the diarist, the important information might instead be when the meat arrived in camp.

Last among the challenges of using the journals for purposes like this book is accumulating as much information as possible. I've devoted years to studying early historical accounts of western wildlife, and I must say that this bear-hunting episode beautifully demonstrates one of the great driving truths of using such anecdotal materials to reconstruct an even vaguely accurate portrait of prevailing wildlife conditions in the past: The more accounts you use, the more you learn. This may seem obvious, but again and again I've seen historical investigators ignore this rule. They will use too few accounts, and—perhaps even more dangerous—they will regard one account of any particular trip or episode to be sufficient even if other accounts by members of the same party exist. The first rule is to use everything you can get your hands on. The more accounts, the better.

Notice how our understanding of the episode grows as we read even these brief accounts. Lewis, Clark, and Ordway tell us only that there were three bears. Whitehouse adds not only that the bears were an old female and two cubs, but also that they were killed on the opposite (the west, in this case) side of the river from the camp. We don't end up with much, but it's a lot more than we would have if we'd read only, say, Lewis's account. In her fine new edition of Patrick Gass's journal, Carol Lynn MacGregor appended a tally of all the animals that Gass's journal reported as having been killed.[6] Gass knew of, or reported, a total of 165 killed elk. This is less than half the number that Ken Walcheck was able to identify by using all of the journals. The expedition split up at times. Individual observers missed information through not paying attention or lack of communication among the men, or perhaps they just forgot to write things down. The more accounts, the better.

Having conducted this exercise once to show you what we are dealing with in excerpting the bear stories from the journals, I do not intend to do so again, though once in a while there will certainly be some interesting (I hope) asides I should offer about differing views of the same event. For the purposes of this book, I have a greater interest in what the journals tell us about bears than in the admittedly fascinating textual minutiae. I suspect and hope that most readers share my view. I will focus more on the essentials of their bear encounters, and therefore perhaps I will slight some of the scholarly intrigues to be found in analysis of the narratives' subtle variations. I go through this little exercise here at the beginning only so that you will know that I have made this choice, and what it means.

⟫•⟪

For weeks after the killing of the sow with two cubs, as the corps worked their way up the Missouri River across present-day Missouri and then northwest where the river forms the present Missouri-Kansas and Missouri-Nebraska boundaries, they seemed to travel through excellent black bear habitat, and the animals were routinely killed. On June 11, Whitehouse said, "Drewyer Killd two bears & One buck." On June 13, at Grand River, Whitehouse said, "our hunters met us there with a bear and Some Venison." On June 15, Floyd reported that "ouer hunters Killed 4 Bars and 3 Deer"; the next day Clark reported that as the party moved up the Missouri, "at about a mile 1/2 we Came to the Camp of our hunters, they had two Bear & two Deer. . . ." On June 17, Floyd said "ouer hunters Returned and Killed one Bar and one Deer." Also on this day, Whitehouse revealed another of the many uses that were made of all these bears. Their skins were used to make "600 feet of Roap."

On June 18, Whitehouse said that "the hunters Killd four deer and Colter one large Bare On the west Side of the River." On June 20, near present Lexington, Missouri, he said the hunters "killd a bear brought the Skin left the Meat as it was poor." And on June 22, he said that "G. Drewyer Killd a large Male Bare weighd Neer 5 hundred Wt."

Clark and Gass agreed that the bear Drouillard killed this day was "fine," or "large," but only Whitehouse made an estimate of its weight. A five-hundred-pound black bear is indeed a large one, perhaps twice the weight of a typical adult black bear in many parts of the country, but five hundred pounds is certainly well within the realm of possibility (the lore of bears is rich with monstrously overestimated bear weights, but these men were accustomed to butchering both domestic and wild animals and should have been reasonably close in their estimates).[7]

Their success at bear hunting continued. On June 23, Whitehouse noted that "G. Drewyer went Out and kill 2 deers and one Bare befor Night which made four deer and One bare Kill in all that day." On June 24, Clark said, "I observed great quts. of Bear Signs, where they had passed in all Directions thro the bottoms in Serch of Mulberries, which were in great numbers in all the bottoms thro which our party passed." He apparently killed one bear that day, though his own journal is somewhat unclear on the point, Ordway said that "Capt. Clark Came to the Boat this morning with a fat Bear."

One of the great joys of reading the journals of long-ago travelers is the discovery of how the writers were either like us or different from us—and the chance to wonder over those differences. When I first read Clark's June 24 entry about "great quts. of Bear Signs," I did a mental double take at what I assume was an unintentional joke. In the nineteenth century, the term *sign* served as a polite euphemism. It could of course mean tracks, but it could just as easily mean feces, which modern naturalists often call "scat." Of the many hundreds of pre-1880 accounts of western wildlife that I have read, even among those unpublished diaries and journals so many travelers seem to keep, I have rarely found any direct mention of scat. No crap, no poop, no droppings, and certainly no shit. A few professional naturalists mention it clearly, but most writers of the period slide past it with a vague mention of "sign" or "traces." I assume this was because there was a firm social convention against such mentions in print. Whatever the reason, this prissy restraint has cost historians an entire category of evidence in the anecdotal record. Fortunately, on many occasions, Lewis and Clark were not reluctant to be candid. Among other blunt terms used to describe various indelicate matters, they used the term *dung* when referring to droppings, so we do often know what they meant.

Clark's restrained language in this case, however, was also entertaining to me. Clark's word "quts." was of course an abbreviation for "quantities," but in my initial scanning of the line it registered in my mind as "great quarts of bear crap," which, based on my experience at looking at quite a few piles of grizzly bear scat, made perfect sense.

Though no bears were reported killed for the next several days, they were abundant. On June 30, Whitehouse said that "the deer was plentifull on the Sand beech as we passd along   all sorts of fowls   likeway the woolves and Bears Every day." On July 8, he said "on the So. West side, a bear was seen & being pursued by one of our hands, it made its escape. . . ."

But somewhere up the Missouri River from present-day St. Joseph, Missouri, in the neighborhood of Mound City, Lewis and Clark noticed that "the deer and bear begin to get scearce and the Elk begin to appear."

On July 27, Whitehouse invites us to consider the vicissitudes of interpreting his journal, or, more accurately, journals. As it happens, the Whitehouse journal exists in two forms. The first, the original from the trip, was dutifully published by Reuben Gold Thwaites in 1905 when he edited his seven-volume set of the *Original Journals of the Lewis and Clark Expedition 1804–1806*. This is the version of the Whitehouse journal that I am quoting from unless I specify otherwise. In 1966, however, a variant was discovered. It seems that Whitehouse, like Gass, had ambitions of publishing his journal, and the 1966 manuscript is apparently a long-lost draft aimed in that direction (there is no known evidence that publication took place). It is written in a different hand, so we can assume that Whitehouse, again like Gass, enlisted the assistance of a more skilled writer, who produced this version apparently in cooperation with Whitehouse. The document, which I will refer to as the paraphrase version, has been well analyzed by historian Paul Russell Cutright, but for present purposes it is enough to say that it does appear to contain a few items of information not in the original. It is somewhat more smoothly and competently written and fleshes out many of Whitehouse's sentence fragments. It is fascinating. But it is also problematic, and I have shied away from using it much. Here is an example of why.

On July 27, in his original journal, Whitehouse made this statement:

> high wood land on S. S. [south shore] G Shannon killed one
> Deer to day. we passed a prarie on The S. S. we passd many
> sand bars, the River very crooked.

The passage continued in that vein. But here is the paraphrase version of the same events:

the land on the South side of the River, being cover'd with Forests, and appear'd very rich, We passed a Priari, laying on the South side of the River where we saw a number of Deer & bear. The River is very Crooked in this days route

This passage continues as well, demonstrating, at the very least, that Whitehouse had not found himself as good an editor as had Gass; the spelling and sentence structure are not much improved. But after reading considerable material from both journals, I conclude that the editor was also careless about information. Notice that in the original journal a deer is killed, but in the paraphrase "a number" of deer and bear were seen. I think the most likely explanation for these changes is that there was in fact no bear seen that day, and that the editor, either in haste or in misunderstanding, converted Whitehouse's original "many sand bars" into bears. Perhaps this happened because the editor was unfamiliar with river terminology or because many people routinely spelled (and may have pronounced) "bear" as "bar." The sequence of the words in this case, in which the sandbars of the original disappear and bears appear in the same place in the paraphrase, seems to me a likely indication of an editorial error.

And, of course, an indication of no bear seen that day.

In any case, as the captains had noted, black bear did indeed largely disappear from sight, and therefore from the journals, for a long time. They were replaced, of course, by the grizzly bear.

"tracks of white bear, verry large"

Grizzly bears eased into the lives and consciousnesses of the Corps of Discovery quite slowly. I have already described Cruzatte's first encounter. It occurred not far south of present Bismarck, North Dakota, and turned out to be the corps's only actual meeting with the grizzly bear that year. But Lewis, Clark, and the rest of the men were given plenty of reason to think about this great and widely rumored carnivore, both as they moved up the river and as they wintered in the Mandan villages.

On August 30 and 31, near present Yankton, South Dakota, the corps met with the Yankton Sioux in an extended parlay, part of their complex and unsuccessful campaign to convince all the river tribes to be peaceful not only with the corps but also with the other tribes. On August 31, during this meeting, Ordway noted an early evidence of the grizzly bears:

> their was Several of the Indians which had Strings of White Bears claws around their necks, which was 3 inches in length, & Strung as close as possable to each other on the String all around their necks.

Except for Cruzatte's exciting encounter, already described, the corps's only evidence of grizzly bears that year would come from this sort of secondhand observation of parts of the animal, or from tales told by the locals. The evidence was clear and often imposing, but it fell short of the real, living thing.

The next day, Ordway said that the corps "passed a chalk Bluff on N. S. where we found pleanty of fine plumbs, little above is a white clift

Little Wolf, a Famous Warrior, *painted by George Catlin in 1844, depicts the* *Iowa Indian wearing a full necklace of grizzly bear claws. Their first sight of the* *tremendous claws of the bear must have given the Lewis and Clark party much to* *think about in their anticipation of meeting this legendary animal.* SMITHSONIAN called the den of the White Bear, we See large holes in the clift which appeared to go Deep into the clift; this clift is about 70 feet high. . . ." We know sadly little about the grizzly bears that inhabited the Great Plains two hundred years ago, but a large, exposed cliff like this seems an unlikely place for a grizzly bear densite, at least a true winter den. Elsewhere in North America, grizzly bears typically dig their dens, to dimensions only slightly larger than their bodies. Preexisting caves are more often used by black bears, though in some special situations grizzly bears will use them as well.[1]

On September 16, Lewis, in a natural history note, rather distantly mentioned that bears were among the species that are fond of eating acorns, but it is not clear which species of bears he referred to. On October 1, in what is now central South Dakota a few miles upstream from the mouth of the Cheyenne River, Clark reported that they met a French trader who informed them that far up that river, close to the "Black mountains" (presumably the Black Hills of western South Dakota), there were "Great number of goats and a kind of anamal with verry large horns about the Size of a Small Elk, White Bear   no bever on the chien [the Cheyenne River]   great numbers in the mountains." This interview was part of the routine information gathering conducted by the captains throughout the expedition. Whenever possible, they reached beyond their own immediate experiences, accumulating secondhand knowledge of regions they could not visit.

A somewhat more personal connection with the grizzly bear occurred for Clark on October 7. At the mouth of the Moreau River in north-central South Dakota (this site, like the mouth of the Cheyenne, is now under the waters of Lake Oahe), Clark said, ". . . We Saw the tracks of white bear, verry large, I walked up this River a mile."

And except for the flurry of journal entries about tracks and especially about Cruzatte's encounter on October 20, that's it. Late in 1804, the corps went into winter quarters at Fort Mandan, north of present Bismarck, North Dakota, with no more mentions of grizzly bears. They had made a start at documenting at least a few useful topics for us, though, perhaps most important being the distribution of the grizzly bear at the time.

The evidence is only suggestive, however. Just because members of the corps saw Indians wearing grizzly-bear-claw necklaces in what is now extreme southeastern South Dakota does not necessarily prove that there were grizzly bears nearby. Tribes throughout the Mississippi River drainage had access to a remarkable trade network by which objects of value traveled many hundreds of miles. But the prevailing view of the historic range of the grizzly bear at the time of first Euro-American settlement places Yankton fairly close to the easternmost edge of that range, which more or less followed the one hundredth meridian from north to south. Most of North and South Dakota, the western half of Nebraska, and the northwestern corner of Kansas were all inhabited by grizzly bears two hundred years ago.[2]

The question this asks is: Why did grizzly bears stop there? And the answer seems to be that they didn't; they once occupied a much larger area. If we take the long view, we see that Lewis and Clark reported on a *stage* of grizzly bear range rather than on some permanent state.

Bears travel. I assume that even as late as 1800 the occasional wanderer might have moved farther east; grizzly bears, especially big males and subadults looking for a place to live, are great explorers, and there is no reason to doubt that now and then a few might have drifted into Missouri, Iowa, or Minnesota when circumstances—mostly food availability—invited them there.

More to the point, we know that grizzly bears had at earlier times inhabited much more of North America than they did when Lewis and Clark crossed the continent. I first became aware of this about twenty years ago, while rummaging through *Forest and Stream,* the granddaddy of modern American sporting periodicals. In 1884 and 1896, *Forest and Stream* ran notes about reports of the existence of grizzly bears in Labrador, east of Hudson Bay in northern Canada.[3] The notes were so seemingly inconclusive that I didn't make much of them, but I did mentally file them away (in the mental folder labeled "really strange little things I'd like to know more about"). But the Labrador grizzly bears were real and survived into surprisingly recent times. In 1975, archaeologists excavating an Eskimo site at Oakak Bay recovered what was unquestionably the skull of a small grizzly bear, thus scientifically confirming long-standing regional traditions about the presence of the bears. The investigators of this site reviewed a considerable body of reports, information, and folklore, concluding that this bear population probably lasted well into the 1900s.[4]

Closer to home—at least the homes of Lewis and Clark—grizzly bear remains have been found in Ontario, Ohio, and Kentucky, all certainly cases of the animals themselves having been there rather than their bones having been brought in by humans from farther west. These remains are much older than the Labrador skull, suggesting to researchers that ten or eleven thousand years ago, grizzly bears included the upper Ohio Valley and southeastern Canada in their range (and further reinforcing the belief in the Labrador bears). Discussing this intriguing former presence of the species in the East, one scientific investigator said that "The eastern boundary of its range has retreated at least 800 miles to the west, presumably in response to climate change."[5]

Archaeology and paleontology can do only so much for us in searches of this sort, but they are not the only tool at hand. Though for many years most scholars tended to discount Native American stories and traditions as little more than "myths" that were historically unreliable to the point of meaninglessness, in recent years at least some investigators have recognized the wealth of information to be found in such traditions.[6] This is not the place for an extended consideration of the crisis of modern anthropology, but the opening up of the storehouses of Native belief to the legitimate consideration of modern scholars is a wonderful gift.

When I think of questions of the eastern range of the grizzly bear, I am reminded of one early report of such a belief. In October 1855, *Harper's New Monthly Magazine* published a long article titled "Bears and Bear-Hunting." No author is given, perhaps because the article seems to be an uncritical sweeping-up of whatever bear-related lore came to hand. It was great fun, though—an appalling mishmash of adventure tales, incorrect natural history, and intriguing episodes. Among these last was the following account of an eastern grizzly bear:

> The home of the grizzly bear is generally confined to the wilds of the Rocky Mountains and the lone wastes of California, yet there can not be a doubt that a solitary specimen has occasionally reached the Atlantic coast. A tradition existed among the New York Indians that some three hundred years ago, a huge monster, which they termed the "Naked Bear," most horrible to behold, and possessed of

naked claws, as large as a man's finger, established himself somewhere among the head-waters of the Hudson, and occasionally falling upon an unprotected town, would destroy with impunity women and children.[7]

The account continues, describing the eventual destruction of the "monster" by a local tribe whose members paraded its head around to the great interest of other tribes.

Whether this is a carefully transcribed Native American belief or not (and I doubt it, considering the informality of the source), the mention of claws "as large as a man's finger" is an almost irresistible anecdotal indication of a grizzly bear. Scientific opinion seems to favor climatic change as the reason that the grizzly bear's range shrank, but I wonder if the east-

Literate travelers in the time of Lewis and Clark would have relied on prevailing natural history works such as Thomas Bewick's A General History of Quadrupeds *(first published in 1790). Though Bewick's information was an improvement on the combination of myth and hearsay of previous centuries, his woodcut portrayal of the brown bear, with its foxlike head, was actually a less accurate portrait than had been provided by Topsell almost two hundred years earlier (see illustration in introduction).*

ern woodlands also became less hospitable to the bears as the Native American human population increased? (Later, we will have reason to ask a similar question about portions of the Pacific Northwest.) Perhaps eastern Native Americans, for reasons of culture, agriculture, technology, or just convenience, were less willing to tolerate the bigger and more aggressive bears in their neighborhood and gave this large competitive predator a nudge in the direction that climate was already suggesting. Black bears are usually a lot easier to live with than grizzly bears.[8]

CHAPTER THREE

Red and Yellow, Black and White

In his indispensable book *Lewis and Clark among the Indians* (1984), historian James Ronda explained that, though President Jefferson had specifically directed the captains to gather ethnographic information of many kinds about the tribes they encountered, such information was often very hard to come by:

> The expedition was to record what the Indians wore, what they ate, how they made a living, and what they believed in. But long before coming to their winter quarters, Lewis and Clark realized that they would have neither the time nor the linguistic ability to ask all of Jefferson's questions. . . . Special attention was given to each Indian group's tribal name, location, population, language, and potential for American trade. Questions about religious traditions, medical practices, or cultural values were quietly dropped from the official list.[1]

This was without question an easy decision to justify at the time. It's one thing to ask, through an interpreter (or two or three interpreters, if such a string of translation was necessary), about straightforward matters like a tribe's size or preferred foods. It is quite another to use even an excellent interpreter to discuss complex matters like moral values and religious beliefs.

A less justifiable aspect of this decision, at least by today's standards, was the hard reality of the captains' disdain for such beliefs. As Ronda put it, "Because the captains were confident of their own cultural superiority, they never doubted the wisdom of judging Indians by white standards."[2] With that bias firmly in place, the captains probably thought that religious and spiritual aspects of Indian cultures were relatively unimportant matters, at least compared to commercial and political issues that might affect future trade relations with the United States.

The effect of these limitations, according to Ronda, was that Lewis and Clark "decided to use their time and resources to gather material on the externals of native life."[3] That winter of 1804–1805, living next door to Mandan and Hidatsa towns, the captains energetically collected all sorts of objects—worked skins, weapons, seeds, and so on—but neglected the kind of information that would flesh out an understanding of Indian culture. Perhaps most important, "nothing was sent back to reveal the rich ceremonial life in Mandan and Hidatsa towns."[4] Throughout their journey, the captains concentrated on gathering and describing *things*—they collected hard evidence rather than ideas, concepts, and beliefs.

This is not to be ungrateful for what Lewis and Clark brought home. Their legacy as documenters of Indian life is a strong one, even if it is somewhat restricted. But it is to express a certain regret that they missed such wonderful opportunities to do more—to add to their baggage the weightless but priceless words of description of ceremonies, intellectual and moral stances, and other aspects of Native culture. I feel this loss especially when I think of bears, animals that have inspired important ceremonial and folkloric traditions in aboriginal people around the world, and that still reach deeply into the psyche of the most urban and modernized humans today.

As Paul Shepard and Barry Sanders said in *The Sacred Paw: The Bear in Nature, Myth, and Literature* (1985), "Modern science makes quite clear what is an animal and what is a man. In popular imagination, however, bears always seem about to transcend that division."[5] It is this irresistible attraction between humans and bears that lies behind a host of cults stretching clear around the Northern Hemisphere.[6] Lewis and Clark were exposed to the rich complexity of a bear cult that winter, but it was out of their reach, practically and perhaps philosophically as well.

And, as much as what was missed in formal ethnography, I regret the stories we missed. Surely in all those months sitting around fires, sharing

This image of an Indian in ceremonial garb was published with no explanation on the title page of George Catlin's relatively obscure book Life Amongst the Indians. A Book for Youth *(1861). The character and richness of the bear ceremonialism witnessed by Lewis and Clark and most other early white western travelers was preserved only in part by a few observers like Catlin.*

meals, hunting, and generally just hanging out with so many Native people, corps members must have heard some great stories. All of us who live in bear country and spend any time at all out looking for them have a few stories. Lewis and Clark were surrounded by people for whom bears were an immediate and often urgent reality—people who must have had many, many adventures, tragedies, and comic mishaps to share. As hard as it might have been for these people to overcome the language barriers between them—members of the corps must have had plenty bear tales of their own to share—I am sure that through a combination of words, gestures, and some hilarious, dramatic, and vigorous theatrics, the stories got told.

Of course specialists in every field of natural science and humanities that somehow relates to Lewis and Clark could express similar regrets about what they wish the corps had spent more time on, and many of these regrets would involve subjects of considerably broader interest and significance than bear lore. The captains and their men had a lot on their minds, and a great deal to do, and their own pressing priorities.

So we must settle for a few brief mentions of bears that first winter. In an undated natural history note written sometime during the Fort Mandan stay, Clark reported that the wild animals found "below the River Platt" included a few "Grisley Bear which is said to be verry dangerous. The Countrey above the Mandans Contain great numbers of those anamils Common below and the White & Rid Bear (The White Bear is larger and more dangerous than eithr the Grey or Rid bear and frequently Kill the Indians, Two of the minetarees has been Killed and eate up this winter on thier hunting parties) The Black Hills is Said abound in Bear of every kind, and in addition to all those animals Common on the Missouri."

The captains would use the names *grisley* (in various spellings) and *white bear* more or less interchangeably. It is pretty well agreed now that by "red" ("Rid") bear they meant to refer to what we now know was the brown or "cinnamon" phase of the black bear. As their journey continued, there would be more comments about the red bear and ruminations on just where it fit in the scheme of bear species. At this stage in their growing knowledge of bears, it is difficult to know precisely what was meant by a "grey" bear.

In early April 1805, as they were preparing their shipment of speci-mens and notes to accompany that part of their party that was about to return to St. Louis, Clark noted that among the items was "the Skin of a yellow *Bear* which I obtained from the *Scious*." In their parlance, a yellow bear was, like a white bear, a grizzly. Like most of the specimens they sent or later brought back, this one has not survived.

The corps set out from Fort Mandan on April 7 and had not long to wait for the first traces of grizzly bears. On April 10, along a stretch of the Missouri River now under Lake Sakakawea, Ordway reported that he "Saw the track of a verry large white bare." On April 11, as he was walk-ing along the shore, Clark also noted "fresh bear tracks." On April 13, after describing "a number of carcases of the Buffale along the shore, which had been drowned by falling through the ice in winter and lodged on shore by the high water," Lewis reported on more bear activity and the corps's interest in making the acquaintance of these famous carnivores:

> we saw also many tracks of the white bear of enormous size, along the river shore and about the carcases of the Buffaloe, on which I presume they feed. we have not as yet seen one of these anamals, tho' their tracks are so abundant and recent. the men as well as ourselves are anxious to meet with some of these bear. the Indians give a very formidable account of the strengh and ferocity of this anamal, which they never dare to attack but in parties of six eight or ten persons; and are even then frequently defeated with the loss of one or more of their party. the savages attack this anamal with their bows and arrows and the indifferent guns with which the traders furnish them, with these they shoot with such uncertainty and at so short a distance, that they frequently mis their aim & fall a sacrefice to the bear. two Minetaries were killed during the last winter in an attack on a white bear. this anamall is said more frequently to attack a man on meeting with him, than to flee from him. When the Indians are about to go in quest of the white bear, previous to their departure, they paint themselves and perform all those supersticious rights commonly observed when they are about to make war uppon a neighboring nation.

Here we receive essentially all the information we ever receive from Lewis and Clark about the relationship between the grizzly bear and the tribes around Fort Mandan. Lewis repeated Clark's note about the deaths of two Indians the previous winter, explained how formidable an adversary the bear was to the hunters, and concluded that the Indians did conduct "supersticious rights" prior to a hunt without elaborating on what those rites might involve. He also offered a first observation on the bear's temperament, obviously not his own but learned from his Fort Mandan informants (who were both Indian and white; a number of trappers and traders passed through the region during the corps's stay[7]). He said that the bears were as likely to attack humans on sight as to flee, which put them in marked contrast to the black bears the men knew so well. Grizzly bears were more aggressive, even belligerent.

More to the point of the corps's own adventure, Lewis described the anticipation that they felt as they awaited their own encounters with the bears. This excitement they felt, similar to that any sportsman might feel before a hunt, would be moderated and enriched over the next few weeks, as the bears revealed themselves to be dangerous, a huge nuisance, and apparently dissimilar in behavior from one to the next.

The captains had their first close experience with grizzly bears on Sunday, April 14, along a creek not far from present New Town, North Dakota. Lewis said that he "walked on shore above this creek and killed an Elk, which was so poor that it was unfit for uce; I therefore left it, and joined the party at their encampment on the Stard shore a little after dark. on my arrival Capt Clark informed me that he had seen two white bear pass over the hills shortly after I fired, and that they appeared to run nearly from the place where I shot." Clark added that "those animals assended those Steep hills with Supprising ease & verlocity. they were too far to discover their prosise Colour & Size—"

On April 17, Lewis was wondering if the grizzly bear was really as great a threat as he had been led to believe:

> we saw immence quantities of game in every direction
> around us as we passed up the river; consisting of herds of
> Buffaloe, Elk, and Antelopes with some deer and wolves.
> tho' we continue to see many tracks of the bear we have seen

but very few of them, and those are at a great distance generally runing from us; I thefore presume that they are extreemly wary and shy; the Indian account of them dose not corrispond with our experience so far. one black bear passed near the perogues on the 16th and was seen by myself and the party but he so quickly disappeared that we did not shoot at him.—

But for the next few days he had little way of improving his perspective. On April 18, Clark, reporting on an inconclusive encounter between some of the men and a bear of unidentified species, said, "we Camped on the SS in an excellent harbor, Soon after We came too, two men went up the river to Set their beaver traps   they met with a Bear and being without their arms thought prodent to return &c." The next day he reported a ". . . Great deal of Sign of the large Bear,—" giving us yet another alternative

Captain Clark and His Men Shooting Bears, *from the 1811 edition of the Gass journal, appears to show the captains in formal attire. This woodcut apparently was intended to illustrate journal entries for late April 1805, when the party was near the mouth of the Yellowstone River near the present Montana–North Dakota border. Contrary to historical reality, there seems to be a large sailboat on the river in the background.* COURTESY OF THE LEWIS AND CLARK TRAIL HERITAGE FOUNDATION LIBRARY, GREAT FALLS, MONTANA label—large—for the grizzly. On the day after, April 20, now near present Williston, North Dakota, he noted more drowned bison, including "2 which had lodged on the Side of the bank & eat by the bears."

This became a common sight, as Lewis noted a week later when the corps would have been crossing the present North Dakota–Montana boundary. He said that "for several days past we have observed a great number of buffaloe lying dead on the shore, some of them entire and others partly devoured by the wolves and bear."

On April 28, now into Montana and probably near the present town of Culbertson, Ordway gave us the most complete account of their day's adventures with bears:

> Capt. Clark had killed one Deer & a goose. he Saw Several bair   proceeded on   towards evening we Saw a large black bair Swimming the River   we went on Shore to head him in hopes to kill him. one man Shot & wounded it but it ran in to thick bushes So that we could not find it. Some of the party Saw Several more bair on the hills, on S. S.

Here again we have to deal with the imprecision of their labels. Lewis said the bears that Ordway reported as being on the hills were four in number and "brown." It appears from Ordway's remark "Some of the party Saw Several more bair" that he was not among those observers.

It is a recurring problem, and a matter worthy of speculation, just what species of bears the corps was seeing in cases like these. The most experienced bear observers I know readily admit—in fact they insist—that it is often very difficult to distinguish grizzly and black bears, especially at a distance. The characteristics that most readily distinguish a grizzly bear, such as a distinct shoulder hump that is as high as the highest point on its rump, large and readily visible claws, and a "dished-in" profile of the face when viewed from the side, are not all that helpful indicators at two hundred yards, especially when the bear is moving over uneven country through brush and other barriers to viewing. Black bears, especially heavy-coated individuals, may have an apparent shoulder hump, though up close it will be revealed as nothing but fur. Grizzly bear claws are sometimes dark in color and difficult to see (though when they are light in color they may be visible at amazing distances). Neither species is especially cooperative about standing sideways to you while you study its profile, and personally I have always found the "dished-in" face profile an almost worthless piece of advice anyway; you hardly ever get that perfect a look at the animal's head from just the right angle, and there is enormous variation in profile among the animals—both species—anyway.

Add to these complications the on-the-ground realities of watching wildlife—extreme distance of the subject, variations in the visual acuity and observational skill of the men, distractions such as trying to draw a bead on the animal rather than study it, and the astonishing differences in apparent bear coat color depending upon the source, direction, and angle of the light.

Then add the equally vexing individual variations in the animals themselves. Both black and grizzly bear come in many shades. I am far from being the world's most experienced observer of bears, but even I have seen black bears, unquestionably specimens of *Ursus americanus,* with the same variations in their coats, such as lighter "saddles" or darker lower legs, that often appear on grizzly bears. I have seen grizzly bears that were for all practical definitions black, and others that a nineteenth-century naturalist might have immediately called "red," or "grey."

On the other hand, outside of Alaska I have yet to see a grizzly bear that would have met my personal definition of the term *yellow* (the straw-colored Toklat grizzlies of Denali National Park are close to what I would call yellow, though straw-colored works better for me). We must also consider the differences among observers over what the name of a specific color actually signifies out there in nature. Generations of hunting writers have described deer as being in their "blue" or "red" phase depending upon the time of year, when in fact most people would say those animals were somewhere between gray and tan. And what are we to make of that most improbable of terms, *white*? Are we really to believe that some of the bears they saw were pure white? How about polar bear white, which is to say a slightly off-white cream? Or are we to recognize in their terminology something we do know from modern experiences, that in certain light, when the animal's guard hairs are most strongly highlighted, a grizzly bear can appear surprisingly, glowingly pale? I suppose that the answer to all these questions is something like "yes." We had best keep a fairly open mind and wait to see how the explorers tried to sort it out themselves.

So if one of the diarists reported a "black bear," we cannot always be sure if he meant that he saw *Ursus americanus,* or just a black-colored bear, or a black-colored bear that might have been a grizzly. We cannot always assume that just because Lewis and Clark seemed to mean *Ursus americanus* when they said "black bear," and seemed to consistently use certain terms to describe a grizzly bear, that the other diarists had the same sensibility. Any "black" bear, or "brown" bear, or bear of any other color could potentially have just been a bear of that color, regardless of species.

This, I think, is one of the great and underappreciated challenges of sorting out Lewis and Clark's bear sightings, and it is a challenge that will be with us through the rest of their journey. If I had to guess, I would say that the four "brown" bears reported by Lewis were probably grizzly bears. Some of them might even have been a family group, perhaps a sow with cubs; it is unclear how many of them were seen individually, or if some were seen together. I would also make a hesitant guess that the "black bear" was indeed a black bear. But I couldn't prove it, and, far more important, the members of the corps probably wouldn't have considered it important enough to worry about.

CHAPTER FOUR

"a turrible looking animal"

inally, on April 29, 1805, the captains not only began to encounter grizzly bears that behaved as advertised but also began to tell us about their experiences at greater length. Near Big Muddy Creek, Lewis for the first time told an entire bear story:

> Set out this morning at the usual hour; the wind was moderate; I walked on shore with one man. about 8 A. M. we fell in with two brown or yellow bear; both of which we wounded; one of them made his escape, the other after my firing on him pursued me seventy or eighty yards, but fortunately had been so badly wounded that he was unable to pursue so closely as to prevent my charging my gun; we again repeated our fir and killed him. it was a male not fully grown, we estimated his weight at 300 lbs. not having the means of ascertaining it precisely. The legs of this bear are somewhat longer than those of the black, as are it's tallons and tusks incomparably larger and longer. the testicles, which in the black bear are placed pretty well back between the thyes and contained in one pouch like those of the dog and most quadrupeds, are in the yellow or brown bear placed much further forward, and are suspended in seperate pouches from two to four inches asunder; it's colour is yellowish brown, the eyes small, black, and piercing; the front of the fore legs near the feet is usually black; the fur is finer thicker and deeper than that of the black bear. these are all the particulars in which this anamal appeared to me to differ from the black bear; it is a much more furious and

formidable anamal, and will frequently pursue the hunter when wounded. it is asstonishing to see the wounds they will bear before they can be put to death. the Indians may well fear this anamal equiped as they generally are with their bows and arrows or indifferent fuzees, but in the hands of skillfull riflemen they are by no means as formidable or dangerous as they have been represented.

Ordway sought to clarify the actual color of the animal, saying, "Capt. Lewis and one hunter who walked on Shore this morning. came to us about 1/2 past 9 oClock had killed a Whiteish bair what is called the white bair, but it is not white but light coullour." Gass likewise struggled with the the color: "The natives call them white, but they are more of a brown grey."

So far, Lewis saw no reason to reconsider his suspicion that the Indians had overstated the danger posed by the grizzly bear. The bear, though it survived his first shot, succumbed relatively easily. While admitting that the grizzly bear was very tough, he seemed confident that his superior weapons would handle it.

But what an interesting, intriguing description he left us, and how many reactions modern bear observers must have to what he said. It is impossible to let these observations go without reflection and speculation.

"we estimated his weight at 300 lbs. not having the means of ascertaining it precisely." I, like many before me, am deeply impressed by Lewis's observational skills. In his classic *Lewis and Clark: Pioneering Naturalists* (1969), historian Paul Cutright said that Lewis "was particularly proficient in seeing the little things so often overlooked, even by the well-trained naturalist. He did this effortlessly and spontaneously."[1] But he was also good at the big things, and his estimates of bear weights amount to a significant big thing because such estimates have always been hard for people to get right. The great twentieth-century naturalist Adolph Murie once wrote that "a bear a long distance from a scale always weighs most," but even that sarcasm doesn't do full justice to the extreme excesses of bear weight estimates.[2] In *The Great Bear Almanac* (1993), my former Yellowstone colleague and longtime national park bear manager

Gary Brown described a survey conducted in Great Smoky Mountain National Park, in which visitors were asked to estimate the weight of black bears. The bears actually weighed "ninety-five to one hundred fifteen pounds." The estimates, on the other hand, ranged from "four hundred to four thousand pounds."[3] There is something about a bear we've seen with our own eyes—much like a fish we caught with our own tackle, I suppose—that magnifies it to monstrous proportions in our minds. Lewis appears never to have succumbed to that conceptual gigantism. His bears remain plausible and typical. Even the largest ones seem to have earned the guesses he made of their weights. Whether this skill was because of his close acquaintance with the butchering of so many domestic and wild animals whose weights were more easily known (an acquaintance very few modern people, such as those visitors to Great Smoky Mountain National Park, would have), or just because he was such a careful observer, the result was an admirable accuracy. When he said that this bear weighed three hundred pounds, we can believe it.

"The legs of this bear are somewhat longer than those of the black, as are it's tallons and tusks incomparably larger and longer." He may have been right that this individual grizzly bear appeared to have longer legs than the black bears he was familiar with. It was April and the grizzly was probably not that long out of its den. It was not far along on its annual summer fatteningup and was probably a little lanky. But there is so much individual variation among bears of both species that it is hard to generalize about which might appear to have longer legs. A thin, young black bear, early in the year, looks almost as leggy as a monkey as it lopes along. On the other hand, the claws of the grizzly are significantly longer than those of the black bear. Very quickly, I suspect, the men learned that this was one of the ways they could distinguish the tracks of the two species: If the tracks were deep and clear enough, the black bear's claw marks, if visible at all, were proportionately much closer to the paw print than were the claw marks of the grizzly bear, whose claws leave distinct little holes in the ground a startling distance in front of the paw print.

"the testicles, which in the black bear are placed pretty well back between the thyes and contained in one pouch like those of the dog and most quadrupeds, are in the yellow or brown bear placed much further forward,

and are suspended in seperate pouches from two to four inches asunder." Journal editor Gary Moulton points out that Lewis was "inexplicably wrong about the testicles."[4] That is true; we may never know for certain what this baffling description was all about. But we do know that grizzly bear and black bear testicles are arranged more or less the same, and that there is only one "pouch."[5] We also know that bears are sometimes injured in fights with one another, and the wounds may be both severe and oddly healed (male readers are welcome to pause and wince in empathy here). We also know, thanks to recent scientific study, that some equally strange anatomical effects are achieved by congenital deformation, and this sounds to me like a possible explanation for Lewis's description of the April 29 bear.[6]

What puzzles me as much as what he described is that he never revised this statement. He looked at many more grizzly bears as the expedition continued, and yet he allowed this mistaken impression, based on one of the first bears he examined, to stand. Perhaps he just forgot he'd written it down.

"it's colour is yellowish brown, the eyes small, black, and piercing; the front of the fore legs near the feet is usually black; the fur is finer thicker and deeper than that of the black bear." We have already considered the question of color descriptions and will have more to do with them later, but here it is worth noting that quite a few grizzly bears do have darker feet, but many more don't. This is not to say that Lewis was necessarily wrong in generalizing, based on only a couple of sightings of grizzly bears, that the color of their feet was "usually" black. For all we know now, that was the most common color pattern on the bears he saw on the plains and along the river. That entire vast regional population of bears is gone now, so we have little way of proving or disproving his generalization. Most modern observers do not say that grizzly bear eyes are black. Gary Brown, who, besides having looked a lot of bears in the eyes, has immersed himself deeply in the bear literature, says instead that the eyes are "various shades of brown."[7] As far as the relative fineness, thickness, and deepness of the fur, that also varies from animal to animal, though of course a big grizzly bear, even a three-hundred-pounder like this one, could well have had thicker fur than most of the smaller black bears the corps had encountered.

"it is a much more furious and formidable anamal, and will frequently pursue the hunter when wounded. it is asstonishing to see the wounds they will bear before they can be put to death." Here's a helpful passage, inspiring a mild "aha!" from the attentive reader. There are generalizations here that appear to be based on more observations and personal experience than Lewis could yet have had. I must wonder if perhaps this passage was written or revised some time after the April 29 encounter occurred. On April 29, Lewis had yet to encounter a grizzly bear that was very hard to kill, but a few days later he would begin to have some stirring experiences with such bears. He may have been updating his account as he learned more. If so, then his earlier generalizations, such as the one about the relative leg length of the two species, or about the "usually" black feet of the bears he saw, would make more sense and have more credibility.

But if so, why didn't he correct that weird remark about their testicles?

We will return to the question of how hard these bears were to kill and the effectiveness of the various firearms of the time, as the corps moves along. Loading the bear's meat on board, they did so, and for the next few days continued to see bison carcasses that had been fed on by the carnivores. On Sunday, May 5, the corps were in the general neighborhood of Poplar, Montana. Whitehouse reported that "At 12 oC. we Saw 4 bair on a Sand beach on S. S." He was the only one of the diarists to report these four animals. We are left to wonder if this was a family group, perhaps a sow with three young or perhaps a group of adult bears attracted to a carcass (we cannot assume that the bears were together, like a family group; they may have been spread out along the beach). But in the middle of the afternoon the corps encountered another grizzly bear, one that lived up to all they had heard about the toughness of these animals, though not what they had heard about their belligerence. Clark was in on the kill:

> The river rising & Current Strong & in the evening we Saw a Brown or Grisley beare on a Sand Beech, I went out with one man Geo. Drewyer & Killed the bear, which was verry large and a turrible looking animal, which we found verry hard to kill   we Shot ten Balls into him before we killed him, & 5 of those Balls through his lights This animal is the

largest of the Carnivorous kind I ever Saw   we had nothing that could way him, I think his weight may be Stated at 500 pounds, he measured 8 feet 7 1/2 In. from his nose to the extremity of the Toe, 5 feet 10 1/2 in. arround the breast, 1 feet 11 Ins: around the middle of the arm, 3 feet 11 Ins. arround the neck his tallents was 4 Inches & 3/8 long, he was good order, and appared verry different from the Common black bear in as much as his tallents were blunt, his tail Short, his liver & lights much larger, his maw ten times as large and Contained meat or flesh & fish only— we had him Skined and divided, the oile tried up & put in Kegs for use.

Lewis said most of the same things (all of the diarists recited Clark's measurements of the bear, indicating a fair amount of copying occurred with this day's entries, but most also added personal comments or insights) but elaborated on the extended death throes of the bear:

Capt. Clark and Drewyer killed the largest brown bear this evening which we have yet seen. it was a most tremendious looking anamal, and extreemly hard to kill notwithstanding he had five balls through his lungs and five others in various parts he swam more than half the distance acoss the river to a sandbar & it was at least twenty minutes before he died; he did not attempt to attact, but fled and made the most tremendous roaring from the moment he was shot. We had no means of weighing this monster; Capt. Clark thought he would weigh 500 lbs. for my own part I think the estimate too small by 100 lbs.

Lewis was also more expansive than Clark about the details of the bear's fate and his species's natural history:

he was in good order, we therefore divided him among the party and made them boil the oil and put it in a cask for future uce; the oil is as hard as hogs lard when cool, much more so than that of the black bear. this bear differs from the common black bear in several respects; it's tallons are much longer and more blont, it's tale shorter, it's hair which is of a redish or bey brown, is longer thicker and finer than that of the black bear; his liver lungs and heart are much larger even in proportion with his size; the heart particularly was as large as that of a large Ox. his maw was also ten times the size of black bear, and was filled with flesh and fish. his testicles were pendant from the belly and placed four inches asunder in seperate bags or pouches.— this animal also feeds on roots and almost every species of wild fruit.

Ordway repeated many of the same basic facts but did add some more interesting details, probably because he was one of the men ordered to do the work of butchering and rendering:

towards evening Capt. Clark and Several more of the party killed a verry large bair which the natives and the french tradors call white but all of the kind that we have seen is of a light brown only owing to the climate as we suppose. we shot him as he was Swimming the River. the place where he dyed was Shallow or perhaps he would have Sunk to the bottom. with the assistance of Several men was got on board a perogue and took him to the Shore on the N. S. and dressed it after taking the measure of him. he was verry old. the tushes most wore out as well as his claws.

After providing the measurements, Ordway added more:

we found a Cat fish in him which he had Eat. we Camped and rendered out about 6 gallons of the greese of the brown bair. he was judged to weigh about 4 hundred after dressed. one of the party went out and killed an Elk, and Saw another brown bair.

And Whitehouse elaborated a little on this additional bear sighting:

> one of the hunters went out and killed an elk & Saw
> another bair nearly of the Same discription.

The paraphrase version of the Whitehouse journal in this case elaborates, saying that this other bear was the "same kind," by which I assume it means species, and was "full as large."

From these descriptions, it is obvious that this bear killed on May 5 was a big, old individual, whose strongest impression on the men was the difficulty of its dying. "Lights" are the lungs; the term is still in use in some commercial livestock circles. "Tushes" are tusks, presumably the prominent, almost fanglike canines that bears use for holding and tearing the meat of their prey. The bluntness of the claws, like the worn teeth, could be another sign that this was an old animal whose most effective tools were now giving out (it might also be that by "blunt" the men meant that the claws were not as sharply curved as the black bear's smaller claws, but I suspect the former interpretation is more likely). We also learn, from Ordway, that the fish they found in the bear was a catfish. Bears are most effective at catching fish in tight quarters, such as during spawning runs or when the fish are confined or stranded in a small stream or pool, but there is no telling what fishing skills this individual bear may have had.[8]

And there was Lewis, talking about strange testicles again. Some of his other observations in this passage are somewhat remote generalizations about grizzly bear life and diet (such as the comment on roots and fruit, which no one else had so far mentioned, and which weren't mentioned as being among the stomach contents of this animal, so early in the growing season), so it is possible that he did not examine this animal closely but only picked up specifics about it from the other men. In that case, he could conceivably have added the comment about testicles just to reinforce his earlier observation—but that seems doubtful in such a conscientious observer. If he did take a close look, then we must accept that there was a second bear on that stretch of the Missouri River with something wrong with its genitals. And if that was so, congenital deformation seems more likely all the time. Two bears with identical injuries of that sort seems too coincidental, while some kind of inherited problem seems slightly more probable. As little as we know about this particular grizzly bear population, I'm still reluctant to entertain even the remotest possibility that it had such a distinct anatomical trait of its own.

Thanks to Whitehouse and Ordway, we know that the party saw six bears this day, including the one they killed. The captains mention only the one, presumably because it was the most exciting, important, and easily discussed one.

On May 6, the day after this animal was taken, Lewis revealed an abrupt change in attitude among the men, who had been quite eager to meet more grizzly bears:

> saw a brown bear swim the river above us, he disappeared before we can get in reach of him; I find that the curiossity of our party is pretty well satisfyed with rispect to this anamal, the formidable appearance of the male bear killed on the 5th added to the difficulty with which they die when even shot through the vital parts, has staggered the resolu tion several of them, others however seem keen for action with the bear; I expect these gentlemen will give us some amusement shotly as they soon begin now to coppolate.

As interesting as his comments on the changed mood of the corps are, I am far more intrigued by his final remark. How did he know that the bears were about to enter their mating season? If he had observed a male bear mounting a female, or even if he'd witnessed the preliminary period during which the male often "courts" the female for days or even weeks waiting for her to be ready to mate, I would have expected him to have described these things, even if in some restrained, gentlemanly fashion. But he never gives an indication that he saw such activity. My only guess is that either he already knew the time of black bear mating and assumed that grizzly bears coincided in this, or, more likely, he learned it from his informants at Fort Mandan—in one of those unreported conversations about any number of subjects that I assume must have occurred during that long and often housebound winter.

He was right, though, about the mating season. As mentioned earlier, grizzly bears in the lower forty-eight states most often mate in May and

June (though there are isolated observations of mating behavior later in the summer).[9] As frequently as the corps were seeing bears, it is not unlikely that some of their sightings were of mated pairs, but the diarists either did not know what they were seeing in that respect (especially if they did not actually see them "coppolate") or were reluctant to describe it.

For all our questions and uncertainties about what Lewis and Clark described on May 5, there is no question that with the death of this bear we come to a crossroads in the life of a species. Altogether, for all their informality and the uncertainties they leave us with, this set of bear observations constitutes a significant, even momentous, historical document. In fact, in the more than three centuries that Euro-Americans have been dealing with grizzly bears, this May 5, 1805, bear must rank among the most important of all. It stands, informally but universally, as the basis for the original scientific description of the North American grizzly bear, *Ursus arctos*. It stands, just as informally and universally, as the beginning of our long and troubled attempts to come to terms with just what kind of creature the grizzly bear might be, and how we are to make it fit in our world.

In 1815, naturalist George Ord, whose work in describing wildlife species was notable enough that he has been called the father of North American zoology, assigned the scientific designation *Ursus horribilis* to the grizzly bear. He published this name, along with his descriptions of many other North American mammals, in the second edition of William Gutherie's two-volume *Geographical, Historical and Commercial Grammar; and present state of the Several Kingdoms of the World* (by the 1890s, only one copy of this edition was known to survive, but a small new edition of Ord's work was published in 1894 and is itself now a coveted rarity).[10]

It is generally agreed that Ord based his description in good part on Lewis and Clark's account of this May 5 bear, but he was clearly aware of at least some of the other bears the corps encountered. By the time Ord wrote his description, the first edition of the Lewis and Clark journals, or rather a narrative based on those journals, had been published. *The History of the Expedition under the Command of Captains Lewis and Clark* (1814) was put into shape for publication by editor Nicholas Biddle, a well-educated and determinedly enthusiastic admirer of the journals.[11] Though a fascinating and important historical document, it was not designed to do

George Ord, known as the father of American zoology, was the author of the original scientific description of the grizzly bear in 1815. This portrait was reproduced in an 1894 edition of his work on North American zoology.

full justice to the natural history discoveries of the explorers. And unlike the exhaustive and masterfully edited compilations of the journals completed by some later editors, Biddle's edition was quite limited. It dealt only with the accounts left by the captains themselves (Gass's volume based on his own journal had preceded it into print, essentially scooping the captains in the market[12]). The Biddle edition appeared in what we now would regard as a very small printing of about fourteen hundred copies, and did not sell well.[13]

In fact, as far as we know, Ord never even saw it. It has been suggested that he also may have had access to a grizzly bear hide brought back by Lewis and Clark, but we do know that Ord based his description primarily on H. M. Brackenridge's book *Views of Louisiana* (1814), which contained material derived from the Biddle edition of the Lewis and Clark journals.[14]

Based on that material in Brackenridge's book, Ord wrote his description. Throughout we can hear the sometimes distorted echoes of the corps's journals. Almost all of the first four paragraphs is a direct quotation from Brackenridge, and then Ord goes on to describe the May 5 bear and to offer his own summary of what Lewis and Clark reported about the species:

> *Grizzly Bear:* "This animal," says Mr. Brackenridge, "is the monarch of the country which he inhabits. The African lion, or the tiger of Bengal, are not more terrible or fierce. He is the enemy of man and literally thirsts for human blood. So far from shunning, he seldom fails to attack; and even to hunt him. The Indians make war upon these ferocious monsters, with the same ceremonies as they do upon a tribe of their own species; and, in the recital of their victories, the death of one of them gives the warrior greater renown than the scalp of a human enemy.
>
> " He possesses an amazing strength, and attacks without hesitation, and tears to pieces, the largest buffalo. The colour is usually such as the name indicates, though there are varieties, from black to silvery whiteness. The skins are highly valued for muffs and tippets; and will bring from twenty to fifty dollars each.

" This Bear is not usually seen lower than the Mandan villages. In the vicinity of the Roche Jaune, and of the Little Missouri, they are said to be most numerous. They do not wander much in the prairies, but are usually found in points of wood, in the neighborhood of large streams.

" In shape, he differs from the common Bear in being proportionately more long and lank. He does not climb trees, a circumstance which has enabled hunters, when attacked, to make their escape."

In the history of the expedition under the command of Lewis and Clark, we have much interesting information relating to this dreadfully ferocious animal. These enterprising travellers made many narrow escapes from the attacks of this monster, who in some instances was not brought to the ground until he had received seven or eight balls through his body. As a wonderful proof of the tenacity of life of this animal, one that was killed on the nineteenth of May, 1805, ran at his usual pace nearly a quarter of a mile, after having been *shot through the heart.*

The Grizzly Bear has long been known to naturalists; but the above travellers were the first to give us a particular account of this monarch of the American forests. One killed by them near the Porcupine river measured as follows:

	Feet	Inches
Length from nose to the extremity of the hind foot	8	7 1/2
Circumference near the fore legs	5	10 1/2
" of the neck	3	11
" of the middle of the fore leg	1	11
Length of the talons		4 3/8

His weight, on conjecture, was between five and six hundred pounds. But this was not the largest Bear that was killed by the party. They give an account of one which measured *nine* feet from the nose to the extremity of the tail;

and the talons of another were six and a quarter inches in length. It is said that this animal when full grown and fat will exceed a thousand pounds.[15]

There are two important legacies here. The less known is the scientific one. Ord formally described the species first. So, though a variety of others offered alternative names in the decades following his publication, and though as the nineteenth century wore on, the whole question of the proper speciation of the bears of North America became quite controversial, Ord's name stuck.[16]

But this original officially designated grizzly bear still lacked a "type specimen"—an actual carcass whose dimensions and features could be measured according to later scientific standards (which Ord's measurements did not satisfy) and thus provide a standard by which other specimens could be classified. This lack was rather boldly remedied more than a century later, by Clinton Hart Merriam, a distinguished biologist and one of the most prominent and forceful mammalian taxonomists of the late nineteenth and early twentieth centuries.

By Merriam's time, a bear's species was formally determined through a series of skull measurements. Lewis and Clark, and thus Ord, recorded none of these for any of the bears they examined, giving later investigators plenty of room to debate just exactly what animal or animals the corps might have encountered.

Merriam was what is now known a "splitter," someone who (as opposed to a "lumper") tended to make more and more species based on finer and finer distinctions between individual animals. In fact, Merriam was pretty much the nation's *leading* splitter, dividing an animal population into ever-subtler and more numerous species based on variations in skull measurements from one specimen to another. Virtually all of his splitting was undone by later taxonomists, and for good reason. By 1918 when he published his monograph, *Review of the Grizzly and Big Brown Bears of North America (Genus Ursus) with a Description of a New Genus, Vetularctos,* he had subdivided the continent's grizzly bears into eighty-six species, and he assumed there were more still to be discovered.[17] It took Merriam only a single bear skull to create a new species, and he energetically gathered the most comprehensive set of grizzly bear skulls ever collected, from all over North America, in his quest to fully define the grizzly and brown bears.

I have a deep and perhaps even overindulgent sympathy for the theories of previous generations of naturalists and biologists. They struggled heroically with the limitations of their knowledge and vision, just as we do today (however reluctant we are to admit it). Today's authorities would be both unwise and unkind to offhandedly fault these earlier investigators for their failure to understand things we now believe we know "for sure." But even I have to admit that it is almost impossible to read Merriam's defense of his system of bear classification without concluding that the man had an irrepressible goofy streak. It was literally possible, by Merriam's system, for three grizzly bear siblings from the same litter to be different enough for each to merit separate species designation. He genuinely believed that an area as small as Admiralty Island, Alaska, was occupied by five distinct and genetically exclusive (noninterbreeding) species of brown bears. He appears to have been a classic laboratory expert, operating almost completely independent of field observation and therefore aloof from the realities of ecology and population biology. His case makes no sense today, and it didn't make all that much more back then. As Theodore Roosevelt (himself a prominent "lumper" who once publicly debated Merriam on the question of creating so many minor species) once put it, "I may as well confess that I have certain conservative instincts which are jarred when an old familar friend is suddenly cut up into eleven brand new acquaintances."[18]

But Merriam was regarded as the leading light in this matter. And he did find a way to solve the problem of Ord's failure to provide the specifics needed to properly support the original species designation of Clark's May 5 bear. In his 1918 monograph, Merriam reported the discovery of a skull that would do the job:

Until recently the absence of authentic specimens from the neighborhood of the type locality, in connection with the presence of several species of grizzly in Montana, caused an embarrassing uncertainty as to which species was entitled to the name *horribilis*. But the slow accumulation of material during the long period in which I have been engaged in a study of the group made it possible to map the ranges of some of the species with some degree of confidence; and finally, through the generosity of Mr. and Mrs. E.S. Cameron, of Marsh, Montana, I have been presented with a splendid skull of an old male *horribilis* from the Breaks of the Missouri, about 100 miles north of Fort Miles, Montana (practically the type locality). This skull proves that the huge buffalo-killing grizzly of the Great Plains bordering the Missouri in eastern Montana and the Dakotas—the "White Bear" of Lewis and Clark—is really the species to which Ord in 1815 gave the name *Ursus horribilis*.[19]

To the extent that it might still matter (and it did matter to many biologists in Merriam's day), this more or less settled and confirmed Ord's rights to patrimony of the species, and seemed to please Merriam no end.

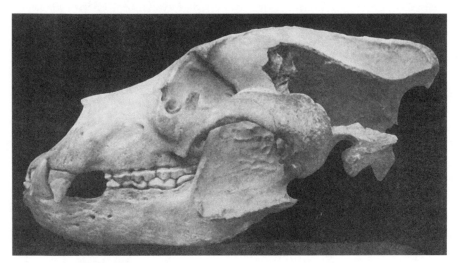

Skull of Ursus Horribilis Horribilis, *an old male "from the Breaks of the Missouri," eastern Montana, as pictured in Clinton Hart Merriam's 1918 monograph* Review of the Grizzly and Big Brown Bears of North America. *In identifying this skull and publishing its photograph, Merriam sought to settle the issue of precisely what "species" of bears was encountered by Lewis and Clark more than a century earlier. Merriam's redefinition of the grizzly bears of North America into dozens of separate species has since been completely undone.*

Today, now that taxonomists have cleared away the rubble of Merriam's species-designation binge, Ord's label remains attached to the surviving kin of that grand, aged, and long-suffering animal killed by Clark and Drouillard on May 5, 1805. The brown bear, worldwide, is designated *Ursus arctos*. Until the last few years, the taxonomy seemed pretty well settled on two subspecies in North America, *Ursus arctos middendorffi* (in Alaska) and *Ursus arctos horribilis*. The latter, still hanging on to Ord's label in its subspecific designation, lived everywhere else in the remaining North American range of the species. It was, and is, the bear of Lewis and Clark.

I say "until the last few years" because the modern biochemical revolution that has allowed us to trace an animal's genetic heritage to a previously unimagined extent reached the world of bear science some years ago, and the previous understanding of world brown bear population genetic lines has been largely overridden by this new work. In the past ten years, genetics researchers, with the wonderful new scientific tools now available, have questioned even the need for a subspecific designation of the giant brown bears of the Alaskan islands.[20]

The second part of George Ord's legacy is the reputation of the bear, a reputation that Ord did so much to establish, and on behalf of which he so enthusiastically invoked the journals of Lewis and Clark. How that reputation sprang from their journals, and to what extent the captains may have contributed to both the misunderstandings and the more accurate elements of the reputation, will concern us frequently as we follow their adventure with this "turrible looking animal."

CHAPTER FIVE

"I do not like the gentleman"

I am sure that I am not the only follower of the Lewis and Clark trail to be struck by the contrast between the sense of the momentous we derive from the diarists' descriptions of certain places and the modest impression those places sometimes make on us when we see them now.

I first saw the Milk River near its headwaters, along the Alberta-Montana border. Being somewhat familiar with its many historical associations, I was reflexively and suitably impressed with what I saw. So much history, it seemed, began here that at least for me this modest stream did have a feeling of the momentous about it. Farther east, where the river arced north into Alberta, I admired its slow, winding course through the remarkable geological, paleontological, archaeological, and historical treasurelands of Writing-On-Stone Provincial Park and again was drawn to both its beauty and its symbolic power (to say nothing of its possibilities as a great place to paddle a canoe).

But when I saw the Milk River as it concluded its long, meandering run across northern Montana and drained unceremoniously into the Missouri, I had an entirely different reaction. Perhaps partly because of those earlier impressions of the upper river, I was somehow almost disappointed, almost embarrassed—this is it? Like any number of other streams and places named by the captains as they traveled from Fort Mandan to the Great Falls of the Missouri, it seemed, well, smaller than I had anticipated. *Modest* was almost too generous a word.

But of course there was no one to be embarrassed on behalf of, unless it was myself for having an inadequate ability to adjust to the realities of a landscape. This was my problem, not the river's. The river was what it was, doing what it did. It was immune to my value judgments, and intellectually I understood its cultural and ecological significance. I have always appreciated the stark, arid, rutted sort of terrain it ran through near its mouth, so I knew it wasn't just a failure of aesthetics. What was wrong here?

Perhaps what I missed was something the river couldn't have provided anyway—I think I must have been hoping for some sort of fanfare. This is partly because I find rivers fascinating enough whether I know anything about their history or not. When a river finishes its long run, when it comes to an end the way countless rivers do all over the world, we should take more note. Something important is happening right in front of us, and we ignore it or take it for granted. And as far as I was concerned, places like the mouth of the Milk River were all the more important because they were discussed, and considered and had an effect on Lewis and Clark.

In part because of Lewis and Clark, the mouths of the Little Missouri, the Yellowstone, the Poplar, Wolf Creek, the Milk, and all the others—big and small, seasonal and permanent—in between them along the Missouri River are places of power in the finest sense of that tired and too-often commercialized word. However humble they might appear at first sight, to those of us who are vicariously exploring the West with the journals in hand, these places are important in the same way that the Cumberland Gap, or Walden Pond, or Lookout Mountain is important. We have done things on these landscapes, and like every human culture before us, we have accumulated memory, myth, and sentiment about them. We have attached and shaped our culture here. In some deep way we have made these places our own.

For Lewis and Clark, these passing river mouths were something like milestones and something like invitations. They were milestones because they were perhaps the foremost consistent landmarks in a new land, sometimes predicted and therefore anticipated, but rarely exactly as expected. They were invitations because they must have taunted the captains with the thought of their unexplored lengths and mysterious headwaters. Again and again, standing on some height of land and gazing up some long, beckoning drainage they had no time to ascend, the captains had to wonder: What kinds of country, inhabited by what people and animals and plants, sheltering what riches and wonders, lay that way? How often do the journals provide us opportunities to imagine Lewis or Clark standing on some riverside eminence to look with longing and curiosity off into hazy distances?

Albert Furtwangler has devoted an entire and very stimulating book, *Acts of Discovery* (1993), to the nature of the process of exploration as it was experienced by the corps.[1] I won't attempt to add to his ruminations in any deep way on this point. But I will say that for me the Milk River epitomizes the complicated quality of their exploration—their puzzling, exciting, frightening, and always instructive meetings-with-the-new that are so matter-of-factly and yet engagingly recorded in the journals. Not far downstream from where the Missouri now runs from the huge artificial reservoir known as Fort Peck Lake, the Milk River quietly reaches the north bank of the big river and demands of me a longer view. The river, like the grizzly bear and the magpie, the cutthroat trout and the swift fox, was an unknown that required knowing. That it could become known through mapping does not seem to make it qualitatively different from the grizzly bear, which only required a different kind of knowing, and which left the hasty explorers with just as many mysteries and questions as did a river known only to them in its last few miles.

I therefore enjoy a certain feeling of symmetry, in my own mind at least, in noticing that it was, coincidentally, in the neighborhood of the Milk River that it must have begun to dawn on the captains that grizzly bears were going to be harder to "map" than most things they encountered. Each new encounter, especially the violent ones, seemed to suggest startling individual variations in these animals. Each additional observation revived questions about what species were represented by these animals, and by their smaller and less fearsome black cousins downstream. Each new encounter, we can now see, exposed the captains to some small additional element of the complexity and mystery of the bear.

On May 11, three days after they passed the mouth of the Milk River and somewhere under the present east end of Fort Peck Lake, Lewis described their next grizzly bear encounter:

> About 5 P.M. my attention was struck by one of the Party runing at a distance towards us and making signs and

hollowing as if in distress, I ordered the perogues to put too, and waited untill he arrived; I now found that it was Bratton the man with the soar hand whom I had permitted to walk on shore, he arrived so much out of breath that it was several minutes before he could tell what had happened; at length he informed me that in the woody bottom on the Lard. side about 1 1/2 below us he had shot a brown bear which immediately turned on him and pursued him a considerable distance but he had wounded it so badly that it could not overtake him; I immediately turned out with seven of the party in quest of this monster, we at length found his trale and persued him about a mile by the blood through very thick brush of rosbushes and the large leafed willow; we finally found him concealed in some very thick brush and shot him through the skull with two balls; we proceeded dress him as soon as possible, we found him in good order; it was a monstrous beast, not quite so large as that we killed a few days past but in all other rispects much the same   the hair is remarkably long fine and rich tho' he appears parshally to have discharged his winter coat; we now found that Bratton had shot him through the center of the lungs, notwithstanding which he had pursued him near half a mile and had returned more than double that distance and with his tallons had prepared himself a bed in the earth of about 2 feet deep and five long and was perfectly alive when we found him which could not have been less than 2 hours after he received the wound; these bear being so hard to die reather intimedates us all; I must confess that I do not like the gentleman and had reather fight two Indians than one bear; there is no other chance to conquer them by a single shot but by shooting them through the brains, and this becomes difficult in consequence of two large muscles which cover the sides of the forehead and the sharp projection of the center of the frontal bone, which is also of a pretty good thickness. the flece and skin were as much as two men could possibly carry. by the time we returned the sun had set and I determined to remain here all night, and directed the cooks to render the bear's oil and put it in the kegs which was done. there was about eight gallons of it.

The other diarists added little to this fulsome description, though Gass and Whitehouse both said it was about the same size as the May 5 bear, and Whitehouse added that it was "fat and good meat." Already, only a few dead grizzly bears into the trip, we can't avoid noticing a consistency in the corps's grizzly bear encounters, which in some important respects just continue the pattern of their black bear encounters. Bears were valuable for their oil, meat, and skins, and they were also exciting to hunt. Throughout the journey, any bear that came within range was probably going to be fired upon. In time, the discretion of the riflemen was heightened about when shooting was wise, but there never seems to have been any deviation from the idea that any bear that can be killed should be killed.

It is important to keep in mind that the corps differed from some later generations in their reasons for killing grizzly bears. By the late nineteenth century, grizzly bears were routinely shot (trapped, poisoned, snared, blown up, deadfall-crushed, set-gunned) because they were not wanted. They competed with hunters for game, they killed livestock, and sometimes they even posed a threat to human safety. They were in the way; they had to go. But bear killing by the corps was usually not that involved. Troublesome bears were killed, especially at the Great Falls of the Missouri, but usually the killing was not because the men had anything against the bears; they just needed the resources that the bears carried in their bodies, and if any additional incentive for shooting was needed, it was provided by the thrill of the chase.

Of course the effect was more or less the same—a lot of dead and wounded bears. Corps members may not have succumbed to the later sentiment that the only good bear is a dead bear, but for their immediate and pressing purposes, a dead bear was certainly a better bear.

This May 11 episode was the second time that Lewis remarked that a grizzly bear could not catch a man because it had been wounded, which suggests that he understood that a healthy grizzly bear could run much faster than a man. Later it becomes clear that he may not have understood just how fast a bear could move when in heated pursuit, but at least his sense of scale was already correct, though we do not learn where he learned this bit of lore. Perhaps he was recalling the two bears that Clark had described on April 14 as racing over a hill with "Supprising ease & verlocity."

We are also given a little more information about what makes these bears so hard to kill. The sturdy skull is further armored by the massive jaw muscles, almost like thick vertical straps on the sides of the head. This extraordinary power is essential for an animal that must be able to crush or grind up such a wide variety of plant and animal foods.[2]

In his journal on May 12, Lewis announced, perhaps as much to himself as to posterity, his new position on dealing with grizzly bears:

> . . . in these excurtions I most generally went alone armed with my rifle and espontoon; thus equiped I feel myself more than an equal match for a brown bear provided I get him in open woods or near the water, but feel myself a little diffident with respect to an attack on the open plains, I have therefore come to a resolution to act on the defencive only, should I meet these gentlemen in the open country.

The espontoon was described by John Bakeless in his one-volume edition of *The Journals of Lewis and Clark* (1964). He said the "espontoon, or spontoon, a kind of halberd—spear and ax combined—was regulation equipment for junior officers and, like the ceremonial saber, occasionally turned out to be a rather practical weapon."[3] It would have been a practical thing to carry for several reasons, most of them the same as the advantages of having a walking stick. It would provide any walker with additional stability on uneven ground, and in a country so generously populated with rattlesnakes and other hazards it must have been nice to have something long and sharp to poke into suspicious grass or brush before venturing there yourself. It would also have provided a steady monopod base from which to fire a rifle. Apparently Lewis figured that under some circumstances (those with either trees or water as an escape route), the espontoon would serve as backup if his rifle did not do enough damage.

A famous photograph of a Yellowstone grizzly bear, taken in the 1960s before park dumps were closed, captures the animal's comprehensively intimidating presence, from the broad shoulders and massive skull to the shining claws. NATIONAL PARK SERVICE PHOTOGRAPH

The difficulty the riflemen had doing damage to bears would be made clear again and again. On May 13, Clark said that "one man Gibson wounded a verry large *brown bear,* too late this evening to prosue him," and on May 14 Lewis told of another exciting adventure in grizzly hunting, this one near the mouth of Snow Creek, which now flows into the south side of Fort Peck Lake not far west of Hell Creek State Park (journal editor Moulton said that they named Snow Creek "Brown Bear Defeated Creek," but the name did not stick[4]):

> In the evening the men in two of the rear canoes discovered a large brown bear lying in the open grounds about 300 paces from the river, and six of them went out to attack him, all good hunters; they took advantage of a small eminence which concealed them and got within 40 paces of him unperceived, two of them reserved their fire as had been previously conscerted, the four others fired nearly at the same time and put each his bullet through him, two of the balls passed through the bulk of both lobes of his lungs, in an instant this monster ran at them with open mouth, the two who had reserved their fires discharged their pieces at him as he came towards them, boath of them struck him, one only slightly and the other fortunately broke his shoulder, this however only retarded his motion for a moment, the men unable to reload their guns took to flight, the bear pursued and had very nearly overtaken them before they reached the river; two of the party betook themselves to a canoe and the others seperated an concealed themselves among the willows, reloaded their pieces, each discharged his piece at him as they had an opportunity. they struck him several times again but the guns served only to direct the bear to them, in this manner he pursued two of them seperately so close that they were obliged to throw aside their guns and pouches and throw themselves into the river altho' the bank was nearly twenty feet perpendicular; so enraged was this anamal that he plunged into the river only a few feet behind the second man he had compelled take refuge in the water, when one of those who still remained on shore shot him through the head and finally killed him; they then took him on shore and butched him when they found

eight balls had passed through him in different directions; the bear being old the flesh was indifferent, they therefore took only the skin and fleece, the latter made us several gallons of oil; it was after the sun had set before these men come up with us. . . .

Whitehouse added some intriguing details, saying that "his feet was nine Inches across the ball, and 13 in length, nearly of the Same discription of the first we killed only much larger his nales was Seven Inches long."

This does sound like a very large bear; all these measurements are well above average. Huge grizzly bear claws are pretty common in popular writing about bears, but in his authoritative book *Bear Attacks: Their Causes and Avoidance* (1985), biologist Steve Herrero said that "a mature grizzly's claws are longer, 1.5 to 3.9 inches, than are its hind claws, 0.6 to 1.8 inches."[5] Herrero measured the claws on a straight line from the upper side of the base to the tip, but even if Whitehouse was describing a claw that had been measured along its outside curve, it was a very big claw and, presumably, a very big bear.

Whitehouse differed slightly with Lewis on one point, saying that nine rather than eight rifle balls were shot into the bear before it died. Either number must have been as impressive—or as alarming—to the men as the ten shots it took to kill the May 5 bear.

Lewis and Clark made their trip at the dawn of an era of incredibly swift evolution in firearms. They were just a little too early to reap the benefits of technological advances that within half a century would place in the hands of mountain men, explorers, and settlers weapons powerful enough to kill both grizzly bears and bison with far less risk of the fire-and-flee theatrics so often performed by the corps.

The corps had weapons that were sufficient for most purposes known to Americans of the time.[6] The U.S. Flintlock, Model 1795, a smooth-bore musket, was regarded as adequate for medium-sized game, perhaps even elk, up to fifty yards, and lethal if progressively less accurate beyond that up past one hundred yards. Reloading took as much thirty often very inconvenient seconds, though some experts could probably accomplish it much faster than that. Some of the corps's men used this musket, but it was not the favorite. Toussaint Charbonneau, being a civilian and carrying his personal weapon (as some of the other men may have), carried a "fuzee." The fusil, usually British made, was a light and therefore more portable musket already favored by trappers and Indians on the upper Missouri when Lewis and Clark reached the area. This was the trade gun referred to by Lewis as "indifferent" for its relative ineffectiveness against large, dangerous game, but in skillful hands it was a trustworthy and effective weapon. Just not for grizzly bears.

The weapon of choice for the captains, and their best hope against grizzly bears, was the rifle. It is believed that some of the men probably carried the "Kentucky Long Rifles" of such lasting legend; certainly the captains would have preferred these more accurate weapons for at least some purposes.[7] Historian Carl P. Russell, in his comprehensive study of mountain man technology, *Firearms, Traps, and Tools of the Mountain Men* (1967), pointed out that the Lewis and Clark Expedition was the first test of the U.S. rifle, Model 1803; at least fifteen of these brand-new rifles (in fact, they were probably prototypes) were requisitioned for the corps, and they seem to have passed this long and most demanding of field tests with high marks. Known as "short rifles," their barrels were likely to be about thirty-four inches long, compared to the thirty-six- to forty-eight-inch barrels of the "long rifles" (barrel length was most important for improving aim rather than in otherwise affecting the killing power of the bullet). Russell concluded that for all the problems they had knocking down grizzly bears with the short rifles, the men had the best weapon of the day:

> The *Journals* reveal that this rifle gave a good account of itself throughout the expedition. Such breakage as occurred was always repairable with the extra parts and special tools that the farseeing Lewis had procured. In this connection, it is to be noted that the wilderness gunsmithing of John Shields was nothing less than phenomenal, considering the adversities with which he contended.[8]

There is no overstating either Lewis's or Shields's contribution in this regard. Not only did Lewis anticipate the needs for extra parts and tools, but he also devised lead containers for the precious powder, so that throughout the long journey the powder stayed dry under the worst of circumstances and it was contained in the material from which shot would be made as needed.

The problem, of course, was that the rifles just weren't up to the task of killing grizzly bears. The great western folklorist, adventure writer, and art historian Harold McCracken compared the corps's weapon to its modern equivalent:

> Most of these early "pea rifles" used bullets that ran about seventy to the pound, with the total amount of lead and powder being the equivalent to less than that contained in the early models of a 33-30 caliber cartridge. The average sportsman of today would consider it little short of personal suicide to tackle a grizzly with the most *modern* type of *repeating* rifle of this caliber— [9]

This is exactly what the corps's hunters did.

We are left, then, with a distinct impression of men doing a job with the wrong tools. It could be argued that the tools were entirely successful. After all, they worked well enough so that for all the bears they killed, the bears didn't kill any of them. But for safety purposes, the bears were so "hard to die" (to use Lewis's term) that the light rifles left little or no margin of error. It amazes me that no one got killed or even seriously mauled.

If I had been a member of that expedition, I would have jumped at the chance to have a more powerful weapon. And yet I suspect that historian Russell was right when, after describing the rapid advances in firearms that occurred in the few decades following Lewis and Clark's trip, he concluded that "Many a mountain man lived to witness these phenomenal improvements and to mourn the quick devastation of the living things in his old haunts brought about by the better guns of his successors." [10]

CHAPTER SIX

Seeking and Sorting Bears

Modern grizzly and brown bear appreciation—that is, most of the activities by which we reveal what we think and feel about the bear—has elements almost completely lacking from the corps's journals. The differences have arisen from the long, violent, and finally more conciliatory history of bear–human relationships during the two centuries since Lewis and Clark were shooting, running, skinning, and eating their way through the Missouri River grizzly bear population.

Through most of the nineteenth century, and in many rural areas well into the twentieth century, the grizzly bear was widely perceived as vermin of the worst sort.[1] It was "good for nothing," which was often enough of a value judgment to cause something to be destroyed, but unlike many "useless" things, the grizzly bear was also unquestionably "bad" in several ways. As mentioned in the previous chapter, grizzly bears sometimes turned stock killers and human killers. I am sure that in my own neighborhood in northwestern Wyoming and southwestern Montana there are still a fair number of people who would just as soon shoot a grizzly bear on sight, either because they perceive it as a threat to some commercial interest of theirs, or because they resent that it competes with them for game animals, or because they believe it is a dangerous animal, or because they think they are doing God's work by killing predators, or because they believe they are honoring some important tradition in their family or culture by doing so, or out of resentment toward the weight and presence of federal and state protection that the bear now enjoys, or just because they feel like it right then. Much more is going on here than might at first appear evident when some man illegally shoots a bear. The shooter and all the others who agree or disagree with him to varying degrees, clear across the opinion spectrum, are products of a sort of perceptual revolution. And much of what is going on in this disagreement would be unfamiliar, perhaps even surprising, to Lewis and Clark and their crew of eminently pragmatic explorers.

In other books and articles, I have pointed out the considerable irony of modern grizzly bear conservation.[2] It starts like this. After Lewis and Clark had long since returned to the East, during the period when the native people, wildlife, and wild country of western North America were being conquered and settled by Euro-Americans—let's say, roughly 1840 to 1900—the bear was a prominent symbol of evil wilderness. Killing predators was part of the necessary job of civilizing the country (a number of writers have pointed out a dismaying parallel—that American Indians and wild predators were subjected to very similar attitudes and treatments).

How that all changed has been documented and described countless times. Thoreau, Muir, Roosevelt, Leopold—just these four names signify a rapidly changing view of our relationship with nature and our feelings about the place of wild country and wild animals in a responsible nation. Hans Huth's *Nature and the American* (1957), Roderick Nash's *Wilderness and the American Mind* (1967), Keith Thomas's *Man and the Natural World* (1987), and Max Oelschager's *The Idea of Wilderness* (1991) are just a few of the many scholarly considerations of how our relationship to nature and wildness has evolved over the centuries.[3]

By all accounts it is an evolution that has accelerated since Lewis and Clark, with a significant effect on grizzly bears. In less than two hundred years, the grizzly has gone from being the symbol of everything in nature that is evil and in need of destruction, to being the opposite. Today, the grizzly bear, at least in the Rocky Mountain West's energetic conservation community, has become one of the foremost symbols of all that is good and deserving of our protection and affection in wild country. In the past few years it may have been displaced as the most publicly appealing such symbol by the wolf, which at least for the moment has proven even more charismatic. (I do not say this cynically; there is no more effective way of making the point than saying that the wolf is the newest and most powerful "poster child" of wild country in this region.) But the grizzly bear is firmly ensconced in our minds as a precious part of what we now think of as our wild heritage.

The result of this swift overhaul of the grizzly bear's public image is evident in many places—in art galleries overflowing with portraits, sculpture, and every other form of fine and commercial iconography that can be applied to wildlife; in local businesses beyond counting that somehow incorporate the bear into their name or trademark; in high school and college athletic teams known as bears, grizzlies, or bruins; and in an overwhelming flood of books, articles, and calendars that keep the bear in front of us and drive it ever more firmly into our consciousness and our consciences. New bear books appear to be published at an even faster rate than new Lewis and Clark books.

But nowhere is the true, personal impact of this new public image more evident than out there in bear country, especially in those special places where people can actually stand and watch real, live, wild bears doing about the same things that wild bears were doing when Lewis and Clark saw them.

Most grizzly bear watching is conducted on public lands, especially those whose ecological integrity is protected closely enough that big predators are not only tolerated but welcomed. I've been able to participate in this relatively recent form of wilderness recreation in four such places: Yellowstone, Glacier, Denali, and Katmai National Parks, all with their own unique biological communities, all with their own unique approaches to facilitating the visual experience of grizzly bears. In some places, the bears are up close. In others, the whole exercise is conducted with high-powered optics, and appreciation involves understanding and enjoying the bears as part of the vast landscape you watch them roam. And though I have yet to tire of the marvels of watching the bears and find wonder in each new sighting, I have also had time to consider the other people who are out there watching, too.

The grizzly or brown bear is now rare enough, and celebrated enough, that for many nature lovers a sighting of one bear is a significant life event. A trip specifically to see bears may be longer planned, and involve more miles, than the Lewis and Clark Expedition. And for all the heightened speed and convenience of the miles, the trip is likely to be just as memorable in the life of the traveler.

Once in sight, the bears are objects of great wonder. They are described as magnificent, beautiful, breathtaking, gorgeous, lovely, grand—the descriptors are nearly rapturous and overwhelmingly positive even if they contain hints of fear (the modern bear experience usually has little room for fear because of the ways in which the bears and the bear-watchers are managed). Each new bear is likewise momentous, adding a whole new dimension to the watcher's experience of this great and complicated symbolic beast.

Besides, out of what Lewis and Clark would no doubt have regarded as a somewhat sterile and remote experience—bears watched from safety, and in no way interacted with—still come cures for that burning need so many of us feel, for our very own bear story. Unlike the bear stories that were common currency in many national parks only half a century ago, in which tourists had colorful and often slightly risky encounters with black bears along roadsides, in campgrounds, or even at garbage dumps, these new bear stories tend to be almost exclusively about the bears. During those often long intervals when no animals are visible, and the people stand around waiting for the show to resume, I've heard these bear stories countless times, all variations on the same theme: what the wild bear—*my* wild bear—did while I watched. "She was just grazing, someone said it was spring beauty, but I don't know, and then all at once here came this big old male out of the trees, and I heard her make this sort of whoofy, barky noise at her yearling, everybody said it was a yearling but I heard from the ranger that it might be small two-year-old, and it took off in the other direction and she slowly kind of backed away from the big male, and he acted like he didn't even know she was there but of course he did, and then. . . ." on and on and on, taking this rare privileged observation into our hearts and working it over with memory and questions to get all we can from it.

Think of it—all this attention, all this deliberation and interpretation, for a bear that Lewis and Clark might have only noted as one of four they saw that day, or that, if they did watch it for a few minutes, they would have concluded wasn't doing anything worth telling about.

Yet as exciting and fulfilling as it might be for the casual tourist, it can be a far more elevated and defined memory for the modern student of bears, the naturalist who is observing them or studying them with more depth. Without a promise of or even interest in any specific reward, much less the imponderable incentive of having been personally directed by the president of the United States to write down lots of notes about everything we see, we may accumulate pages of notes about a single bear on a single day. We note how often he fed, how long he napped, where he moved after the nap, how he jumped back when he was suddenly startled by a noise from a nearby stand of trees (a noise that we, two miles away looking through a spotting scope, couldn't hear). Some serious professional bear observers have developed handheld computer systems, coded shorthand for many of the more common log entries, that allow them to document every specific move the bear makes. Later they can compile time-motion studies of elegant precision.[4]

Think of this, too—all this attention for a bear that Lewis and Clark might only have noted as one they could see at a distance but couldn't get a good shot at, so they hurried on.

None of this is to slight the corps for their lack of interest in what we now consider priceless details, or for their apparent insensitivities to the beauty and magic we now find in a wild bear. They were not us, and we are certainly not them, however much we may enjoy playing at being them when we wander into some wilderness that is new to us and imagine ourselves making discoveries that are anything other than personal.

When it comes to bears, the lesson of our differences from Lewis and Clark is one of scale and scope. For all practical, biological purposes, they saw the same bears we see today, but we must not forget how differently they perceived and imagined them. Their bears were so common that they were a nuisance, sometimes even a hazard. Our bears are so rare that any risk they may represent to humans is seen as sufficient cause for us to change *our* behavior and *our* use of their habitat in order to avoid troubling *them*.

Their bears inspired awe, fear, curiosity, and perhaps even amazement, but their bears did not stand for more than a small part of what our bears do. Their bears were specimens; our bears are symbols.

Their bears were puzzling for the peculiar complications of deciding what species they were. Our bears are intriguing for all we know about them, from their unique regional cultural histories right down to DNA portraits of each population and their relatives around the globe.

Their bears were primarily interesting for what practical resources they might provide the corps or for what risks encountering them might entail. Our bears are primarily interesting for what they might do for the individual soul and the collective spirit.

The more I study what the corps's diarists wrote about bears, and the more I think on these differences in our perspectives, the more it impresses me that we can get anything out of their journals at all, and the more I am convinced that most of what we get isn't quite what they intended when they wrote.

There are times, as several Lewis and Clark scholars have noted, when the corps's diarists (Lewis more than Clark) admitted that they were experiencing emotional or aesthetic reactions. Most of these occasions seemed to involve grand scenery or other natural spectacles, but it is easy enough to read between the lines and imagine how often the men were moved by what they saw or did. The elation or satisfaction of reaching the Great Falls of the Missouri or the Pacific, of turning for home, of escaping tedium or danger or shortage of food, of finding accessible women, of an exceptionally good feast after too long on grim rations, of a happy fiddle tune—these and many other emotional responses are obvious and regularly evident, even if the diarists rarely came right out and described their feelings.

But the scope of emotion is much narrower in their descriptions of bears, and the emotions they did feel are left even more to our imaginations. Only those bears with which they had some frightening or otherwise unusual encounter tended to get more than a few words. Most of the time the observing and killing of bears went well, and was noted only in passing. After the first few bears, the ones whose descriptions were obliged by the captains' mandate to study and note what they saw, the accounts got brief except when someone had a mishap or misadventure and generated a good bear story. The modern bear story—with all its fear and violence, humor and humanity—emerged as a full-blown literary form in this country in the decades well before the Civil War.[5] But for all the businesslike tone of the corps's diarists, we can see the glimmerings of the form now and then in their clipped little recountings of a few episodes, usually those in which things got good and scary.

Most of the time they didn't get scary at all, or, if they did, not scary enough to report on. On May 15, Lewis reported that they "saw three bear one of which they wounded." Two days later, he said that "the party with me killed a female brown bear, she was but meagre, and appeared to have suckled young very recently." This could have been a female that had for one reason or other just lost her cub or cubs (big males will kill young bears if they catch them unprotected, as will other predators), or who had just dismissed them in order to mate again. Of this same bear, Ordway (May 17) said, "towards evening I and Several more of the party killed a femail brown bear, the first female we killed."

On May 19, they received another course in grizzly bear stamina when Clark reported that "I walked on Shore with two men we killed a white or grey bear; not withstanding that it was Shot through the heart it ran at it's usial pace near a quarter of a mile before it fell." From the context of previous and later comments on how they hunted bears, I assume that the bullet through the bear's heart was not the only one it was carrying when it ran. From the context of Clark's statement, I also surmise that the bear ran away from the hunters when shot. If it had run toward them for a quarter mile it must have either been more than a quarter mile from them when shot, which seems unlikely considering the limited range of their rifles, or been less than a quarter mile from them and run right past them, which seems even less likely (surely Clark would have noted such a thing). So in this case, a wounded bear did not attack its attackers but fled. Ordway added that it was "a young brown bear, on the S. Shore." Whitehouse elaborated further, that "about 10 oClock we killed a Small female brown bear on S. S. we took on board the meat & Skin and proceeded on." It was their second female, then.

On May 22, now upstream of the mouth of the Musselshell River, Whitehouse reported that "we wounded a brown bear in the River," but the animal escaped. Later in the day, he said that "towards evening Some of the hunters killed a large brown bear. we Saved the Skin & greese." Contrast Whitehouse's report with Lewis's:

> We encamped earlyer this evening than usual in order ren-
> der the oil of a bear which we killed. I do not believe that
> the Black bear common to the lower part of this river and
> the Atlantic States, exists in this quarter; we have seen nei-
> ther one of them nor their tracks which would be easily dis-
> tinguished by it's shortness of tallons when compared with

the brown grizly or white bear. I believe that it is the same species or family of bears which assumes all those colours at different ages and seasons of the year.

Lewis did not mention the grizzly bear that got away, the one they wounded in the morning. Neither did Clark, Ordway, or Gass. But Lewis also continued his intermittent deliberations on the species issue, tentatively concluding that the black bear didn't live here at all (probably too broad a generalization, considering how versatile and adaptable black bears are), and that the various bigger bears, which we now know were all grizzly bears and which he continued to list under multiple names or colors in his uncertainty, were in fact all representatives of one species. In his closing sentence, he appears to be suggesting that the colors of the bear might change as it aged and as it passed through the seasons of the year. The former contention, that a single bear might change color over the course of its life, is to some extent true, especially in particulars such as the pale "collar" that quite a few grizzly bear cubs have but lose by the time they are adults. The latter contention I assume to refer to such well-known factors as the bleaching or fading of the coat in the summer sun. Many large mammals experience this to some extent or other; the magnitude of the change is often most evident when they are shedding their old winter coat and the underlying new coat is exposed in darker contrast. If, on the other hand, Lewis was proposing that different colors consistently represented different ages in the lives of all bears, then he was wrong. But I doubt that he meant that.

On May 23, they lost a bear. Lewis reported, "We killed a large fat brown bear which took the water after being wounded and was carried under some driftwood where he sunk and we were unable to get him. Saw but few buffaloe today, but a great number of Elk, deer, some antelopes and 5 bear." Were I attempting to compile as accurate as possible tally of how many bears they observed, I would have to assume that the bear that sank was among the five total bears that they "saw" this day, just to be on the conservative side. But I think it entirely possible that the total of five that were only seen could exclude the one that they killed.

On May 25, while discussing the habits of the bighorn sheep that so fascinated many early western travelers, Lewis said that "the places they gerally celect to lodg is the cranies or cevices of the rocks in the faces of inacessable precepices, where the wolf nor bear can reach them." His correct assumption that bears would prey on the sheep was apparently a matter of intuition on his part. He never reported having seen such pursuit or predation.

On May 28, Lewis said, "One of the party saw a very large bear today but being some distance from the river and no timber to conceal him he did not think proper to fire on him." On May 29, the day they passed the mouth of the Judith River, Lewis described at considerable length a recently used buffalo-jump site, where Indians had driven a herd of bison over a cliff to their deaths. Lewis complained that the leftover remains of more than one hundred bison "created a most horrid stench." He said that the corps "saw a great many wolves in the neighborhood of these mangled carcasses." Again, however, Whitehouse seemed to provide details missed or neglected by the others:

> we passed high Steep clifts of rocks on the N. S. where the natives had lately drove a gang of buffaloe off from the plains. they fell So far on the uneven Stone below that it killed them dead. they took what meat they wanted, & now the wolves & bears are feasting on the remains, which causes a horrid Smell. Capt. Clark killed a wolf with a Sphere near that place. we Saw Several brown bear on the mountains on the S. Side.

Whitehouse added bears to the "Gangs" of scavengers that he saw at the buffalo jump and seemed also to indicate that several other grizzly bears were seen along the route that day. Editor Moulton explained that by "Sphere" Whitehouse meant Clark's espontoon. (Thwaites suggested that he meant "spear.")

Incidentally, buffalo jumps figure in a minor way in modern bear conservation debates. The grizzly bear ecology study conducted by John and Frank Craighead in Yellowstone National Park in the 1960s resulted in a still-simmering controversy over how best to manage the bears. There were a number of points of contention, but one of the most interesting involved the park's long-used garbage dumps, where grizzly bears gathered in great numbers for the easy feeding.[6] For many years after the park service closed the last Yellowstone dump, in 1970, the Craigheads argued that the closure was a mistake because the dumps concentrated the bears away from people during the busiest tourist season. Whether this was a sound assumption was also debated, but out of the debate grew the Craighead idea of an "ecocenter," a place of unusually rich opportunities that tended to concentrate bears. Salmon streams are perhaps the most famous modern ecocenters for bears, but anyplace where food is sufficiently abundant to cause a considerable aggregation of bears meets the Craighead definition for the term. In *The Grizzly Bears of the Yellowstone Ecosystem* (1995), John Craighead and his colleagues argued that having garbage dumps in Yellowstone had a certain ecological legitimacy because they were ecocenters similar to those found at buffalo-jump sites, where bears also found an easy bonanza of leftovers.[7] The argument wasn't entirely convincing (for one thing, buffalo jump sites did not provide the kind of consistent quantities of food, either through a summer season or from year to year, that a modern garbage dump does).[8] But it does remind us of a potentially important way in which grizzly bears and humans were interrelated in Lewis and Clark's America.

On May 31, Whitehouse was the only person to report that "we Saw a brown bear on the N. S. Some of the hunters went out in order to kill it." But he did not tell us whether or not they succeeded.

On June 2, Lewis said that he

> walked on shore most of the day with some of the hunters for that purpose and killed 6 Elk 2 buffale 2 Mule deer and a bear. these anamals were all in good order we therefore took as much of the meat as our canoes and perogues could conveniently carry. the bear was very near catching Drewyer; it also pursued Charbono who fired his gun in the air as he ran but fortunately eluded the vigilence of the bear by secreting himself very securely in the bushes until Drewyer finally killed it by a shot in the head; the shot indeed that will conquer the farocity of those tremendious anamals.—

On June 4, while the captains struggled with the critical decision over whether to follow what we now call the Marias River or to continue up what we now know to be the Missouri, Clark said that "at the river near our camp we Saw two white Bear, one of them was nearly catching Jospeh Fields who could not fire, as his gun was wet   the bear was So near that it Struck his foot, and we were not in a Situation to give him assistance, a Clift of rocks Seperated us   the bear got allarmed at our Shot & yells & took the river.—" This time it was Gass who fleshed out the story:

> In the evening we went towards the river to encamp, where one of the men having got down to a small point of woods on the bank, before the rest of the party, was attacked by a huge he-bear, and his gun missed fire. We were about 200 yards from him, but the bank there was so steep we could not get down to his assistance; we, however, fired at the animal from the place where we stood and he went off without injuring the man.

Gass did not give us the man's name, but he clarified the topography, the distance, and the tactic used by the corps to drive the bear away from their threatened comrade. Whitehouse, catching up on this episode in his June 6 journal entry, added that the attacking bear was an "old hea bear."

On June 5, while scouting up the Missouri to determine if it really was the Missouri, Clark reported that ". . . about the time we were Setting out *three* white bear approached our Camp   we killed the three & eate part of one & Set out." Later that same day he said, "I Saw great numbers of Elk & white tale deer, Some beaver, antelope mule deer & wolves & one bear on this little river."

On June 10, as they prepared to head up the river that they had correctly decided was the Missouri, Lewis said that they cached (buried in a pit, in this case) many items, including "3 brown bear skins." On June 12, the day before Lewis reached the Great Falls of the Missouri, the party "met with two large bear, and killed them boath at the first fire, a circumstance which I beleive has never happend with the party in killing the brown bear before. we dressed the bear, breakfasted on a part of one of them and hung the meat and skins on the trees out of reach of the wolves." I think it most likely that he does not mean it took only one shot to kill each bear, but that the first fusillade of firing from several men killed them both, each bear presumably getting multiple wounds.

Later the same day, near their camp, he saw "a great number of tracks of the brown bear; these fellows leave a formidable impression in the mud or sand I measured one this evening which was eleven inches long exclusive of the tallons and seven and 1/4 in width."

And on June 13, he continued his ruminations on the species question, and the relative distribution of the black and grizzly bears:

> I am induced to believe that the Brown, the white and the Grizly bear of this country are the same species only differing in colour from age or more probably from the same natural cause that many other anamals of the same family differ in colour. one of those which we killed yesterday was of a creemcoloured white while the other in company with it was of the common bey or rdish brown, which seems to be the most usual colour of them. the white one appeared from it's tallons and teath to be the youngest; it was smaller than the other, and although a monstrous beast we supposed that it had not yet attained it's growth and that it was a little upwards of two years old.   the young cubs which we have killed have always been of a brownish white, but none of them as white as that we killed yesterday. one other that we killed sometime since which I mentioned sunk under some driftwood and was lost, had a white strip or list of about eleven inches wide entirely around his body just behind the shoalders, and was much darker than these bear usually are. the grizly bear we have never yet seen. I have seen their tallons in possession of the Indians and from their form I am perswaded if there is any difference between this species and the brown or white bear it is very inconsiderable. There is no such anamal as a black bear in this open country or of that species generally denominated the black bear.

Here, he seems to be toying with the idea that color is related to age, but he can't quite make a direct correlation based on his observations so far. The lighter band that encircles some grizzly bears immediately behind the front legs had now come to his notice. He is still waiting to see something that meets his personal definition of a grizzly bear, though he realizes that it may just amount to a color phase of the species he has been observing since April. He is still puzzled over these bears and their speciation, but his confidence seems to be growing that this question is sorting itself out in a very simple way—there is one species of big bear, whether it is called brown, yellow, white, grizzly, grey, or some combination of terms. He is still not sure, but he is on the right track.

CHAPTER SEVEN

Courage

On June 14, 1805, Lewis spent most of the day alone, reconnoitering the Great Falls and a possible portage route. It was painfully evident that the portage was going to be a lot longer and more involved than his Hidatsa informants had suggested back at Fort Mandan the previous winter. With so much on his mind, perhaps his carelessness in the following bear episode is more understandable. He was approaching what he called the Medicine River, which we now know as the Sun River. It flows into the Missouri immediately north of the Tenth Avenue Bridge on the west side of Great Falls, Montana. This grizzly bear encounter occurred in what is now West Bank Park, a long narrow band of lawns and picnic areas the city maintains along the west side of the river. A small interpretive site commemorates the encounter.

If you have been to Great Falls and visited this pleasant park, you might enjoy imagining the malls, fast-food places, and other businesses and suburban sprawl to the west evaporating, and those same low, rolling slopes covered instead by a scattered and dusty herd of bison.

Or maybe you wouldn't. I wonder which scene Lewis, so self-consciously leading the nation into the West, would prefer?

> I decended the hill and directed my course to the bend of the Missouri near which there was a herd of at least a thousand buffaloe; here I thought it would be well to kill a buffaloe and leave him untill my return from the river and if I then found that I had not time to get back to camp this evening to remain all night here there being a few sticks of drift wood lying along the shore which would answer for my

fire, and a few sattering cottonwood trees a few hundred yards below which would afford me at least a semblance of a shelter. under this impression I scelected a fat buffaloe and shot him very well, through the lungs; while I was gazeing attentively on the poor anamal discharging blood in streams from his mouth and nostrils, expecting him to fall every instant, and having entirely forgotten to reload my rifle, a large white, or reather brown bear, had perceived and crept on me within 20 steps before I discovered him; in the first moment I drew up my gun to shoot, but at the same instant recolected that she was not loaded and that he was too near for me to hope to perform this opperation before he reached me, as he was then briskly advancing on me; it was an open level plain, not a bush within miles nor a tree within less than three hundred yards of me; the river bank was sloping and not more than three feet above the level of the water; in short there was no place by means of which I could conceal myself from this monster untill I could charge my rifle; in this situation I thought of retreating in a brisk walk as fast as he was advancing untill I could reach a tree about 300 yards below me, but I had no sooner terned myself about but he pitched at me, open mouthed and full speed, I ran about 80 yards and found that he gained on me fast, I then run into the water   the idea struk me to get into the water to such a debth that I could stand and he would be obliged to swim, and that I could in that situation defend myself with my espontoon; accordingly I ran haistily into the water about waist deep, and faced about and presented the point of my espontoon, at this instant he arrived at the edge of the water within about 20 feet of me; the moment I put myself in this attitude of defence he sudonly wheeled about as if frightened, declined the combat on such unequal grounds, and retreated with quite as great precipitation as he had just before pursued me. as soon as I saw him run of in that man- ner I returned to the shore and charged my gun, which I had still retained in my hand throughout this curious adventure. I saw him run through the level open plain about three miles, till he disappeared in the woods on medecine river; during the whole of this distance he ran at full speed, sometimes appearing to look behind him as if he expected pursuit. I now began to reflect on this novil occurrence and indeavoured to account for this sudden retreat of the bear. I at first thought that perhaps he had not smelt me before he arrived at the waters edge so near me, but I then reflected that he had pursued me for about 80 or 90 yards before I took the water and on examination saw the grownd toarn with his tallons immediately on the impression of my steps; and the cause of his allarm still remains with me misterious and unaccountable. so it was and I felt myself not a little gratifyed that he had declined the combat. My gun reloaded I felt confidence once more in my strength; and determined not to be thwarted in my design of visiting medicine river, but determined never again to suffer my peice to be longer empty than the time she necessarily required to charge her. I passed through the plain nearly in the direction which the bear had run to medecine river, found it a handsome stream. . . .

This is perhaps the most famous single episode in the Lewis and Clark adventure with bears. It has been quoted and retold countless times, usually just for the thrill of the tale but sometimes to penetrate deeper into its meanings. Albert Furtwangler, in *Acts of Discovery: Visions of America in the Lewis and Clark Journals* (1993), devoted nine pages to an inquiry into the lessons, for us today, of Lewis's brief, enervating account with this grizzly bear. Furtwangler agreed that the story is well known for its excitement:

But in its full details this story also points to other meanings. On the one hand, it brings out the fragile defenses these early explorers had for the unpredictable world into which they were intruding. Technologically, they were closer to Christopher Columbus than to pioneers who would cross the plains and mountains just a few decades

after them. And on the other hand, this story gives historical body to an ancient legend, the encounter of a hero with
monstrous spirits of the wilderness. How, with such crude
implements as he had, could Meriwether Lewis come to
terms with the "misterious and unaccountable"?[1]

Furtwangler was rare among scholars in attempting fully to put this
episode in the greater context of what must have been one of the weird-
est days of Lewis's life. After the odd episode with the bear, Lewis encountered an animal he didn't quite know what to call—it has been suggested
that it was a cougar, or a wolverine—that also seemed to threaten him
until he shot at it and it disappeared, and then he was unaccountably
approached from a great distance by three bull bison. It was during this
third strange encounter that Lewis began to wonder what had happened
to the world, and if he'd slipped into some alternate state of reality:

The Bear Pursueing His Assailant, *from the 1813 edition of the Gass journal, pur-
ported to show Lewis fleeing the grizzly bear on June 14, 1805. Apparently the small
stream toward which he is walking (running?) was intended to be the Missouri River
near the mouth of the Sun River. The artist seems to have lacked the ability to
portray the bear and man actually running; the bear appears to be standing still (the
1847 edition of the Gass journal shows this same scene, redrawn with both bear and
man in awkward motion, and with the banks of the stream made steeper).* COURTESY OF
THE LEWIS AND CLARK TRAIL HERITAGE FOUNDATION LIBRARY, GREAT FALLS, MONTANA

It now seemed to me that all the beasts of the neighbourhood had made a league to distroy me, or that some fortune
was disposed to amuse herself at my expence, for I had not
proceeded more than three hundred yards from the burrow
of this tyger cat, before three bull buffaloe, which wer feeding with a large herd about half a mile from me on my left,
seperated from the herd and ran full speed toward me, I
thought at least to give them some amusement, and altered
my direction to meet them; when they arrived within a hundred yards they mad a halt, took a good view of me, and
retreated with precipitation.   I then continued my rout
homewards passed the buffaloe which I had killed, but did
not think it prudent to remain all night at this place which
really from the succession of curious adventures, wore the
impression on my mind of inchantment; at sometimes for a
moment I thought it might be a dream, but the prickly pear
which pierced my feet very severely once in a while, particularly after it grew dark, convinced me that I was really
awake, and that it was necessary to make the best of my way
to camp.

One of the great advantages of having scholars from so many disci-
plines study the journals of Lewis and Clark is the fresh impressions they
bring to stories we think we know well. Furtwangler approached the journals as literature— "a heretofore neglected American literary classic, some
of whose features compare in intriguing ways with outstanding works by
William Wordsworth, Mark Twain, Wallace Stevens, and others."[2] Like
others before him, Furtwangler wondered if the journals are in fact an
authentic epic tale that might "have to be understood in epic terms."[3]
And as a literary scholar, he found the tale of the bear that chased Lewis
into the river ripe for such an interpretation. Likening Lewis to the
unfortunate Old Navigator in Coleridge's *The Rime of the Ancient
Mariner*, Furtwangler saw a greater theme in Lewis's bewildering day:

He may have been a young explorer rather than an Old
Navigator, but he too had violated a new territory by killing

one of its peculiar animals. He had cruelly shot an entire buffalo for his own dinner and was watching it die a bloody death when the bear charged him and drove him from the scene.[4]

But Furtwangler concluded that for all the dangers, inadequacies of their technology, and mysteries of the wild world they were witnessing at the Great Falls, Lewis and Clark were fundamentally unperturbed in their confidence and reluctant to succumb to such compelling portents as Lewis's day of "enchantment."

> In approaching and passing the Great Falls and their grizzlies, then, Lewis and Clark bore witness to a modern confidence in European ways of thinking, even when their guns and compasses failed or were slapped away. When monsters and prodigies appeared and even drove them to the brink of death, the explorers were deterred or confused for a moment, perhaps, but not for long. They recorded these phenomena, searched for natural explanations, and explicitly rejected mystery or superstition. They kept their journals for the eyes of civilized readers.[5]

The behavior of the bull bison, it might be added, does not seem as mysterious as some of the other events of Lewis's day. Though they lack the intense urge to investigate everything that an omnivore like the bear has, large grazing animals are necessarily curious about unfamiliar things. I have on a few occasions seen adult elk cautiously approach a grizzly bear that was digging or crossing through an area. They showed no interest in getting especially close to the bear, but they significantly lessened the distance between themselves and the grizzly, apparently in order to get a better look at it. I assume that making certain they understand the nature and location of a possible threat is important enough to these ungulates, and their confidence that they can outrun any pursuit is strong enough, that they will occasionally make such investigations. It could be that the bull bison that approached Lewis were engaged in a similar reconnaisance.

Or, as the saying goes, not.

It in no way reduces the strength of Furtwangler's inquiry into these events that Lewis probably misunderstood the grizzly bear's intentions anyway. What mattered—what shaped Lewis's behavior and tested his determination to remain a civilized observer of things—was what he believed was happening. He believed the bear wanted to kill him. Thus it is that modern bear authorities find this episode interesting as much for what Lewis thought the bear was doing as for what it probably was doing instead.

We have to consider the setting. Lewis said that the bear was about twenty steps from him before he noticed it. It sounds as if it continued to approach while Lewis decided what to do—raising his rifle, then, realizing it was not loaded, considering his options. So let's say the bear was at least fifty feet from Lewis when he reacted and began to run. At that point, according to Lewis, the bear also began to run toward him at full speed. Lewis then ran about eighty yards before realizing that he could not escape that way, so he waded into the river.

It sounds as if Lewis was running parallel to the shore, following a course not dissimilar to today's modern (if less excited) joggers on the park's riverside path. Thus as soon as he saw that running wasn't going to work, he was able to get into the water right away. When he was up to his waist, he faced the bear and presented it with the point of his espontoon. The bear, arriving at the edge of the water about twenty feet from him, immediately turned and ran away, continuing to run for three miles or so, apparently in a southerly or southwesterly direction, and finally disappearing into the cottonwood groves along the Sun River. Lewis was apparently able to watch it most or all of that time and distance, which suggests to me that it must have stayed relatively close to the river, in the level bottomlands. That area is not perfectly flat, so it is hard to imagine that the bear was always in sight over the whole distance.

Can we make any more of this than Lewis did? Probably, and yet we will end up only a little less mystified than he was.

The most important point is that it is hard to believe that this grizzly bear was determined to catch and kill Lewis. Even with a fifty-foot head start, Lewis almost certainly could not have outrun this bear for eighty yards if it really wanted to catch him.

Lewis had by this point in the journey probably seen some grizzly bears run. He also had Clark's description of the two April 14 bears running with "Supprising ease & verlocity." So Lewis had reason to believe that bears could run fast. But that may not have been enough information; a properly motivated grizzly bear can go amazingly fast, sprinting more or less as fast as a horse. Lewis would have been caught.

He would have been caught, that is, if the bear really wanted to catch him. It took most of a century for a few of the most savvy bear observers to realize that just because a bear is coming toward you, even running toward you, does not mean it intends to attack you. Several twentieth-century hunters and writers, with a more diverse grizzly bear experience than most earlier people, observed that a bear running toward you might just be rushing up for a closer look. And since more formal bear behavior studies have been conducted in the past forty years, it has become clear that the "false charge" or "bluff charge" is an important element of bear behavior when the animal is alarmed.[6] Such rushes allow bears to make their mood clear without actually engaging in combat.

I don't for a minute mean to imply that Lewis should just have stood there and waited to find out what the bear's intentions were, any more than I would ever recommend that anyone should run from a grizzly bear today. What Lewis did worked well enough to keep him alive. But it is important to recognize that Lewis, lacking the hard-earned awareness we now have of grizzly bear behavior, was making assumptions based on regrettably incomplete information and was very likely to misunderstand any bear he met.

Bears are curiosity personified. As omnivores, it is to their advantage to check things out. Poking around, nosing this and that, loping over to get a better look at something unfamiliar—these are essential attributes of an animal that lives by investigation as much as the bear does. They are inveterate detectives and experimenters. After more than three decades of almost continuous scientific scrutiny in the 1960s, 1970s, and 1980s, the grizzly bears of Yellowstone were still surprising researchers by eating foods no one had ever seen them eat before. If you're a full-time carnivore that lives primarily on a few species of other animals or an herbivore that lives on a few species of plants, life is a lot more straightforward than if you're a generalist omnivore not as specifically adapted to any kind of food. Each year, the omnivore's available choices vary. One year maybe two or three of your favorite plants don't flourish, or a harsh winter and other hunters (including those annoying humans) take a larger share of your favorite prey species, or something else in your environment changes, and life gets more complicated. It is always to your advantage to be open to new things, especially if they might either provide food or taste good themselves.

There were, no doubt, humans using the Great Falls area now and then in 1805; there must have been for thousands of years. Perhaps this bear associated people with carrion, such as piles of butchered bison that the scavengers were enjoying at the buffalo jump Lewis described on May 29. Or perhaps the bear had in fact never even seen a human firsthand and was just curious. Perhaps the bear really was considering that this man might be a meal, but wanted to give Lewis a nudge and see how hard he'd be to catch. Or perhaps the bear itself didn't know quite what it was going to do next and was letting Lewis dictate its next move. Ultimately, when it comes to a specific case rather than the comforting generalizations of scientific findings, we have to admit that we really have little more idea than Lewis did why this bear acted the way it did when it ran away.

Lewis's choice of response to being approached by a bear was perfectly predictable and was one many of us would probably lean toward, but it was exactly the wrong one according to all modern professional advice on the subject.[7] For many years, bear managers have been advising people who find themselves in this situation not to run. Running, they say, triggers a chase response in the bear, just as it will in a dog. If the bear really hadn't decided what it would do, Lewis probably helped it make up its mind. At least that is one arguable reading of what happened when, as Lewis said, "I had no sooner terned myself about but he pitched at me, open mouthed and full speed." Up until Lewis turned, the bear may have been only curious; now it was curious and probably kind of excited. But Lewis's presumption that the bear intended to catch him and kill him is still just that—a presumption.

The lore of bear–human encounters is full of unexpected twists and turns. Bears don't think or react as we do, nor for the same reasons. Their incentives are different. Lewis, a man of his times, seems to have assumed that when he faced the bear down, his tactical advantages—standing in the water holding a sharp espontoon—registered in the mind of the bear as they would have in a human mind, as if the bear thought, "Whoa, this is a well-armed opponent on favorable ground, so I'm out of here!" But wild predators, unencumbered by our sensitivity to issues of valor and discretion, make their decisions for other reasons that, I suspect, often have nothing to do with what we could call reason. Something suddenly spooked this bear, and it ran off. It could have been visual, perhaps to do with Lewis's stance or his silhouette against the low horizon, or it could have been something in the bear's own mental wiring. It's fun to wonder about it, but again we do not know.

Whatever it was, the result was a major spooking—three miles is a very long run for any animal that is not being chased. Perhaps Lewis was right, and the bear finally figured out that he was a human. But unless the bear had some painful personal experiences with humans, it is hard to understand why that revelation would cause such a dramatic and long retreat. As we will see, many of the other grizzly bears in this neighborhood had no such fear of people, making this one's behavior all the more intriguing.

What underlies Lewis's view of the bear, and what is most important about this episode for the grizzly bear legacy bequeathed to us by the corps, is Lewis's presumption that the bear must be attacking. Whether or not Lewis personally believed that grizzly bears reflexively attack humans on sight, that is the conviction that so many writers, bear hunters, and naturalists inherited from the corps. It is in this that the legacy of Lewis and Clark became muddled and is still problematic.

To explore this issue, we need to jump ahead about a century, to the popular magazine *Recreation,* specifically the edition published in September 1902. A contributor introduced only as "The Old Cattleman," writing in a colloquial dialect style that was much more popular in those days than now, explained how grizzly bears had changed during the nineteenth century. I realize that this excerpt is a bit of a slog, but stick with it; it's a striking reflection of values, attitudes, and state-of-the-times knowledge.

> Courage is frequent the froots of what a gent don't
> know. Take grizzly b'ars[.] Back 50 years, when them squir-

rel rifles is preevelant; when a acorn shell holds a charge o' powder, an' bullets runs as light and little as 64 to the pound, why son! you-all could shoot up a grizzly till sundown an' hardly gan his disdain. It's a fluke if you downs one. That sport who can show a set o' grizzly b'ar claws, them times, has fame. They're as good as a bank account, them claws be, an' entitles said party to credit in dance hall, bar room an' store, by merely slammin' 'em on the counter.

At that time the grizzly b'ar has courage. Whyever does he have it, you asks? Because you couldn't stop him; he's out of hoomanity's reach—a sort o' Alexander Selkirk of a b'ar, an' you couldn't win from him. In them epocks, the grizzly b'ar treats a gent contemptous. He swats him or he claws him, or he hugs him, or he crunches him, or he quits him accordin' to his moods, or the number o' them engagements which is pressin' on him at the time. An' the last thing he considers is the feelin's o' that partic'lar party he's dallyin' with. Now, however, all is changed. Thar's rifles burnin' 4 inches o' this yere fulminatin' powder, that can chuck a bullet through a foot of green oak. Wisely directed, they lets sunshine through a grizzly b'ar like he's a pane o' glass. An' son, them b'ars is plumb onto the play.

What's the finish? To-day you can't get close enough to a grizzly to hand him a ripe peach. Let him glimps or smell a white man, an' he goes scatterin' off across hill an' canyon like a quart of licker among 40 men. They're shore apprehensife of them big bullets and' hard-hittin' guns, them b'ars is; an' they wouldn't listen to you, even if you talks nothin' but bee-tree an' gives a bond to keep the peace besides. Yes, sir; the day when the grizzly b'ar will stand without hitchin' has departed the calendar a whole lot. They no longer attempts insolent an' coarse familiar'ties with folks. Instead of regyardin' a rifle as a rotten cornstalk in disguise, they're as gunshy as a female institoote. Big b'ars an' little b'ars, it's all sim'lar; for the old ones tell it to the young, an' the lesson is spread throughout the entire nation of b'ars. An' vere's where you observes, enlightenment that a-way means a-weakening of grizzly-b'ar courage.[8]

There is much here to consider, and most of it has to do with Lewis and Clark. But we will confine ourselves to two primary points. The first is that by the time of this article it was almost universally believed that grizzly bears had once been much more "brave" around humans, which was to say that grizzly bears would attack humans much more readily. The second is that over the course of the nineteenth century, grizzly bear behavior changed dramatically as the bears learned that humans were getting better and more powerful weapons and could stand them off more easily. In this chapter, we will deal with the first point, and save the second for later (see chapter 9).

Of course labeling a wild animal "brave" or "cowardly" or "noble" or any of the other human character traits we sometimes apply to other crea-

The Grizzly, *from Colonel Randolph B. Marcy's* Thirty Years of Army Life on the Border *(1866). Much was written by contemporary observers in the nineteenth century about how improvements in firearms changed the relationship between grizzly bears and humans. Perhaps of almost equal importance in this shift was the horse, which provided hunters with a highly mobile and relatively safe platform from which to hunt. Lewis and Clark, however, met most of their grizzly bears while afloat or on foot.*

tures is a dubious practice in the first place. The grizzly bear does not adhere to any set of human values, Judeo-Christian or otherwise. It is a wild animal, doing what it needs to do to get by. "Good" behavior is behavior that keeps it alive and well fed. More important, its aggression or timidity around humans is not a reflection of some failing in its moral character. The Old Cattleman quoted above humanized wild processes and had some fun in doing so, but that's all it is—a shallow way of personalizing something only poorly understood.

As we have seen so far, and as the rest of the journal entries on grizzly bears will demonstrate, Lewis and Clark were rarely attacked, and only occasionally even approached, by grizzly bears unless the bears were shot first. Remember George Ord's quotation of H. M. Brackenridge's description of the grizzly bear? "He is the enemy of man and literally thirsts for human blood. So far from shunning, he seldom fails to attack; and even to hunt him." That became a prevailing view of the grizzly bear, but it was not the Lewis and Clark experience.

It was not the experience of their successors in the western wilderness either. Few early western travelers bothered to interview the Indians at much length on this subject, so we are left with a fairly difficult-to-use set of secondhand accounts of Indian–bear violence. But we have a wealth of firsthand accounts, or detailed secondhand accounts, of "fights" between early Euro-American travelers and grizzly bears. I've been gathering and studying these accounts intermittently for many years, and I have found them to be similar to the reports of Lewis and Clark.

One of the most thorough published collections of the earliest written accounts of interactions with grizzly bears is Fred Gowans's exceptional compilation, *Mountain Man and Grizzly* (1986).[9] Here is a mother lode of eyewitness reports of what it was like to meet the grizzly bear of the Great Plains, the Rocky Mountains, and the Pacific Coast states before the Civil War. For the purposes of this chapter, I made a quick scan of the actual episodes of violence in the Gowans book. I wanted to keep score on these encounters. I necessarily eliminated a number of incomplete stories or passing mentions of events in which it is impossible to determine whether the person or the bear was the initial aggressor. I also did not count vague references by any person who reported that he had killed a total of several, or dozens, or however many bears. I concentrated instead on reports of encounters in which the details are specific enough to allow identification of some probable or likely cause of the trouble.

In about seventy cases, the person or persons attacked the bear first. In fourteen others, the bear initiated the violence without being shot or shot at. But only a few of these fourteen could be considered as even a possible premeditated attempt by the bear to prey on a person. Almost all of the fourteen involved one or more of the following: person(s) surprising a bear at very close quarters, as in a willow thicket; person(s) surprising a sow with cubs; person(s) surprising a bear on a carcass: person(s) inadvertently attracting a bear into camp with the scent of freshly killed or cooked meat. In only one or two instances is it unclear what caused the bear to rush the person(s). I am uncertain about calling even these actions true charges, but they may have been.

So out of more than eighty episodes, we have one or two possible cases in which bears, for reasons of their own and without known human action, attacked people. That doesn't suggest that these bears were all that aggressive and certainly doesn't support the notion that they harbored a constant craving for human blood.

Bear managers in the lower forty-eight sometimes recommend that you stay a minimum of one hundred yards from a grizzly bear, to avoid pushing up against its "fight-or-flight" threshold.[10] For the bear's sake and the people's sake, I suspect a larger distance would be better, if only to ensure that the bear is not made restless by the presence of people and drifts out of view. Bear safety manuals always emphasize the special danger of surprising a bear at a short distance and the even more extreme danger of surprising a bear that has something it feels a need to defend, whether meat, a mate, or cubs.

With that background in mind, the bears in Gowans's book sound a great deal like the bears in modern national parks and forests. Indeed, though a very few early observers assumed the bear would attack on sight, quite a few others saw the bear as shy or tolerant. Naturalist John Townsend crossed the Rockies in 1834 and in his memoir a few years later said that the grizzly bear was like a "cowardly burglar" in the presence of humans.[11] Trapper Osborne Russell, whose journal of his adventures in the Rockies in the 1830s and 1840s is among the most popular of all mountain man diaries, had his share of harrowing encounters with large mammals but generally thought the grizzly bear could be gotten along with:

> In going to visit my traps a distance of 3 or 4 mils, early in the morning I have frequently seen 7 or 8 [grizzly bears] standing about the clumps of Cherry bushes on their hind legs gathering cherries with surprising dexterity not even deigning to turn their Grizzly heads to gaze at the passing trapper but merely casting a sidelong glance at him without altering their position.[12]

What we get from these firsthand accounts is, predictably, a mix of opinions. There was general (but not unanimous) agreement that grizzly bears were very hard to kill, and the accounts of the battles with bears are full of admiring language about the animal's incredible durability, its "sagacity," and its status as the most formidable wild adversary to be found in the American West. But whether the men said so or not, the documentary record of bear–human encounters in this early period provides strong if not conclusive evidence that the bear of Lewis and Clark's West was much like today's bear—fairly cautious. We would know more if all those men who shot grizzly bears on sight had not done so and had instead allowed the bears to see them approach from some reasonable distance. As it is, we are left doubting The Old Cattleman's assessment of the grizzly bear as an animal that was once much more aggressive, and we can see that Brackenridge was simply wrong in his assertions about the almost invariable tendency of the grizzly bear to attack.

How did this story go so wrong? How did public belief get so misdirected? Probably several things occurred. The Biddle edition of the Lewis and Clark journals was not widely distributed; it must have been much easier to come by popular interpretations of it, like Brackenridge's (Ord's publication of the species description, with its lengthy quote from Brackenridge, was apparently too obscure to have been widely read). It was, and is, easy to carelessly read what happened to Lewis and Clark as proof of an almost pathological belligerence on the part of all grizzly bears. Lewis and Clark provided more than enough encouragement, even (as we will see later) specifically claiming that at least some of the grizzly bears along their route had an unhesitating tendency to attack. The even less careful interpretations of their journals piled up, one upon another, in the decades after Lewis and Clark returned. This can't be much of surprise, considering the public's great appetite for lurid stories. It was an exciting discovery, this great, terrifying animal, and what popular writer is going to downplay all that delicious dread and gore?

William Wright, in *The Grizzly Bear, The Narrative of a Hunter-Naturalist* (1909), the first great American bear book, complained that this excitement was the principal reason why even as distinguished and careful a naturalist as John James Audubon could overlook "all the testimony relating to the grizzly bear's wariness and disinclination to fight unless pressed. . . . Lewis and Clark's observations are the basis of it, repeated with slight variations and considerable embellishments in regard to ferociousness and bloodthirstiness by each after writer. Occasionally one of these adds an original observation or a hearsay anecdote. Then these in turn are repeated and embellished."[13]

Wright pinned down what may have been an even more important part of the creation of the legend of the ferociously aggressive grizzly bear—adventure fiction:

> Meanwhile, the grizzly had been seized upon as a literary godsend in another quarter. To the romancers, the discovery of an *Ursus horribilis* was like the throwing open to settlement of a new territory, and there was a regular stampede to locate quarter sections. Captain Mayne Reid was the hero of the movement. Jenkins, Lawrence, and a host of others preceded and followed him. Kit Carson wrote reliably and was not listened to. Jim Bridges [Bridger] told whoppers and was believed.[14]

Mayne Reid, who specialized in thrilling adventure tales for children in the 1850s, could count among his enthralled readers generations of later hunters, naturalists, and adventurers, not the least of whom was Theodore Roosevelt.[15] Just as the creators of Pooh, Yogi, and countless other twentieth-century bears firmed up the image of the bear as the children's pal, so did nineteenth-century writers firm up the worst possible ideas about bears, especially grizzly bears, as monsters (of course, the writers of "dime novels" were doing a similar sensationalizing disservice to practically every other aspect of the American West at the same time). It is hardly fair simply to fault creators of fictional bears for the bad public image of the grizzly bear. After all, the public does have some responsibility for discriminating between fantasy literature and trustworthy natural history, and Pooh, Yogi, and their kind are justifiably beloved in American culture. Readers must share considerable responsibility for buying improbable or unrepresentative tales of bears.

Wright could have added popular art to his complaint about what went wrong for the grizzly bear's public image. It is hard to find more than a very few published images of the grizzly bear in the nineteenth century that do not portray it as a ravening, snarling, bloodthirsty beast, the perfect visual counterpart to the monster that Brackenridge told us was so valiantly battled by Lewis and Clark.

There is a very practical reason to be careful in our assumptions about what a bear is doing when it rushes at you, and here again the lessons of Lewis and Clark may be interfering with getting it right. Lewis believed that this bear—and indeed many of the bears they encountered on the upper Missouri—closed with him with intent to kill, and that became a part of the expedition's legacy. It was a long time before observers began to understand that a bear might only be making a false charge, or rushing up for a closer look, and in the meantime we killed a lot of bears. Even now, when we have alternative deterrents available to us, we may be misunderstanding what's happening. The relatively recent development of powerful pepper spray devices that can give a bear a good blast of capsaicin has changed the way we deal with bears in wild country. But as years of experience have accumulated, and as bear sprays are reported as successfully driving off "attacking" bears, we again must wonder. Some bear authorities are now suggesting that at least some of these apparently successful efforts to turn a bear's charge may instead have only been instances when the bear was going to stop its rush anyway, either because it was just bluffing a charge or because it was now close enough to see what it wanted to see.[16] Modern hikers with their shiny cans of bear spray are in a situation not unlike Lewis's, though: How are they to tell if the charge is real, and how close must they let the bear come before they decide? Bears move amazingly fast, and at close quarters, under the formidable duress of the situation, the person must make the right judgment call almost reflexively.

The better course—one that would probably have been available even to Lewis had he not been so inattentive—is to keep far enough from the bear so that it never feels the need to run at you in the first place. But even that is not always possible in the convoluted landscapes of bear country.

CHAPTER EIGHT

The Great Falls Bear Crisis

O ne of the great joys of following Lewis and Clark on their journey across the country is the number of fine museums and interpretive centers that are springing up along the way. It would be impolitic and probably impossible for me to name a favorite, but I would be hard pressed to name a more impressive one than the Lewis & Clark National Historic Trail Interpretive Center overlooking the Missouri River on the northern edge of the city of Great Falls. And I would likewise be hard pressed to name a more convincing part of the exhibit at this facility than the portrayal of the men wrestling one of their heavy canoes up a steep slope. As often as the difficulties and strains of the portage have been written about, this exhibit still makes the point with a fresh power. It was brutally exhausting work for the men and an exasperating delay for the captains, who had far to go before the snows came. Indeed, had they known just how far they had to go, exasperation might have easily enough edged over into despair before they even reached the Rocky Mountains.

Though much of the almost eighteen miles of the portage route is now under cultivation or the city and suburbs of Great Falls, it is immediately obvious how taxing the portaging of canoes and equipment would have been even if the only challenge was crossing the topography. But add the rattlesnakes, the prickly pears, hailstones, mosquitoes, and it was about as awful a stretch of travel as any early western explorer ever faced. Add the grizzly bears and it was something worse.

By all accounts, the weeks that the corps spent in the arduous labors of portaging around the Great Falls were the intensive peak of their

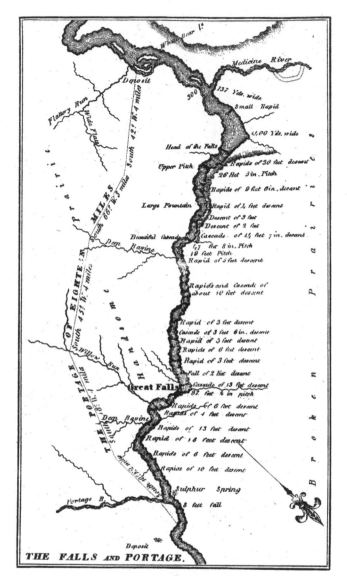

The Falls and Portage, *map of the portage route around the Great Falls of the Missouri River, from Elliott Coues, editor,* History of the Expedition Under the Command of Lewis and Clark *(1893), volume 4. The eastern, or downstream, end of the portage is at the bottom. The dotted line along the left side of the map is the portage route. The Upper Portage Camp, at the top of the map, is opposite the White Bear Islands in the river. Lewis's close call with the grizzly bear, described at the beginning of chapter 7, occurred near the mouth of the Medicine River (now the Sun River), upper right, just opposite the present town of Great Falls. Note also the location of Willow Run, east of the Great Falls. It was where the portage route crossed Willow Run that Hugh McNeal had his fight with a grizzly bear on the expedition's return trip in 1806 (this encounter is described in chapter 13).*

acquaintance with the grizzly bear and the low point in their relationship with this big carnivore. For the first time the bear became a regular hindrance to their progress, and for the first time the captains had to launch an attack on bears that was motivated by reasons other than the need for natural resources or the urge for sporting adventure.

On June 14, 1805, Ordway was one of a group who "passed a bottom on N. S. where Capt. Lewis & men had Camped 1 night & killed 2 bears & one Deer & left the Skins & fat for us to take on board." These would have been the bears Lewis reported killed on June 12. On June 15, in their combined comments, the captains noted that "The Brown or grizzly bear begin to coppolate."

Modern North American grizzly bears have been observed mating as early as April and as late as August, with most activity from late May to early July, so this is a reasonable observation by the captains.[1] We can only wonder, though, if they saw mating bears. Courtship often lasts several days, and even a couple of weeks, so they could easily have been seeing mated pairs even if they did not observe actual copulation. Considering how candidly the captains sometimes spoke of the sexual exploits of their men among the women of the various Indian tribes, it seems improbable the captains were reluctant to speak graphically about such an indelicate topic as sexual intercourse among other species.

On June 17, Lewis, in discussing the many dead bison washed ashore in the area, said that "their mangled carcases ly along the shores below the falls in considerable quantities and afford fine amusement for the bear wolves and birds of prey; this may be one reason and I think not a bad one either that the bear are so tenatious of their right of soil in this neighborhood." This is the first mention of something unusual going on with the local bears. Clark's duties the same day added more details on the scene by the river, as well as including a specific bear sighting: "we Saw one Bear & inumerable numbers of Buffalow, I Saw 2 herds of those animals watering immediately above a considerable rapid, they decended by a narrow pass to the bottom Small, the rier forced those forwd into the water Some of which was taken down in an instant, and Seen no more." There is certainly no question that there was a huge quantity of handy meat for scavengers near the falls.

On June 18, Clark and a party of the men worked their way up along the south shore of the Missouri, viewing the various falls, discovering Giant

Spring (now a refreshing little park managed by the Montana Department of Fish, Wildlife and Parks), and finally camping a short way north of the mouth of Sand Coulee Creek. This camp, known now as the Upper Portage Camp, would be the destination of the men laboring across the open country with the canoes and equipment. It faced the White Bear Islands, where various adventures awaited the men (from the general area of Upper Portage Camp today, it is very difficult to identify actual islands like those described in the journals; according to editor Moulton, the islands of 1805 have "virtually disappeared, merging with the banks of the Missouri. . . .").

passed an Island of [apparently missing word here] and a little timber in an Easterly bend at 1 mile, passed Some timber in a point at 2 mile at or near the lower point of a large Island on which we Shot at a large white *bear*. passed a Small Island in the middle and one close to the Lard Shore at 3 miles behind the head of which we Camped. those 3 Islands are all opposit, Soon after we Camped two ganges of Buffalow crossed one above & the other below we killed 7 of them & a calf and Saved as much of the best of the meat as we could this evening, one man A Willard going for a load of meat at 170 yards distance on an Island was attact by a white bear and verry near being Caught, prosued within 40 yards of Camp where I was with one man I collected 3 others of the party and prosued the bear (who had prosued my track from a buffalow I had killed on the Island at about 300 yards distance and chance to meet Willard) for fear of his attacking one man Colter at the lower point of the Island, before we had got down the bear had allarmed the man and prosued him into the water, at our approach he retreated, and we relieved the man in the water, I Saw the bear but the bushes was So thick that I could not Shoot him and it was nearly dark, the wind from the SW & Cool killed a beaver & an elk for their Skins this evening.

This does appear to be a more assertive and confident bear than the one that fled from Lewis and his espontoon on June 14. Again, though, freshly killed meat was involved. The account does not tell us if Willard was with the meat, or was actually carrying it, when he was "attact by a white bear." Ultimately the bear retreated when confronted with four men approaching him, even though they did not fire. I doubt that this bear's "attack" on the men was independent of its interest in the meat they were spreading around.

Lewis's June 19 entry explained that camp life was getting tense, especially at night:

> After dark my dog barked very much and seemed extreemly uneasy which was unusual with him; I ordered the sergt. of the guard to reconniter with two men, thinking it possible that some Indians might be about to pay us a visit, or perhaps a white bear; he returned soon after & reported that he believed that the dog had been baying a buffaloe bull which had attempted to swim the river. . . .

There was a lot of wildlife nearby, and it certainly could have been a bison that upset the dog so much. But it appears that the longer the men spent in this area, and the more they needed to kill animals for food and thereby scatter fresh carcass parts around, the greater the likelihood of bears visiting them and becoming a nuisance and a danger.

There is no additional mention of bears in the corps's journals until June 25, when Gass wrote that one of the men (Joseph Fields, though Gass did not name him) "went up the river to look for elk. When he had gone about three miles, he was attacked by 3 brown bears, that were near devouring him; but he made his escape by running down a steep bank into the water. In this adventure he fell, injured his gun, and hurt one of his hands; therefore returned to camp." Gass was the only one of the diarists to mention this encounter, for which we must be grateful, but again it is frustratingly incomplete if we are trying to understand just how aggressive these bears were. If the three bears were together, it seems unlikely that Fields would have fired on them unless two were small and unthreatening, which easily could have been the case. Most of the year one would not expect to encounter three adult bears together, unless Fields had wandered into a good berry patch or had encountered a sow being courted by two males.

Ordway appears to be the only one to tell us about a hunt made by some of the men on June 26, when they "went with Capt. Lewis on a Small Island below the Camp to hunt for a white bear which had been about the Camp the night before and cut Some meat near the tents &C." But Lewis's journal (June 27) does reinforce the concern he now had about bears around camp, at the conclusion of an account of another bear adventure had by the returning hunters:

> They had killed 9 Elk and three bear during their absence; one of the bear was the largest by far that we have yet seen; the skin appear to me to be as large as a common ox. while hunting they saw a thick brushey bottom on the bank of the river where from the tracks along shore they suspected that there were bare concealed; they therefore landed without making any nois and climbed a leaning tree and placed themselves on it's branches about 20 feet above the ground, when thus securely fixed they gave a hoop and this large bear instantly rushed forward to the place from whence he had heard the human voice issue, when he arrived at the tree he made a short paus and Drewyer shot him in the head. it is worthy of remark that these bear never climb. the fore feet of this bear measured nine inches across and the hind feet eleven and 3/4 in length exclusive of the tallons and seven inches in width. a bear came within thirty yards of our camp last night and eat up about thirty weight of buffaloe suit which was hanging on a pole. my dog seems to be in a constant state of alarm with these bear and keeps barking all night.

Unfortunately, the captains were evidently now less interested in recording a full set of measurements on the bears that were killed. It seems a little odd that they still took a few measurements but not a full set. And though the literature of bears is sparsely inhabited by accounts of grizzly bears that did climb trees, Lewis was also right on that point. Most adult grizzly bears don't climb (exceptions usually prove this rule, as grizzly bears have been observed climbing the most easily climbable trees, such as those with conveniently laddered branches that don't require the embracing grip of the trunk that black bears employ when they climb).

Lewis's observations about bears around camp are interesting. At least some of these bears were confident enough to ease right into the edge of the camp and make off with fresh meat, a behavior occasionally reported in the diaries and other writings of western travelers during the next few decades.

On June 28, Lewis continued to express alarm over the boldness of the bears around the Upper Portage Camp:

> The White bear have become so troublesome to us that I do not think it prudent to send one man alone on an errand of any kind, particularly where he has to pass through the brush. we have seen two of them on the large Island opposite to us today but are so much engaged that we could not spare the time to hunt them but will make a frolick of it when the party return and drive them from these islands. they come close arround our camp every night but have never yet ventured to attack us and our dog gives us timely notice of their visits, he keeps constantly padroling all night. I have made the men sleep with their arms by them as usual for fear of accedents.

On June 30, in a journal entry that seems to be a catching-up of several days' events, Whitehouse said that there were "bear about the Camp everry night, and Seen on the Islands in the day time." In a more fulsome statement that appeared in the paraphrased version of his journal, he said that "The bears are plenty along the upper Camp every night, and we see them in great plenty on the Islands in the day-time." This suggests greater numbers of bears than suggested by the original version; was it an accurate remembrance by Whitehouse passed along to his editor, or was it a little added drama introduced by the editor himself?

By July 1, Lewis had had enough and decided to act: "the bear were about our camp all last night, we have therefore determined to beat up their quarters tomorrow, and kill them or drive them from their haunts

Grizzly Bears overhauling us, *from George Catlin's* Life Amongst the Indians. A Book for Youth *(1861), shows the willingness of grizzly bears to investigate the camps of travelers. Such encounters, often brought on by the presence of freshly killed game that attracted the bears, were a frequent and harrowing part of early western travel long after the experiences of Lewis and Clark at the Great Falls of the Missouri.*

about this place." On July 2, Gass reported that "In the evening, most of the corps crossed over to an island, to attack and rout its monarch, a large brown bear, that held possession and seemed to defy all that would attempt to besiege him there. Our troops, however, stormed the place, gave no quarter, and its commander fell. Our army returned the same evening to camp without having suffered any loss on their side." Clark explained that "Capt. Lewis my Self & 12 men Crossed to an Island on which we Saw a bear the evening before," so they apparently assumed that this individual was one of the ones causing them so much trouble. Ordway added that they "Saved the Skin and Greese."

And abruptly, their trouble with the bears of Great Falls was past. It was July 14 before the corps finally was ready to head on up the Missouri, but in the intervening twelve days they mention no more bear encounters or problems.

Since the 1969 publication of Paul Cutright's *Lewis and Clark: Pioneering Naturalists,* the most important book to deal with the ecological and biological issues of the expedition is Daniel Botkin's provocative *Our Natural History: The Lessons of Lewis and Clark* (1995).[2] I am happy to admit that it was Botkin's book, especially his thoughtful chapter on grizzly bears, that finally convinced me that I should go ahead and write this book. Among many other challenges to conventional wisdom he offered, Botkin questioned the extreme characterizations of grizzly bear abundance that have grown from the corps's journals during their trip. He singled out their experiences near the Great Falls of the Missouri as a good example of what he considered a misinterpretation of the journals on this question of bear abundance.

He made a good point. If you count the actual reported sightings of specific bears, they are not numerous. Having spent so much time already stressing the importance of hearing what the diarists actually said rather than what so many later writers said about them, I am quick to agree with Botkin's insistence that we be careful about this.

On the other hand, one thing I've noticed in my reading of early accounts of western wildlife is that there is sometimes an inverse relationship between wildlife abundance as it approaches superabundance and the number of times such abundance was reported. Once animal numbers reach certain levels, some observers feel less obliged to write about it. If they've told you in one diary entry that such-and-such a creature is simply over-running the landscape, they don't feel especially compelled to tell you again the next day.[3] The condition becomes simply a fact of life. For example, on July 24, 1806, while traveling down the Yellowstone River on the return trip, Clark said that the animals were so numerous that he would be "silent on the subject further." Unfortunately for the modern reader, such observers do not always feel in the least compelled to alert you the day that the creature in question is no longer so common (and, in fact, though Clark said he would let it go, he kept enthusing about the abundance of animals in subsequent journal entries).

To some extent, something like this could have occurred at the Great Falls. Once Lewis told us that the bears were so abundant that he would not send the men out alone, and once the diarists said that the bears were numerous at night around camp and on nearby islands, they may have, at least in their own minds, passed beyond the point of needing to report on each individual sighting. At least I am certain that such a scenario happened to other early trappers and travelers in the early-nineteenth-century West. Lewis's vaguely stated conviction that there were lots of bears around, and Whitehouse's comment that there were bears "in great plenty," cannot be lightly disregarded.

The cynically glib might point out that it doesn't take very many grizzly bears to make a lot, especially when they're right beyond the reach of your campfire, or when you practically have to shoulder them out of the way to get to your meat supply. But these were not men who let their ability to report their adventures be dramatically affected by fear or alarm. They have been celebrated for the consistency of their Joe-Friday "just-the-facts" narrative presentation. It seems unlikely that they would have significantly overstated the seriousness of their situation. They were just really vague when it came to telling us how many bears there were.

On yet the other hand, killing one bear on July 2 seemed to make a huge difference. From that day on, after all their concerned reports of nightly troubles, the journals switch abruptly to no mention of concern, or of sightings of bears, at all. Perhaps there really were very few bears left around the Great Falls; after all, the corps killed six and shot at a couple of others during their time there. Or perhaps the corps still had some trouble after July 2 but did not feel a need to mention it again. Perhaps they killed just the right bear on the island, and its colleagues somehow got the message. Perhaps after the portage was concluded, the men had less reason to encounter bears and may have been less likely to attract them.

Without doubt, the time at the Great Falls was the corps's most continuous and contentious period of grizzly bear interactions and constitutes the heart of their grizzly bear adventure. At no other point in the trip did the bears have such a determined effect on the activities of the men or so threaten their plans. Still, Botkin's call for moderation in our assessment of bear numbers seems more than justified. And as we contrast the bear behavior reported by the corps at the Great Falls with that of the bears upstream, it becomes a little more plausible that the Great Falls grizzly bears may indeed have been somewhat different.

CHAPTER NINE

Shy Bears

After the excitement and close calls of the corps's early encounters with bears, and the sustained tension of the Great Falls bears hanging around camp and along the portage route, the men must have been relieved by the easier time they had with the big carnivores as they moved upstream. For the rest of July and well into August, little was said about dangerous encounters with bears.

But the bears were there. They were occasionally sighted, their tracks were common, and they were still on the minds of the men. On July 18, not far upstream from the mouth of the Dearborn River, Lewis observed bighorn sheep on cliffs across the river, stating, "this anamal appears to frequent such precepices and clifts where in fact they are perfectly secure from the pursuit of the wolf, bear, or even man himself." While not specific evidence of bears in that very area, it is a contribution to the useful bear lore accumulated by the corps, as it suggests that bears had something to do with the sheep's adaptation to steep terrain.

On July 22, on the home stretch of the upper Missouri River and only a few days from the Three Forks, Lewis devoted journal space to a summary of the species and seasonality of the vegetation, including four colors of currants. He concluded that "the bears appear to feed much on the currants." This seems to suggest that Lewis, in his wanderings along the shore, saw bear scat composed primarily of freshly processed currants. Again, I tend to wonder if polite discretion (and his probable assumption that such specificity was unnecessary) prevented him from mentioning feces directly.

On July 24, now less than a day from the Three Forks, Lewis reported that "we saw a large bear but could not get a shoot at him." The two variant Whitehouse journals complicate this episode. In his original journal,

Whitehouse said only, "a white bear Seen." But in the paraphrased version, he disagreed with Lewis's account and noted that "The hunters killed this day a White or brown bear." It seems most probable to me that the disagreement between the Whitehouse accounts over whether or not the July 24 bear was killed arose during the rewriting.[1] As historian Paul Cutright said in his analysis of this rewrite, sometimes Whitehouse's ghostwriter "goes wrong" and muddles the information.[2] Considering how many bears were seen, shot at, and missed or hit, it is impressive that so few such confusions arise in our readings of the written record of the expedition.

On July 25, the day the smaller advance party under Clark reached the Three Forks, Lewis and the main group passed the area of the present Tosten Dam. Lewis said that "in the forenoon we saw a large brown bear on an island but he retreated immediately to the main shore and ran off before we could get in reach of him. they appear to be more shy here than on the Missouri below the mountains." If there is any doubt, Whitehouse helpfully clarified the species, as a "large white bear," so it was certainly a grizzly bear.

On July 26, Clark was at the mouth of the Jefferson River (then still known as the North Fork), where "we killed 2 bear which was imediately in our way. both pore." This time Lewis elaborated on species, saying that "they killed two brown or Grisley bear this evening on the island where they passed the N. fork of the Missouri." In this case, at least, Lewis meant "brown" and "Grisley" to be interchangeable. This seems to be his habit by this time. So far in the journals, only black-colored bears were known to be referred to as "black bears." But we still must worry that these observers might simply have referred to a brown-colored black bear simply as a "brown bear," and thus we have to wonder at least a little about each bear given that name. As a further puzzle, Ordway, in his July 27 entry mentioned that Clark's party killed one bear, a cub. This is a rare mention of what apparently was a subadult grizzly bear.

Lewis reported that during the night of July 29–30, he "was awakened by the nois of some animal runing over the stoney bar on which I lay but did not see it; from the weight with which it ran I supposed it to be either an Elk or a brown bear. the latter are very abundant in this neighbourhood." Journal editor Gary Moulton, in footnoting this mention of a "brown bear," assumed that Lewis was referring to a "Black bear, *Ursus americanus.*"[3] Though there were probably black bears in the neighborhood as well as grizzly bears, it appears to me from the context that Lewis meant this to be a grizzly bear. The party's other mentions of grizzly bears being common in the area seem to reinforce the idea that in this case he was thinking of a grizzly.

On July 31, Lewis said, "this evening just before we encamped Drewyer discovered a brown bear enter a small cops of bushes on the Lard. side; we surrounded the place an surched the brush but he had escaped in some manner unperceived but how we could not discover." According to Ordway, the bear was shot: "our hunter on Shore wounded a White bear, but did not kill it dead." On August 1, Clark "saw a large Bear eateing currents this evining." Lewis said that "They saw a large brown bear feeding on currants but could not get a shoot at him." Whitehouse and Ordway both said this was a white bear, again confirming that it was a grizzly.

By now the party was anxiously looking for the Shoshone Indians, from whom they hoped to acquire both horses and guidance for the trip across the mountains to the headwaters of the Columbia River. On August 2, Lewis reported that "we also saw many tracks of the Elk and bear. no recent appearance of Indians." The next day, Clark reported "Some Deer Elk & antelopes & Bear in the bottoms." Whether because of the actual scarcity of large animals, or because they were preoccupied with more urgent matters in locating the Shoshone and starting their trek over the mountains, almost three weeks would pass before they reported even a trace of a bear along their route.

To whatever extent the men may have been relieved not to encounter bears as bold as those at the Great Falls, it is kind of a relief as a reader not to hear about quite so many bears being shot. That sort of action is pretty hard on the modern sensibility. Today, with grizzly bear populations in the lower forty-eight states reduced to a few small remnants of their former spread, we are not accustomed to thinking of this many bears as being expendable. Environmental historian Dan Flores, in *The Natural West: Environmental History in the Great Plains and Rocky Mountains* (2001), probably spoke for many modern readers of the Lewis and Clark journals in this exasperated outburst:

Absorbing the mounting tension of these journal entries almost two centuries later, you're almost prompted to shout aloud at Meriwether Lewis, "Christ Almighty, order them to stop shooting up grizzly bears!"[4]

I agree; at times the journals get to be pretty bruising reading. Even though we know how vitally important bear meat, grease, and hides were to the men, and even though we must resist cramming our own values down the throats of people who lived in a very different world, after a while it's hard not to wince when the sentence begins, "They saw a large bear . . ."—or to relax a little when the bear gets away.

Indeed, after the excitement of the Great Falls, even though the men continued to blaze away at every bear they thought they could reach, the bears themselves seemed to get harder to find and, as Lewis put it, more shy. Shyness in bears, as the corps's members described it here, is as intriguing a notion as the aggression they believed they were encountering earlier, and it brings us necessarily back to the tale told by "The Old Cattleman" in chapter 7.

There were two central ideas in The Old Cattleman's rant about bears. The first, that the bears used to be more "ferocious," we dealt with in chapter 7. The second, that over the course of the nineteenth century grizzly bears learned to fear men and guns, comes up now.

This was and still is an opinion of great popularity and durability in hunting circles, and today it applies to wildlife species besides bears. In several parts of the country today, where wild carnivore populations are growing and even expanding, this is an important issue because the public faces increased (if still quite low) risk of attack. In any region with a resident population of large predators, you may hear local hunters and even game managers assert that hunting is important to keep those animals wary and fearful of people. Otherwise, the grizzly bears, black bears, cougars, coyotes, or whatever will get familiar, bold, and aggressive.

In saying this, the local hunters do have a point. Human hunting may actually have an effect on the behavior of the animals in question. But the process is somewhat more complicated than might at first appear. I've attempted to address this question in previous books, most notably *The Bear Hunter's Century* (1988), and my answer goes something like this.[5]

First, The Old Cattleman was in the best of company in his belief that grizzly bears had learned to fear guns. In *Hunting Trips of a Ranchman* (1885), Theodore Roosevelt, one of turn-of-the-century America's most distinguished authorities on large game animals, held precisely the same view, which he expressed rather more intelligibly:

> But the introduction of heavy breech-loading repeaters has greatly lessened the danger, even in the very few and far-off places where the grizzlies are as ferocious as formerly. For nowadays these great bears are undoubtedly much better aware of the death-dealing power of men, and, as a consequence, much less fierce, than was the case with their forefathers, who so unhesitatingly attacked the early Western travellers and explorers. Constant contact with rifle-carrying hunters, for a period extending over many generations of bear life, has taught the grizzly by bitter experience that man is his undoubted overlord, as far as fighting goes; and this knowledge has become an hereditary characteristic.[6]

Again and again, bear authorities have said that the bears *learned* this new behavior. The first question that I, and modern managers of bears, must ask about this line of reasoning is this: Exactly what did the bear you just killed learn from the experience?

The second question is then obvious: How is that new information passed along from the dead bear to the other bears so that they, too, become "wary"? Killing bears seems a poor way to teach them anything useful.

The "learning" was more likely a populationwide enterprise that took at least a few generations. Several things were happening at once. Perhaps a bear that was only wounded or "dusted off" did learn to be more shy. Perhaps a yearling bear whose siblings or mother were shot was ever after more cautious around people. Perhaps some bears escaped traps, or only became sick rather than died when poisoned, or otherwise caught on to the wisdom of avoiding people.

No doubt these things happened. But in a more important way, through a haphazard, inefficient, and often far too destructive process,

Bears On All Sides, *from Anne Bowman's* The Bear-Hunters of the Rocky Mountains *(1862), captures all the elements needed to thrill young readers 140 years ago: One grizzly bear, in the foreground, appears to have been killed already, while another is hugging the probable shooter as three men close in to save their companion. In the background, just to make sure the romantic imagery is dense enough, Indians approach. Scenes similar to this, in which whites and Indians fought it out with grizzly bears, were common enough in reality in the West to encourage a sizable adventure literature, to which the Lewis and Clark tales were easily adapted and attached.*

the entire bear population was changed by the killing. The hunters—whether they were out there for sport, or to protect their livestock, or simply to eliminate a dangerous animal—probably weren't really teaching individual bears all that much. Instead, they were unintentionally participating in what we might today call selective culling. The most aggressive bears—the ones most likely to venture into pastures and take a steer, or to approach people closely, or to otherwise put themselves at risk—were the most likely ones to be shot. No doubt plenty of shy ones were shot, too, but unless the hunting was so wholesale that it wiped out the whole population (which it eventually did almost everywhere in the United States), its effect was to create a pretty shy bunch of bears.

Interestingly, and by contrast, such culling might also single out extraordinarily savvy individual bears. These individuals somehow combined shyness with an exceptional ability to get in and out of trouble without being killed. Many parts of the West look back on such stock-killing, trouble-causing, near-legendary bears, which were in fact singing the swan song of aggressive tendencies in the local population (the wolf eradication undertaken by stockmen and government agents in the late 1800s and early 1900s helped produce equally famous and crafty animals). In fact, they may have hastened the demise of the population, because stockmen's organizations were skilled at publicizing such animals as justifying ever more effort at comprehensive predator eradication.[7]

Of course, shy bears teach their young to be shy, too. Here is where Roosevelt's "hereditary characteristic" changes actually come into play, and here is where much of the "learning" actually occurs. In a few generations, the bears do indeed become more wary of people.

Biologist Steve Herrero, certainly one of the world's foremost authorities on bear–human interactions, has described the eventual extreme consequence of this kind of accidental reengineering of grizzly bear behavior, where "problem bears" were progressively removed from the population for many generations without wiping out the bears completely:

> I studied bears in one such area, Abruzzo National Park
> in the Appenine Mountains of central Italy. Here the bears
> did not have an aggressive bone in their bodies, at least with
> regard to human beings. Superficially they looked like little

grizzly bears. Our work left me with the impression that the bears seldom left cover and that much of their foraging took place during twilight or nighttime. (Because we did not use radiotelemetry we could not confirm this supposition.) Studies done on an even smaller number of bears in northern Italy did use telemetry and found that there the bears almost never left cover except during darkness or twilight.[8]

This is a remarkable example of adaptation. Here we have one of the world's most famous predators—a tremendously successful carnivore of enormous potential power—that after centuries of competition with humans has converted itself, behaviorally at least, into a timid black bear. What striking evolutionary plasticity, and what a statement about the subtleties and forcefulness of bear–human interactions! (A few years ago, long after listening to Steve describe these bears, it was my good fortune to spend some time with some Abruzzo Park staff members while they were touring the United States, and the story became more extraordinary as they told it. They also have wolves in their park, living the same cautious lives. Though not as readily tolerated as the grizzly bears, the wolves still survive.)

Any mention of shy bears reminds me of these descriptions of Abruzzo, and the capacity of a bear population to change over time, or to vary from place to place. Remember that Lewis quickly developed a theory to help explain the aggressive bears in the Great Falls area. He concluded that the great abundance of bison carcasses "may be one reason and I think not a bad one either that the bear are so tenatious of their right of soil in this neighborhood." It may be. On the other hand, the tremendous abundance of a rich, reliable food source in another setting—Alaskan salmon streams—has tended to make those bears more tolerant of humans. They are frequently referred to as "mellow" and under careful management have learned to tolerate people at much closer quarters than would seem possible for bears in settings without so much easy food.

The difference between the bison and salmon as food sources that affect bear behavior might have to do with timing. Perhaps the real glut of bison carcasses didn't last as long as the salmon runs, and the bears were eager to make the most of the bison and therefore more defensive of this short-lived bonanza than they might be along a salmon stream.

Or the difference between the bison and the salmon as food sources may have to do with the size of the individual unit of food. Even when bison were very common, a bear could take considerable risks to acquire a carcass, but once in possession there was an enormous amount of food available in that package. When I discussed this recently with Steve Herrero, he repeatedly emphasized what must be a primary axiom in the life of a bear, obviously understood by Lewis: A carcass is worth defending. That is, several hundred pounds of meat, even if replacement carcasses are readily available, will naturally inspire stronger proprietary feelings in a bear than will a ten-pound salmon.

After leaving the Great Falls, and especially after passing the Three Forks on their way up the Jefferson River, Lewis and Clark reported far fewer bison. There was no barrier to bison movement upstream to the Three Forks and beyond into the valleys of the Gallatin, Madison, and Jefferson Rivers, but they happened not to be there when Lewis and Clark came through. On August 2, in the lower Jefferson River Valley near present Silver Star, Lewis said that "the bones of the buffaloe and their excrement of an old date are to be met with in every part of this valley but we have long since lost all hope of meeting with that animal in these mountains." Sacagawea would later tell Clark that bison had also once been common in the Gallatin Valley, two drainages over to the east. Some combination of factors, certainly including the timing of seasonal migrations and Indian hunting (Sacagawea mentioned hunting as the major factor in the Gallatin Valley), had at least temporarily left the area without large numbers of bison.

If bison were only occasionally available to the grizzly bears upstream of the Great Falls, it certainly could have had an effect on the bears' behavior. The Canadian hunter-naturalist Andy Russell, author of *Grizzly Country* (1967), one of the authentic classics of grizzly bear literature, made the case this way in discussing the aggressive bears of the Missouri River:

> These were plains grizzlies described in the journal so far, bears which ranged the prairies with buffalo in great numbers at that time. Doubtless, having met only primitively armed

Indians, they were not much afraid of white men and reacted either in anger or curiosity upon seeing them. These bears were bison-eaters. The migration routes of buffaloes ran at right angles to the big rivers, and while crossing them, the millions of big grazers suffered much mortality. Many were drowned, bogged in quicksand, and injured and killed while climbing up steep banks from the bottoms to the plains above. Consequently there were easy pickings for the bears. Undoubtedly many grizzlies learned to kill mature animals. It was small wonder that these bears were arrogant, fearless animals not particularly inclined toward self-effacement at human intrusion.[9]

The point I find most helpful about Russell's discussion is the scale of the landscape. Even if bison were present, the headwater rivers of the Missouri above the Three Forks simply couldn't create this kind of natural carnage. For one thing, they didn't have the power to stack great numbers of bison bodies along the banks in high water. Besides, though no doubt bison lived in those smaller upstream valleys, Russell was talking about the huge main tides of migration—millions of animals clomping along and wallowing right into the swollen Missouri River. The only venue for that big a show was out on the prairies well to the east. It was a different world, and it almost had to generate a somewhat different bear.

What should make us most nervous about this sort of theorizing—all our attempts to mentally reconstruct a missing animal and its world—isn't what the bears might have been able to do under different circumstances. Grizzly bears are incredibly adaptable, and we should never underestimate their gift for fitting in anywhere they go. What worries me instead is the risk we run whenever we attempt to draw firm conclusions about these animals based on so little information.

Consider the situation. Lewis and Clark traveled across North Dakota and Montana in about as much of a hurry as they could manage. True, they conscientiously wrote down what they saw. True, they were exceptionally good observers. For some specific purposes, such as understanding river drainage systems, they took a lot of time to get it right. But most of what they told us about grizzly bears (or any other species of plant or

The relationship of the grizzly bear with the bison in Lewis and Clark's West was more involved than merely that of a carnivore and a huge food supply. It may well have been that the availability of such quantities of meat had important effects on the behavior of the grizzly bears when they first encountered the Corps of Discovery. In the lower forty-eight states today, the only vestiges of that relationship between bear and bison now survive in Yellowstone National Park, where this photograph was taken.

NATIONAL PARK SERVICE PHOTOGRAPH

animal, for that matter) was based on hasty observation under considerable stress. They didn't spend a lot of time just watching bears be bears; if the animals were in range, they shot at them.

As Daniel Botkin pointed out, Lewis and Clark specifically referred to very few grizzly bears in the neighborhood of the Great Falls. Likewise, from the Great Falls to the head of Jefferson River, though they mentioned tracks or other evidence of bears a few times, they only reported seeing about half a dozen actual bears. In both cases, a casual impression is given of a great abundance of bears, but actual reported observations of bears are remarkably few. It is impossible for us to know how many other bears were around. Upon this thin observational evidence, those of us who study the informational legacy of Lewis and Clark have tended to build a mighty theoretical edifice about the relative aggressiveness of what were closely affiliated, neighboring groups of bears. Scientists might object to this confident a conclusion on several grounds, most of all that these are pitifully small "sample sizes" about which to conclude anything.

Considering the exceptional variability in bear personality (remember the grizzly that ran from Lewis when he first got to the Great Falls?), what do we really know? We know that Lewis and Clark tended to shoot at any bear that came within range, and that many of those bears took this treatment hard and tried to fight back. We know that this trait of bears apparently showed itself more clearly in the country around the Great Falls, and that the men were in constant fear of the bears. We know that some number of bears—apparently more than one, but how many we are not told—were even bold enough to come into camp to steal the raw meat lying around. We know that while they were at the Great Falls, the corps moved slowly enough and set up camps that were permanent enough, that for extended periods of time they provided bears with some irresistible attractants.

But we also should keep in mind that had only one or two bears behaved differently than reported, either at the Great Falls or upstream, the impression left us about aggressive bears versus shy bears would be a different one. If even one or two of the bears they shot or shot at upstream from the Great Falls had turned and charged them, or tried to swim out to the canoes, Lewis might not have made his comment about them being shy. Can we really assume that the half dozen or so bears they reported seeing upstream of the Great Falls accurately represent the prevailing temperament of all the bears of that region? Perhaps, but I doubt it.

We're counting even more heavily than Lewis and Clark did on educated guesses. And as it happens, we will find ourselves engaging in much more conjectural biology as we go along. These exercises in interpreting slight information into bigger stories are great fun and are sometimes even important in modern wildlife management, but let's not get too sure of ourselves here.

In this context, it would be useful to hear from another great western traveler, Francis Parkman. In 1892, writing a new preface to his masterpiece of western adventure, *The Oregon Trail,* Parkman looked back down the long decades since his trip west in 1846 and reflected on the reported change in the grizzly bear's behavior:

> It is said that he is no longer his former self, having found, by an intelligence not hitherto set to his credit, that his ferocious strength is no match for a repeating rifle; with which discovery he is reported to have grown diffident, and abated the truculence of his more prosperous days. One may be permitted to doubt if the bloodthirsty old savage has really experienced a change of heart; and before inviting him to single combat, the ambitious tenderfoot, though the proud possessor of a Winchester with sixteen cartridges in the magazine, would do well to consider not only the quality of his weapon, but also that of his nerves.[10]

CHAPTER TEN

Rare Bears

On August 12, 1805, Lewis first reached the Continental Divide at today's Lemhi Pass, in extreme southwestern Montana. Crossing that divide, the corps moved not only onto the Pacific Slope and beyond the boundaries of the United States but also into some of the least hospitable landscapes of the trip. After having reached well into the Rocky Mountains by following the river valleys, they were now confronted with the high country itself.

In *Passage through the Garden: Lewis and Clark and the Image of the American Northwest* (1975), John Logan Allen's magnificently researched study of the geographical theorizing that preceded and grew from the Lewis and Clark Expedition, we learn the extent to which centuries of hope and imagination had misled the captains about these mountains.[1] Prevailing ideas about continental geography, combined with ardently wishful thinking, had led most theorists, including President Thomas Jefferson, to assume that the crossing would probably be easy. Some theorized that it would involve merely carrying the canoes across a level "height of land." At most, it would require a day or two of travel over a single range of mountains probably less high and formidable than the Appalachians. Advice received by the captains at Fort Mandan only encouraged such hopes, which stemmed as much from the needs of the young republic as from any trustworthy facts. The future of the nation's trade, political unity, and military defense were all seen as depending in part on proving this heartfelt dream of a "short portage."[2] Of course the dream was doomed. The trip was awful, through rugged terrain with little food to be found.

On August 21, still at Camp Fortunate, Lewis devoted considerable diary space to information about the habits and material lifeways of the

Shoshone Indians with whom they were camped. He explained that some of their ornaments were acquired "from their friends and relations who live beyond the barren plain towards the Ocean in a S. Westerly direction."

> these friends of theirs they say inhabit a good country abounding with Elk, deer, bear, and Antelope, and possess a much greater number of horses and mules than they do themselves; or using their own figure that their horses and mules are as numerous as the grass of the plains.[3]

Lewis noted that bear claws had great value, and the hunting of the bear was perceived as a great challenge—his comments on the Shoshone echoed those made by corps members about other tribes far down the Missouri River. Throughout the grizzly bear's range, its physical and spiritual power was universally recognized:

> the warriors or such as esteem themselves brave men wear collars made of the claws of the brown bear which are also esteemed of great value and are preserved with great care. these claws are ornamented with beads about the thick end near which they are peirced through their sides and strung on a thong of dressed leather and tyed about the neck commonly with the upper edge of the tallon next the breast or neck but sometimes are reversed. it is esteemed by them an act of equal celebrity the killing one of these bear or an enimy, and with the means they have of killing this animal it must be a really serious undertaking.

Virtually all depictions of nineteenth-century Indians wearing bear-claw necklaces show them with the claw points facing "down," or toward the chest. Lewis suggested not only that the claws might point up or down but also that the point-up style was most common. At least that is how this seems to be stated—that the "upper edge of the tallon," which I take to mean the outside curve of the claw, rested against the person's skin. This would cause the points of the claws to arc up away from the skin.

Clark, camped that same day west of the divide near the Salmon River, noted that the local Shoshone Indians' tools and clothing were made from parts of many animal species:

> They have only a few indifferent knives, no ax, make use of Elk's horn Sharpened to spit their wood, no clothes except a Short Legins & robes of different animals, Beaver, Bear, Buffalow, wolf Panthor, Ibex (Sheep), Deer, but most commonly the antilope Skins which they ware loosely about them.

On August 23, while he was in the process of discovering the impassability of the Salmon River, Clark complained that "we have but little and nothing to be precured in this quarter except Choke Cheres & red haws not an animal of any kind to be seen and only the track of a Bear."

On August 24, Lewis again was moved to comment on the Shoshone perception of bear hunting as one of the greatest of honors, explaining that "those distinguishing acts are the killing and scalping an enemy, the killing a white bear, leading a party to war who happen to be successful either in destroying their enemies or robing them of their horses, or individually stealing the horses of an enemy."

By early September the party was on its way again, leaving Camp Fortunate and moving across the divide into present Idaho, then north and back into present Montana, in the drainage of the Bitterroot River, reaching Traveler's Rest (near present Lolo, Montana) on September 9. Back in Idaho, on September 1, Clark reported that ". . . one man Shot two bear this evening unfortunately we Could git neither of them." Whitehouse elaborated that "the hunters killed a Deer and wounded two bear at dark but could not get them." We are left to assume that the bears escaped wounded, perhaps aided by the failing light, but we are given no hint of their species.

Whitehouse also gave us the most detailed discussion of a Salish Indian "medicine tree" that the party sighted, apparently on Lolo Creek, when they left Traveler's Rest on September 11:

> passed a tree on which was a number of Shapes drawn on it with paint by the natives. a white bear Skin hung on the

Same tree. we Suppose this to be a place of worship among them.

Anthropologist Patricia Robins Flint, in a brief article about another such tree in Montana, said that "the ethnographic Salish in Western Montana used trees as shrines and offering places. Token gifts were placed on medicine trees to [here she cited Granville Stuart's 1925 memoir, *Forty Years on the Frontier*] 'invoke the aid of the Great Spirit to make game plentiful and make them successful in their enterprises.'"[4] James Ronda, author of the milestone *Lewis and Clark among the Indians*, quoted earlier, saw such a tree in the recent past:

> In the early 1980s Gary Moulton and I were part of a L&C Trail Heritage Foundation trip up over Lemhi Pass and then up to Travelers Rest. In those now-long-gone days it was possible to get the entire L&C group into one yellow school bus! Anyway, once over the pass we headed north toward Travelers Rest. On the way, Edrie Vinson (then secretary of the Foundation) pointed out a large tree known locally as the medicine tree mentioned in the L&C journals. We all stopped, got out, and looked at what was indeed a very grand tree. I seem to recall that there were some bits of "offering cloth" still on the tree; and somewhere in the house I think there is a photo of me standing by the tree. As I recall there was no marker by the tree and when last I was up in those parts (summer, 1999) I must have missed seeing the tree.[5]

This may have been another tree than the one Whitehouse mentioned; along the route north into the Bitterroot Valley, before the East Fork of the Bitterroot River joins the West Fork, it receives the waters of a stream called Medicine Tree Creek. In any event, the explorers did not take this opportunity to explore Indian use of bear parts in tribal spiritual life, and we are left with only this brief description of the site.

In the crossing of the mountains from Traveler's Rest, the corps found early snows, rugged country, and little to eat. On September 17, now well into present Idaho, Whitehouse was disappointed to report that "one of the hunters chased a bear in a mountn but killed nothing." On September 18, now nearly over the worst part of the mountains, Lewis reported that the corps's rations were a combination of horsemeat and the prepared soup mix they had hauled all this way but had little interest in actually eating:

> we dined & suped on a skant proportion of portable soupe,
> a few canesters of which, a little bears oil and about 20 lbs
> of candles form our stock of provision. . . .

Bear oil was worth mentioning; it must have been one of the few comforts available at such times, that they could enrich whatever poor fare they had with some bear grease.

Though their food improved as they reached the Nez Perce villages on the west side of the mountains—the Nez Perce were quite generous—the corps had left the glorious wildlife abundance of the Great Plains behind. From Camp Fortunate on, they frequently mentioned the shortage of good food, either among their party or among the Indians they met. Though they were never in serious danger of starvation during the following winter on the west slope, they were never especially happy with the available food and by the end of winter looked forward with great enthusiasm to their return to buffalo country.

But one more matter must be dealt with before leaving the mountains behind. Thanks in good part to the accounts that Lewis and Clark and their men left of their difficult and hungry crossing of the mountains, another piece of indestructible folklore has arisen. It is the notion that the Rocky Mountains—not just the stretch of the Bitterroot Mountains the men crossed in late August and September, but the whole mountain range generally—were essentially devoid of large animals prior to the coming of white men.

It is not a simple notion or one susceptible to simple analysis. There are many variant opinions out there. Some seem to hold that these mountains could not support large animals, period—that there just wasn't enough food. Others suggest that even if the mountains were hospitable enough to support some animals, there were more than enough Indians

Medicine tree, Bitterroot Valley, western Montana, as described by James Ronda in the text. PHOTO COURTESY OF J. I. MERRITT.

in the area to keep the wildlife populations down close to zero. Others suggest that the mountains could support some animals in the summer but that the grazing species all migrated to lower winter ranges when the snow came.

Perhaps the most interesting of the interpretations that arose from early accounts like those of the corps is that the Rocky Mountains were indeed without large animals, but that the settlement of the lower country near them forced the animals that lived there to retreat to the higher elevations. In other words, white people caused the animals to live where they had not lived before and turned the starvation country of Lewis and Clark into big-game habitat. Stephen Ambrose, in his deservedly popular chronicle of the expedition, summed up this remarkable change like this:

> [Lewis and Clark] were in what is today prime big-game country; out-of-state hunters pay hundreds of dollars for a license and an outfitter to hunt elk and bear in these mountains. But in 1805, such animals were down on the plains and meadows; they were driven into the mountains by the coming of the ranchers and farmers.[6]

This concept, like the notion that grizzly bears "learned" to fear white men with guns, has been under discussion for many years among wildlife biologists and managers. And like the grizzly bear question, it has revealed greater and greater levels of complexity.

The idea that these large mammals were driven into previously unoccupied high-country habitats is still widely believed. I suspect that among local people who have any reason to think about historic wildlife populations in the Rocky Mountain West, the majority believe that the mountains used to be largely unoccupied and were only filled up with mammals when the low country was settled by white humans. But this belief is so problematic and has been called into question so often, I wonder that any modern writer still uses it with confidence.

It might help us to begin at the beginning of the reign of the present set of wildlife species that inhabit the West. The large mammals of the West have been the resident fauna there for more than ten millennia—ever since the spate of extinctions at the end of the Pleistocene restructured

North American ecosystems by removing dozens of ancient species, including mastodons, short-faced bears, dire wolves, and many other spectacular creatures. For many years, scientists have debated what caused these extinctions—changing climate and the arrival of large numbers of human predators are the most frequently argued-over causes of this extraordinary shuffling of the evolutionary deck.

Whatever caused the extinctions, the surviving species had more than ten thousand years to find every available niche. If there was anything good to eat, and anyplace good to live, they had millennia to learn about it. During all those years, climatic changes certainly compelled these species to adjust to changing food regimes and the like, but the species held out and made themselves at home wherever homes could be made.

Because of this longtime residence and familiarity with the land, the idea that suddenly, in the nineteenth century, these animals could be forced to live in places that up until then had been inhospitable to them is somewhat shaky and unconvincing. If there was livable habitat, they were using it. If it was not livable, how could they suddenly go live there?

But these questions are themselves somewhat simplistic. Animals must have found the best habitats and used marginal ones when the circumstances (such as an extended drought, for example) required them to. Over the course of so many centuries, they developed seasonal migratory routes that took them to the best foods, calving areas, wintering areas, and other habitats that their region could offer. We think of bison as the great wanderers, but all the large ungulates migrate as need be, sometimes for considerable distances. Elk, for example, are often determined migrators, with seasonal migration routes of fifty or more miles in length.[7] Some deer and pronghorn are known to move as far at times.[8] Obviously none of these animals would stay in the harsh high-elevation areas when the snow was several feet deep, any more than they would ignore rich high-elevation meadow forage in the late spring and summer. No doubt throughout the Rocky Mountains elk and other ungulates developed migratory patterns uniquely adapted to each locale, and no doubt predators accommodated their own annual rounds to those patterns. Subtlety, complexity, and change were everywhere.

On that very involved ecological system, with its many subtleties and flexibilities, humans could have many influences. Native Americans had at least ten thousand years (and perhaps much longer; the arrival date of humans in North America is also subject to heated debate) to influence these animals, and they did so in many ways, from directly killing them, to outcompeting them for certain resources, to selectively burning preferred habitats to enhance forage production, drive game, or accomplish other local aims.

Then, about five hundred years ago, Euro-Americans arrived on the continent. Their influences were far-reaching almost from the beginning. European disease epidemics raced far ahead of white settlers and travelers, progressively decimating many if not most tribes and thereby affecting their use of the land and their impacts on wildlife. Other European diseases affected native wildlife species, some of which were just as susceptible to catastrophic death tolls as were Native humans. Euro-Americans pushed eastern Indians off their lands, setting off a chain reaction of successive displacements as tribes moved west and forced other tribes to move as well. European settlement, trade incentives, horses, and technology forever changed the way tribes used the land and its wildlife. By shifting the balance of military or economic power among the tribes, these things introduced tremendous political and environmental turmoil into vast regions where white people had barely even visited yet.[9]

By the time Lewis and Clark came west, all these factors were at play along their travel route. We will have more to do with the implications of all this European influence on the West as we continue the journey, but for now it is enough to say that these influences alone should suggest that nothing so involved as the long-distance migrations of large numbers of wild animals across a mountainous landscape can be summed up in a sentence about game being pushed back into the mountains. Much more was going on.

When white settlers actually got to the various parts of the West and set up shop—fencing land, raising livestock, shooting wild animals, and doing everything else they did so successfully—no doubt they had instant and dramatic effects on the local wildlife. Most significant, they tended first to wipe out or greatly reduce the resident animals, especially predators.

But Euro-American settlements had other, more far-reaching effects as well. Perhaps most significant of these, if you were an elk or deer, was the restriction or simple elimination of portions of your migratory range.

This has been noted, again and again, as one of the biggest wildlife conservation failings of the system of national parks and national forests in the West: Because these federal lands were set aside after most valleys were claimed or settled, they tend to protect only the high-country summer ranges. As the valleys continue to fill up with ranches, suburbs, and other developments, the native wild animals have fewer and fewer places to go to spend their winters. Thus, though these animals were not "driven into the mountains" by settlement, the mountains are all that is left to them.

The prominent western forester Elers Koch took on this issue as long ago as 1941. In an extended article in *The Journal of Wildlife Management,* Koch reviewed the journals of Lewis and Clark, as well as those of other early western travelers, and concluded that a misunderstanding had arisen that had misled several generations of citizens, biologists, and managers:

> The theory has been developed, and to a considerable degree accepted by field naturalists, that before the coming of the white man the mountains were very thinly populated with game, particularly elk and buffalo, and that it was only through persistent hunting in the plains and valleys that these animals were driven back in the mountains for refuge. This theory is based to a large extent on Lewis and Clark's record of the scarcity of game in the Bitter-root Mountains, and on a half dozen accounts of early exploration of the Yellowstone Park, from 1870 to 1875.
>
> I am unable to accept this theory. It is probably based on relative rather than actual numbers of game animals in the mountains as compared with the plains country.
>
> To a man accustomed to the daily sight of hundreds of animals on the plains, the ordinary mountain occurrence of game would seem scarcity. . . .
>
> The general statement is correct that the elk and buffalo were primarily plains animals in the sense that they occurred in vastly greater numbers in the plains country, with some timber or mountain shelter, than they did in the higher mountain country, and likewise mountain sheep were far more abundant in the breaks of the Missouri River,

or in steep, cliffy country low down along the Clark Fork River than they ever were in the high timberline country. But there is ample evidence that these animals also ranged the high mountain country in probably considerably greater numbers than have occurred at any time since the valleys were settled. In other words, the plains animals were killed off, not driven back in the mountains, and the rough mountain country continued to give some refuge to the animals that were already there.[10]

There will probably always be disagreements over just how scarce or abundant large animals were in various parts of the West, how much Indians may have influenced population sizes and distributions, and what we should do about it today. The careless or cavalier interpretation of the Lewis and Clark journals on this point has had a lasting and powerful legacy. Wildlife managers in many parts of the West have long attempted to understand their local wildlife herds at least in part through the window provided by Lewis and Clark—which is to say through the window provided by secondhand interpretations of what Lewis and Clark saw.

It is no accident that Koch singled out Yellowstone National Park, because Lewis and Clark's accounts of their travels through the Bitterroot Range have been used countless times to "prove" that the park—hundreds of miles away, with significant ecological differences from the Lewis and Clark route—was either devoid of large animals prehistorically, or had them only in small numbers. The controversy over just what the "appropriate" number of elk, bison, and other species is for the park has been rolling along for nearly a century.[11] Indeed, Lewis and Clark's accounts were recently reactivated by people opposed to wolf restoration in and around Yellowstone. They argued that Lewis and Clark's journals demonstrated that large grazing mammals such as elk did not live in the mountains and then reasoned that if there were no large grazing mammals in the park, there certainly couldn't have been predators there, either. A thorough review of the historical record, as well as of archaeological and paleontological evidence, established the pre-Euro-American presence and abundance of both prey and predators in the park area, but debates continue over just how numerous the animals were and how they used the land compared with today.[12]

The use of Lewis and Clark to support various interpretations of wildlife abundance or scarcity in the Rocky Mountains recently came home to the very route they traveled. The corps's journals have been invoked in opposition to the plan to restore grizzly bears to the Bitterroot Ecosystem. It is a testament to the extraordinary authority of their journals that what Lewis and Clark said about their quick if laborious passages through one narrow portion along one edge of the Bitterroot Ecosystem has been used to "prove" something about grizzly bear use of more than five thousand square miles of Rocky Mountain wilderness.[13] Whatever this may say about the wisdom of the people interpreting the journals of Lewis and Clark, it says worlds about the continuing power of the Corps of Discovery in our imaginations.

Pacific Slope Bears

Most of us who care about the fate of the grizzly bear are heartily sick of the many maps that show the bear's shrinking range. Typically on these maps, a crosshatched pattern labeled something like "grizzly bear range in 1492" or "grizzly bear range at the time of Lewis and Clark" stretches the length and breadth of western North America. Another, darker pattern, labeled "grizzly bear range today," still shows substantial continuous range in western Canada and Alaska, but in the lower forty-eight states there are just a few forlorn little blobs, representing the last stand of the species in a few northwestern states.

The older, larger pattern on the map is most interesting, and not just because it indicates a more prosperous bear population. It is interesting, even intriguing, for what it says about where bears *didn't* prosper, even long ago. One of the most authoritative early maps of the grizzly bear's range appeared in Ernest Thompson Seton's monumental *Lives of Game Animals* (1926). Seton was and still is criticized for his anthropomorphism—his tendency to humanize wild animals at the cost of scientific objectivity. But there is no questioning the thoroughness of his patient gathering of information. He was a tireless correspondent, researcher, and reader, and his accounts of the lifeways of American mammals are nothing if not exhaustive accumulations of loosely organized anecdote, insight, and inquiry. As informal and undisciplined as they may sound to the modern ear, they were about as complete as this kind of information got in his day.

This makes his map especially appealing. The "ancient range" of the grizzly bear, according to Seton, included virtually all of California, Nevada, and Utah, and most of Colorado, New Mexico, and Arizona.

Seton's dark pattern of original grizzly bear habitat dipped well into the north-central highlands of Mexico, and north from there, taking in West Texas, the very northwest tip of Oklahoma, and various percentages of the Great Plains states of Kansas, Nebraska, South Dakota, and North Dakota. Occupied grizzly bear habitat even reached the extreme western edge of Minnesota before turning northwest and slanting all the way up into the high Yukon. There is even a thoughtful elongated blob, complete with question mark (suggesting Seton's own capacity for skepticism), in northern Labrador.[1]

This is a huge, unruly range, embracing an amazing array of habitats, from desert to rain forest and from baking heat to arctic cold. Grizzly bears seemed able to live anywhere they chose, and this might make us wonder, as we scan the edges of Seton's range map—why did they stop where they did? Why weren't they everywhere else? And perhaps just as interesting, were those boundaries stable or changing? Were grizzly bears retreating, as we have already seen they seem to have been from the East? Were they advancing in other places? Or were they just holding their own?

A perhaps even more intriguing question arises along the western edge of this sprawling habitat blob, in the Pacific Northwest. Not far north of the California border, along the southern Oregon coast, the line of occupied grizzly bear habitat suddenly swings inland, arcing across southern Oregon clear into southwestern Idaho, and then angling back to the northwest to encompass the northeastern and north-central part of Washington. The line appears to take in the Cascade Range of the northern half of Washington, including present North Cascades National Park. But it leaves conspicuously unoccupied a large reach of land on both sides of the Columbia River. Far back from both shores, the entire length of the river where today it forms the boundary between Washington and Oregon was shown by Seton as having been grizzlyless country.

Offhand, this does not seem to make much sense. The foremost biological spectacle in Columbia River history has been its prodigious salmon runs. Early observers of the river and its tributaries marveled at the seemingly endless, inexhaustible numbers of huge fish.[2] And no species of animal is more closely associated with the grizzly or brown bear than the salmon; at many places farther north, even today, bears fishing for salmon are a kind of nature cliché, a tourist attraction of great power,

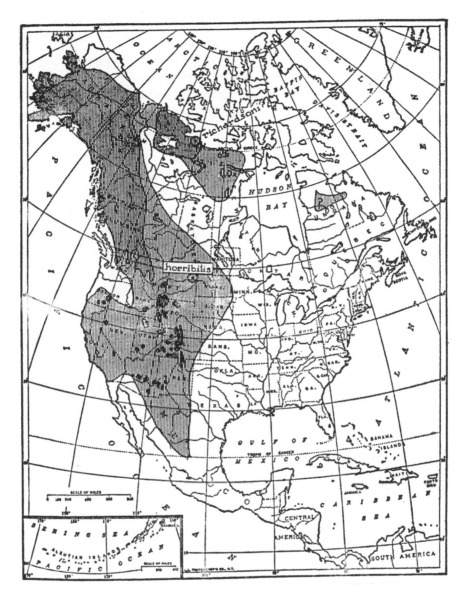

Ranges of the Grizzly-Bears and of the Barren-Ground Bear, *from Ernest Thompson Seton's* Lives of Game Animals *(1926). With the assistance of the United States Biological Survey, Seton prepared this then-authoritative map showing the known former eastern extent of the grizzly bear's range, as well as its pocket population in northern Labrador and the curious absence of the species from the lower Columbia River drainage in Washington and Oregon.*

and an indication of the boundless appetites of bears and the irresistible determination of salmon.

So why did this great natural pairing fail to materialize along the Columbia? Bears are not especially adept at taking salmon from deep, open, water like the main river itself, but the many tributaries of the lower and upper Columbia, with their countless feeder streams, must have provided opportunities galore for successful fishing by bears.

Lewis and Clark did not find it to be so. Once across the Rocky Mountains and into the main drainage of the Columbia, they had nothing more to say about grizzly bear sightings and precious little to say about bears of any kind. On October 25, 1805, just upstream of the Short Narrows (now drowned by The Dalles Dam), they met with some Wishram-Wasco Indians. Whitehouse said that "they had deer & bear meat with them the head chief had on a jacket that was made of Some kind of worked Splits which would defend off the arrows. our Capts. gave him a meddle, then he gave our Capts. Some bears oil and a fresh Sammon."

On October 26, near the present site of the city of The Dalles, Oregon, Clark said that "one man giged a *Salmon trout* which we had fried in a little Bears oil which a Chief gave us yesterday and I think the finest fish I ever tasted." The same day, he said that "our hunters Saw Elk & bear signs to day in the white oake woods." On October 30, downstream from present Hood River, Oregon, Clark reported that "The bottom above the river is about 3/4 of a mile wide and rich, Some deer & bear Sign." On December 8 and December 10, Clark reported bear tracks in the general vicinity of the site of Fort Clatsop, which they were just then starting to build in a sheltered site near what is now called the Lewis and Clark River.

And that is the extent of their bear reports for the entire length of their downstream transit of the Columbia. On the whole route, they did not report seeing a single live bear, and it seems to be generally agreed that the bear meat, bear tracks, and bear grease they were discussing, unless left over from the mountains, were almost certainly from black bears.

If we had only Lewis and Clark's accounts of the lower Columbia River to go on, we would still have at least three good reasons to be cautious in assuming that the evident lack of bears was a reflection of a genuine scarcity. The first reason is the same one mentioned earlier, in relation to their observations at the Great Falls of the Missouri. Their observations of bears were incidental to other missions, and they were not formally conducting surveys of the animals. We should not overstate the meaning of their occasional observations of this species.

The second reason is at least as important and has to do with the timing of their visit. Lewis and Clark were, after all, *wintering* at the mouth of the Columbia River, and in most parts of their range, bears den during the cold season, which makes them essentially invisible to all observers.

The third reason is that once the corps approached the Pacific Coast, they spent more and more of their time in forested environments, in which wildlife sightings would necessarily be more difficult.

But we are not dependent solely upon Lewis and Clark. As Seton and later writers reported, historical evidence of grizzly bears is indeed sparse to nonexistent in the lower Columbia River area, though somewhat better the farther you get from the river. In my documentary study of the early historical record (roughly 1833 to 1897) of wildlife in the Mount Rainier area (north of the Columbia River, in present Washington), I was struck by the extreme scarcity of nineteenth-century observations of grizzly bears in that part of the Cascades.[3] In the many firsthand accounts of the park area and the nearby valleys, wildlife was sometimes described as abundant, and bears were sometimes said to be common. Species was rarely mentioned, but black bears seem to have been intended. One writer said that "brown" bears were present, but as usual it is impossible to know what the writer meant by that term. Still, I did not find a single bear sighting that could be confidently described as a grizzly bear, leaving me with the distinct impression that grizzly bears were uncommon in the Mount Rainier area during the period I studied.

On the other hand—and providing further indication of the difficulty of using these early anecdotal sources—several other early travelers through western Washington stated that all large animals were scarce. Some specifically said or implied that the scarcity was due primarily to Indian hunting. Some gave the impression that these scarcities were a relatively new thing. The more early opinions I gathered, the more puzzling the situation seemed.[4]

Without question, the historical presence of grizzly bears in the Cascade Range north of Mount Rainier has been satisfactorily confirmed by historical research. In his study of the early historical record in the area in and around North Cascades National Park (near the Canadian border), researcher Paul Sullivan quoted early reports of actual sightings. He also reviewed early-nineteenth-century fur-trade records maintained at two Hudson's Bay Company posts near the present park area in Washington and British Columbia.[5] Sullivan found that low numbers of grizzly bear hides appeared in the fur-trade records in the decades before the Civil War. The most hides traded in any one year at Thompson's River, B.C., was eleven in 1851. Apparently four hides turned up at Fort Nisqually, near present Tacoma, Washington, over a period of many years. Of course there is no knowing how far a hide was carried from the bear's carcass to where it was traded, but from the combination of trading records, early accounts, and archaeological evidence, there is sufficient reason to indicate that grizzly bears did live in the Cascades of central and northern Washington.

Perhaps as interesting, Sullivan found that much higher numbers of hides came in to the post at Fort Colville, in eastern Washington, far from the Cascades but nearer the Rockies. The peak year in the grizzly bear hide trade there was 1849, when 382 hides came through. It seems safe to assume that these bears were from that region rather than from the much farther distant Cascades.

Fort Nez Perce, near present Walla Walla in southeastern Washington, had its peak year in the grizzly bear hide trade in 1846, when thirty-two hides came through. Fort Nez Perce was only about thirty miles east of the Columbia River where that river begins its duties as the Oregon-Washington boundary. Again, it seems most likely that these bears were taken in southeastern Washington or in the mountains of nearby Idaho.

From a variety of evidence like this—and including a certain amount of archaeological information—we have indications that grizzly bears did inhabit several parts of present Washington and certainly were scattered widely in the Cascade Range of that state, and that they were very scarce or absent from the Columbia River corridor farther south.

We likewise know, from much more abundant historical evidence, that grizzly bears thrived through much of California, not only in the Sierra Nevada but also in the lower river valleys all the way to the coast. Tracy Storer and Lloyd Tevis's *California Grizzly* (1955), a thorough literary reconstruction of this state's vanished grizzly bear population, has established the bear's abundance and widespread distribution.[6]

Which leaves us with this puzzling gap between California to the south and Washington to the north. Why weren't grizzly bears there?

By all accounts, the foremost reason was people. The entire length of their trip down the Columbia, Lewis and Clark were in daily contact with people, often in large numbers. The journals of the corps in that period feature a regular recitation of meetings, tradings, tensions, and other dealings with many humans who were well settled and obviously of lengthy local residence. While it is not safe to assume that this situation had been stable or even similar over several thousand years, it is clear that humans were there in great numbers and were making the most of the salmon runs. At no other point in their entire journey would the captains encounter such dense human populations. They estimated that the Columbia River tribes totaled eighty thousand people.[7]

People in that number, settled in established villages, would have had a low tolerance for free-ranging predators that were not only dangerous but also competed for the salmon. It is reasonably well established that Native Americans had little trouble displacing grizzly bears from preferred sites. For example, it has recently been suggested that some of Alaska's premier brown bear viewing areas, where bears gather by the dozen to feed on spawning salmon, probably don't replicate the scene of several hundred years ago at those sites. Prior to the arrival of whites, such gatherings of bears may not have happened as consistently, if at all. Archaeological evidence at Brooks River, in Katmai National Park, where such salmon-fishing bears are now a well-established visitor attraction, suggests that Native people used that site for thousands of years and probably would not have been willing or able to risk sharing the fish with huge, ungenerous bears.[8] So it seems perfectly imaginable that a similar condition existed along the Columbia. Once people staked out the good fishing spots—places where for one reason or another the fish were easiest to take—the bears would have had a hard time of it. As the human population grew, the bears would have to go or adjust to human presence in some way.[9]

The presence of large numbers of humans must have had other effects. People would necessarily hunt other animals as well as take salmon, thus further reducing the prey base for bears. Though some large mammals—elk, deer, and black bears—did exist along the river and around Fort Clatsop, their numbers seemed low to Lewis and Clark.

On the other hand, the Columbia tribes did have large numbers of horses. One recent estimate gave a possible range of between fifty thousand and five hundred thousand horses owned by the Columbia River tribes.[10] That many horses would have competed with native ungulates for food, further reducing the ungulate prey base for bears and other predators (horses, being quite similar to money, would have been more closely guarded and difficult to kill to have simply replaced the wild ungulates as bear food). Horsemeat (and dog meat) were very common in the corps's diet during their sojourn on the Pacific Slope.

As their dreary winter wore on at Fort Clatsop, the men occasionally mentioned bears. On January 15, 1806, Lewis, while dutifully reporting on the habits of the local Indians, mentioned that they used their bows and arrows for most purposes, but "Their guns and ammunition they reserve for the Elk, deer and bear, of the two last however there are but few in their neighbourhood." He also noticed that for arrow storage, "the quiver is usually the skin of a young bear or that of a wolf. . . ."

On February 9, Lewis said that "in the evening Drewyer returned; had killed nothing but one beaver. he saw one black bear, which is the only one which has been seen in this neighbourhood since our arrival; the Indians inform us that they are abundant but are now in their holes."

On February 15, Lewis returned briefly to his continuing rumination on the issue of bear species, having at least temporarily resolved the question of how many species there were to his own satisfaction. At the beginning of a list of the various mammals of the West, he stated that "The quadrupeds of this country from the Rocky Mountains to the pacific Ocean are 1st the *domestic animals,* consisting of the horse and the dog only; 2cdly the *native wild animals,* consisting of the Brown white or grizly bear, (which I beleive to be the same family with a mearly accedental difference in point of colour) the black bear. . . ."

The next day, he pursued the matter more fully:

The brown white or grizly bear are found in the rocky mountains in the timbered parts of it or Westerly side but rarely; they are more common below the rocky Mountain on the borders of the plains where there are copses of brush and underwood near the watercourses. they are by no means as plenty on this side of the rocky mountains as on the other, nor do I beleive that they are found at all in the woody country, which borders this coast as far in the interior as the range of mountains which, pass the Columbia between the Great Falls and rapids of that river. the black bear differs not any from those common to the United states and are found under the rocky Mountains in the woody country on the borders of the great plains of columbia and also in this tract of woody country which lie between these plains and the Pacific Ocean. their oconimy and habits are also the same with those of the United States.

From then until their departure upriver, the only bear-related remarks made by the journalists involved Lewis's observations on March 19 that local Indians used bearskins, among other kinds, to make robes, and that "the men sometimes wear collars of bears claws." This was the first mention of what were most likely black bear claws being used for this ornamentation, and it might indicate that a certain amount of valor or heroism was associated with taking black bears (it is not impossible that coastal Indians also wore grizzly bear claws acquired in trade from upstream tribes).

CHAPTER TWELVE

Variagated Bears

On March 23, 1806, the corps set out from Fort Clatsop on their return trip. They would move as a single group until they reached Traveler's Rest, and then split up to broaden their earlier explorations. The first part of the journey, up the Columbia and across the mountains, seems to have been as arduous as their trip out the previous year. Bears continued to be a routine part of the adventure.

On April 1, as the party neared the mouth of the Willamette River (at present Portland, Oregon), Lewis said that one of the hunting parties reported "much sign of the black bear." The next day Gass said that "Myself and 4 men went below the mouth of Sandy river, and killed an elk, some deer and a black bear." The Sandy, which the men also knew as the Quicksand, flows into the Columbia from the Oregon shore just upstream of Portland.

On April 4, apparently describing a hunt that occurred the previous day, Lewis said that "Sergt. Gass and party brought the flesh of a bear and some venison. they informed us that they had killed an Elk and six deer tho' the flesh of the greater part of those animals was so meagre it was unfit for uce and they had therefore left it in the woods. Collins who had killed the bear, found the bed of another in which there were three young ones; and requested to be permitted to return in order to waylay the bed and kill the female bear; we permitted him to do so; Sergt. Gass and Windsor returned with him." In his April 4 journal entry, Gass said that "Four men were sent on ahead this forenoon in a canoe to hunt; and I went out with two more to the den where we saw the cubs, to watch for the old bear; we stayed there until dark and then encamped about a quarter of a mile off, and went back early in the morning; but the old one was not returned; so we took the cubs and returned to camp." The next day, Lewis reported on the outcome of this little cubnapping enterprise, saying that "this morning at 10 OClock Sergt. Gass returned with Collins and Windsor   they had not succeeded in killing the female bear tho' they brought the three cubs with them. the Indians who visited us today fancyed these petts and gave us wappetoe in exchange for them. Drewyer informed me that he never knew a female bear return to her young when they had been allarmed by a person and once compelled to leave them."

Drouillard had a more sophisticated understanding of black bear behavior than many people, then or now. The defensive ferocity of mother bears is legend, and many people assume that any mother bear will fight to the death to protect her young. But there is an evolutionary advantage in the discrete withdrawal; a sow that dies defending her young can have no more young, but a sow that lives to breed again may produce several more offspring, thus ensuring the survival of her genetic heritage. These experiences further highlight the importance of the men fully understanding the difference between black and grizzly bears—the explosive defensive reaction of female grizzly bears to any perceived threat to their young is deservedly legendary, but black bear females rarely attack humans to defend their cubs.[1]

Now that many studies have been conducted of black bears, we know that their feelings about humans meddling with their young are not simple, either. Since at least the 1930s, naturalists have been invading black bear dens, handling the cubs (for measurements), and returning them to the den. Sow black bears do not abandon their cubs merely because humans have handled them.[2]

On April 7, Lewis, looking toward their upcoming crossing of the Rocky Mountains and the provisions they might acquire from the Nez Perce, said that "in the neighbourhood of the Chopunnish we can procure a few deer and perhaps a bear or two for the mountains." The next day, Lewis noted that "we have seen the black bear only in this quarter," and Clark said, ". . . we Sent out Drewyer, Shannon Colter & Collins to hunt with derections to return if the Wind Should lul, if not to Continue the hunt all day except they killed Elk or bear Sooner &c." Later in that day's entry Clark noted that "Collins Saw 2 bear but could not get a Shot at them."

Over the next four weeks, the only mention of bears in the journals was a brief mention of bear tracks in the vicinity of The Dalles. It wasn't until the party had returned to the Nez Perce and were impatiently waiting for the snow to melt out the pass over the Rockies that both Lewis and Clark commented on bear-claw necklaces being common among their hosts. It was also during their interval of waiting among the Nez Perce that they met Hohots Ilpplip, the chief named for the grizzly bear. According to journal editor Gary Moulton, the name "referred to a red, or bleeding grizzly bear, his spiritual animal helper or guardian."[3]

On May 14, still waiting for the snow to melt in the high country, Lewis had time to indulge his interest in the bear species question some more, as well as to record the details of some local cuisine:

> Collins killed two bear this morning and was sent with two others in quest of the meat; with which they returned in the evening; the mail bear was large and fat the female was of moderate size and reather meagre. we had the fat bear fleaced in order to reserve the oil for the mountains. both these bear were of the speceis common to the upper part of the missouri. they may be called white black grizzly brown or red bear for they are found of all those colours. perhaps it would not be unappropriate to designate them the variagated bear. we gave the indians who were about 15 in number half the female bear, with the sholder head and neck of the other. this was a great treat to those poor wretched who scarcely taist meat once a month. they immediately prepared a brisk fire of dry wood on which they threw a parsel of smooth stones from the river, when the fire had birnt down and heated the stones they placed them level and laid on a parsel of pine boughs, on these they laid the flesh of the bear in flitches, placing boughs between each course of meat and then covering it thickly with pine boughs; after this they poared on a small quantity of water and covered the whoe over with earth to the debth of four inches. in this situation they suffered it to remain about 3 hours when they took it out. I taisted of this meat and found it much more

tender than that which we had roasted or boiled, but the strong flavor of the pine destroyed it for my pallate. Labuish returned late in the evening and informed us that he had killed a female bear and two large cubbs, he brought with him several large dark brown pheasants which he had also killed. . . . The indians after their feast took a pipe or two with us and retired to rest much pleased with their repast. these bear are tremendious animals to them; they esteem the act of killing a bear equally great with that of an enimy in the field of action. I gave the claws of those which Collins killed to Hohâstillpilp.

On May 15, the hunters gave Lewis more cause to ponder the speciation of bears:

This morning early Reubin Fields in surching for his horse saw a large bear at no great distance from camp; several men went in pursuit of the bear, they followed his trail a considerable distance but could not come up with him. Labuish and Shannon set out with a view to establish a hunting camp and continuing several days, two others accompanyed them in order to bring in the three bear which Labuish had killed. Drewyer and Cruzatte were sent up the river; Shields R. Feilds and Willard hunted in the hills near the camp they returned in the evening with a few pheasants only and reported that there was much late appearance of bear, but beleived that they had gone off to a greater distance. at 11 A. M. the men returned with the bear which Labuich had killed. These bear gave me a stronger evidence of the various coloured bear of this country being one speceis only, than any I have heretofore had. The female was black with a considerable proportion of white hairs intermixed and a white spot on the breast, one of the young bear was jut black and the other of a light redish brown or bey colour. the poil of these bear were infinitely longer finer and thicker than the black bear their tallons also longer and more blont as if woarn by diging roots. the white and redish brown or bey coloured bear I saw together on the Missouri; the bey and grizly have been seen and killed together here for these were the colours of those which Collins killed yesterday. in short it is not common to find two bear here of this speceis precisely of the same colour, and if we were to attempt to distinguish them by their collours and to denominate each colour a distinct speceis we should soon find at least twenty. some bear nearly white have also been seen by our hunters at this place. the most striking differences between this speceis of bear and the common black bear are that the former are larger, have longer tallons and tusks, prey more on other animals, do not lie so long nor so closely in winter quarters, and will not climb a tree tho' ever so heardly pressed. the variagated bear I beleive to be the same here with those on the missouri but these are not as ferocious as those perhaps from the circumstance of their being compelled from the scarcity of game in this quarter to live more on roots and of course not such much in the habit of seizing and devouring living animals. the bear here are far from being as passive as the common black bear they attacked and faught our hunters already but not so fiercely as those of the Missouri. there are also some of the common black bear in this neighbourhood.

Lewis may have hoped that with "variagated" he had come upon a term that would finally be accepted as doing justice to the full array of shades and colors worn by grizzly bears. If so, it was a forlorn hope. The term did not catch on, and I am not sure any other early traveler ever used it (and what chance did it stand, against such a glorious word as *grizzly?*). Even Clark did not seem to favor it.

Lewis's speculations about the bears of western Idaho and eastern Washington being less aggressive because of their diet are especially interesting. In recent years, stable-isotope analysis of bone and hair from old specimens (killed between 1890 and 1931) have shown that grizzly bears in the upper Columbia River drainage relied heavily on salmon.[4]

As much difficulty as early white western travelers had sorting out bear speciation issues, readers back east must have been even more baffled by the animals depicted in publications of the time. Sensational popular adventure books, such as W. H. Davenport Adams's The Hunter and Trapper in North America, *published in London in 1875, showed grizzly bears in a variety of stylistic deformations. These misshapen animals were almost certainly the result of the distance between the engraver and the actual animals. The effect in this case is a portrayal of what could just as easily be two very uncomfortable men with really large feet in a badly padded bear costume.*

As mentioned in chapter 9, salmon-eating bears in Alaska are regarded as less aggressive than their ungulate-eating counterparts in other habitats. Perhaps this also had an effect on the bears Lewis and Clark encountered during their layover in western Idaho.

In any case, the men continued to find bears and shoot at them, species notwithstanding. On May 16, Lewis reported on more bear hunting by his men and elaborated some more on Nez Perce hunting:

> Hohâstillpilp and all the natives left us about noon and informed us that they were going up the river some distance to a place at which they expected to find a canoe, we gave them the head and neck of a bear, a part of which they eat and took the ballance with them. these people sometimes kill the variagated bear when they can get them in the open

plain where they can pursue them on horseback and shoot them with their arrows. the black bear they more frequently kill as they are less ferocious. . . . at 5 P. M. Drewyer and Cruzaate returned having killed on deer only. Drewyer had wounded three bear which he said were as white as sheep but had obtained neither of them.

I see no reason to doubt that Drouillard at the very least believed he had seen three bears that were truly white. Whether or not they really were (he was apparently unable to kill them and thus did not get to examine them up close or let Lewis have a look at them, too) I simply cannot know. But the persistent appearance in the journals of the words *white bear*, written by smart, capable observers like Drouillard, leads me to assume that the grizzly bear population of this region, and perhaps of the Missouri River as well, contained some extremely fair-haired individuals.

On May 17, after their chronometer was accidentally soaked in the rain, Lewis revealed yet another application for the ever-valuable bear grease they were constantly seeking:

> I opened it and founded it nearly filled with water which I carefully drained out exposed it to the air and wiped the works as well as I could with dry feathers after which I touched them with a little bears oil.

That same day, he also reported on another bear hunt and implied that even if the local bears were somewhat less belligerent than the Missouri River bears, they were still formidable:

> at 9 A. M. Sergt. Pryor and Collins returned, Sergt. Pryor brought the Skin and flesh of a black bear which he had killed; Collins had also killed a very large variegated bear but his horse having absconded last evening was unable to bring it. they had secured this meat perfectly from the wolves or birds and as it was at a considerable distance we did not think proper to send for it today. neither of these bear were in good order. as the bear are reather ferocious and we are

obliged to depend on them pincipally for our subsistence we thought it most advisable to direct at least two hunters to go together, and they accordingly paired themselves out for this purpose.

The next day, May 18, another variation, or variegation, on the grizzly bear presented itself to Lewis's inquiring eye:

> Potts and Whitehouse accompanied Collins to the bear he had killed on the 16th inst. with which they returned in the afternoon. the colours of this bear was a mixture of light redish brown white and dark brown in which the bey or redish brown predominated, the fur was bey as well as the lower portion of the long hairs, the white next succeeded in the long hairs which at their extremites were dark brown, this uncommon mixture might be termed a bey grizzle.

Lewis also reported that another party of hunters had "scowered the country between the Kooskooske [Clearwater River] and Collins's Creek [Lolo Creek] from hence to their junction about 10 miles and had seen no deer or bear and but little sign of either." On the nineteenth, Lewis said they were eating "lean bear meat" (Clark called it "pore"), and that "a little after dark Sheilds and Gibson returned unsuccessfull from the chase. they had seen some deer but no bear." On the twentieth, Lewis said that the late spring snows continued to plague even their bear hunters:

> Shannon and Colter came in unsuccessfull, they had wounded a bear and a deer last evening but the night coming on they were unable to pursue them, and the snow which fell in the course of the night and this morning had covered the blood and rendered all further pursuit impracticable.

On May 25, still waiting for the snow to melt, and still accumulating bear-color lore, Lewis reported that "Joseph and Reuben Feilds passed the river in order to hunt on the opposite side some miles above where the natives inform us that there is an abundance of bear and some deer." He then said that "Gibson and shields returned this evening having killed a Sandhill Crain only. they had wounded a female bear and a deer but got neither of them. Gibson informed me that the bear had two cubbs one of which was white and other as black as jett."

The same day Clark said that "one of our men purchased a Bear Skin of the nativs which was nearly of a Cream Colored white. this Skin which was the Skin of an animal of the middle Size of bears together with the defferent Sizes colours &c. of those which have been killed by our hunters give me a Stronger evidence of the various Coloured bear of this country being one Species only, than any I have heretofore had." He then continued, paraphrasing Lewis's April 15 observations on the color differences of the bears—an interesting twist on using an older journal entry from a colleague to reinforce a personal observation.

On May 28, Lewis noted that a hunting party returned: "deer were very abundant they informed us, but there were not many bear." On May 31, Lewis seemed to be describing the same bearskin already reported by Clark:

> Willard brought with him the dressed skin of a bear which he had purchased for Capt. C. this skin was an uniform pale redish brown colour, the indians informed us that it was not the Hoh-host or white bear, that it was the Yâck-kâh. this distinction of the indians induced us to make further enquiry relative to their opinions of the several species of bear in this country. we produced the several skins of the bear which we had killed at this place and one very nearly white which I had purchased. The white, the deep and pale red grizzle, the dark bron grizzle, and all those which had the extremities of the hair of a white or frosty colour without regard to the colour of the ground of the poil, they designated Hoh-host and assured us that they were the same with the white bear, that they ascosiated together, were very vicisious, never climbed the trees, and had much longer nails than the others. the black skins, those which were

black with a number of intire white hairs intermixed, the black with a white breast, the uniform bey, brown and light redish brown, they designated Yâck-kâh; said that they climbed the trees, had short nails and were not vicious, that they could pursue them and kill them with safety, they also affirmed that they were much smaller than the white bear. I am disposed to adopt the Indian distinction with rispect to these bear and consider them two distinct speceis. the white and the grizzly of this neighbourhood are the same of those found on the upper portion of the Missouri where the other speceis are not, and that the uniform redish brown black &c of this neighourhood are a speceis distinct from our black bear and from the black bear of the Pacific coast which I believe to be the same with those of the Atlantic coast, and that the common black bear do not exist here. I had previously observed that the claws of some of the bear which we had killed here had much shorter tallons than the variagated or white bear usually have but supposed that they had woarn them out by scratching up roots, and these were those which the Indians called Yâck-kâh. on enquiry I found also that a cub of an uniform redish brown colour, pup to a female black bear intermixed with entire white hairs had climbed a tree. I think this is a distinct speceis from the common black bear, because we never find the latter of any other colour than an uniform black, and also that the poil of this bear is much finer thicker and longer with a greater proportion of fur mixed with the hair, in other ispects they are much the same.

Here Lewis takes a step backward from an accurate understanding of the bear species—seeming to conclude that there were three—but we should go easy on him for his misunderstanding. The brown-colored black bear, often known as the "cinnamon bear," continued to confuse naturalists for many years. As late as 1961, biologist Raymond Burroughs could write that "reputable zoologists still disagree about the scientific status of the cinnamon bear which has at various times during the past hundred years been shifted from a subspecies to a distinct species; from a subspecies to a mere color phase of the black bear; and recently has been restored to the status of a subspecies."[5]

Lewis and Clark were familiar only with the eastern black bears, all of which were in fact black (as far west as Minnesota, 94 percent of the black bears are in fact black, the rest brown[6]). But a sizable percentage of bears in the West—in some cases more than half—are brown. Again, studies of fur-trade records are helpful. As far as the bears Lewis and Clark were seeing on the Pacific side of the Rockies, Washington biologists Richard Poelker and Harry Hartwell summarized one large study of bear hides traded before 1938:

> Of 19,228 black bear pelts recorded from posts along coastal British Columbia, 7 percent were of the brown color phase. Records at Ft. Vancouver showed 21 percent of the brown phase. This figure was no doubt influenced by pelts brought down the Columbia River from interior areas. An east-west gradient of brown phase incidence was shown when looking at trading post records in the Rocky Mountains where only 37 percent of the black bear were of the black phase. This percentage increased to 100 percent as one moved to the Pacific Coast. A north-south gradient similar to that found along the foothills of the Cascade Mountains in western Washington was found in Idaho where the frequency of black phase bear increased from 37 percent in southern Idaho to 93 percent in what was then New Caledonia.[7]

No wonder the precise relationship of these bears was unclear.

Ultimately, the question over the possible distinctness of the cinnamon bear as a race or strain was much like similar doubts over how many grizzly bear species there were. Today, thanks to more advanced genetic analysis, taxonomists agree that there are only two species of bears in this part of North America—the grizzly bear and the black bear. The frequent observation of black bear mothers of any color—from darkest black to palest blond—accompanied by a litter of cubs that are each a different color should instantly call into question the validity of designating bear species or subspecies on the basis of color.

Color in black bears seems more likely to be an evolutionary response to habitat differences. Black, for example, may be just the color for a murky coastal rain forest, but not as helpful in an arid, open environment. The mixture of black bear colors found in the Rockies today suggests that nature hasn't settled on any one color as the best, and maybe nature never would have, even if we hadn't showed up and started wondering about it all. Perhaps "variagation" would work best for the black bear, just as it has for the grizzly.

On June 3, Lewis continued to note details of bear color: "Colter, Jo. Fields and Willard returned this evening with five deer and one bear of the brown speceis; the hair of this was black with a large white spot on the breast containing a small circular black spot." Clark elaborated on this animal: "(this Species of bear is Smaller than our Common black bear) this was a female bear and as our hunters informed us had cubs last year, this they judged from the length and Size of her tits &c. this bear I am Confident is not larger than the yerlin Cubs of our Country." Black bears much more commonly have white markings on their chests, a variety of dots and circles and other marks. And, though both Lewis and Clark say that this bear was of the "brown species," which through most of the trip meant "grizzly," I agree with journal editor Moulton, who said this was a "cinnamon" bear—in other words, a brown-colored black bear.[8]

By "yerlin," Clark meant "yearling" and was suggesting that the local bears were quite small. On June 5, Lewis reported that "In the evening R. Feilds Shannon and Labuish return from the chaise and brought with them five deer and a brown bear." In this case we have no certain way of knowing which species this was; the captains, under the influence of local Indian explanations of the cinnamon bear as a separate species, may have at this point begun to call them brown bears. Lewis was showing greater allegiance to his "variagated" terminology for the grizzly bear, and may have considered abandoning "brown" as a descriptor for the grizzly. Compelled to guess, I would say that this June 5 bear was a black.

This guess is reinforced by Lewis's entry on June 11. The party had moved to Weippe Prairie in anticipation of an imminent assault on the mountains: "All our hunters were out this morning by daylight; Labuish

Head of Grizzly Bear, Shot September 13, 1884, *from Theodore Roosevelt's* Hunting Trips of a Ranchman *(1885). Though many early grizzly bear illustrations were woefully inaccurate, they did improve in the later nineteenth century. In the hands of a capable artist, in this case the famous sporting illustrator J. C. Beard, the grizzly bear became a believable, finely constructed creature of fearsome reality.*

and Gibson only proved successfull, the former killed a black bear of the brown speceis and a very large buck, . . ." Editor Moulton and I again agree that this was a black bear, and Ordway, sticking with traditional terminology, reassures us in this interpretation when he says that "Labuche killed a black bear."[9]

The rest of June, as they waited some more and then struggled over the mountains to Traveler's Rest, was a recitation of bears hunted and bears shot. On June 12, Gass reported that "There are a good many deer here, and some bears, but they are very wild, as they are much pursued by the natives." On June 15, the day the party tried the mountain trail but were turned back by deep snow, Lewis said that members of the party "had seen two large bear together the one black and the other white." This would have been the mating season for both species, so these could have been two very differently colored grizzly bears "together." On June 18, still waiting, Lewis said that "the hunters saw much fresh appearance of bear but very little of deer." The next day Clark went hunting and saw "some bear Sign." On June 20, Lewis said that "R. Feilds killed a brown bear the tallons of which were remarkably short broad at their base and sharply pointed this was of the speceis which the Chopunnish call *Yah-kar.* it was in very low order and the flesh of the bear in this situation is much inferior to lean venison or the flesh of poor Elk." This brown bear was also certainly a "cinnamon" black bear.

On June 22, Ordway reported that "about noon all the hunters came in had killed in all eight deer and two brown bear. towards evening the hunters turned out again and Collins killed a black bear." This seems like a successful day considering that on June 23, Clark complained that "the indians pursue the game So much on horse back in this neighbourhood that it is very Shye." On June 24, Lewis said that "Colter joined us this morning having killed a bear, which from his discription of it's poverty and distance we did not think proper to send after."

On June 26, they finally started on their trip over the pass, and the next day Lewis complained that "our meat being exhausted we issued a pint of bears oil to a mess which with their boiled roots made an agreeable dish." By June 29, now nearly to Traveler's Rest, they were in desperate condition: "near the River we found a Deer which the hunters had killed and left us. this was a fortunate Supply as all our bears oil was no exhosted, and we were reduced to our roots alone without Salt."

On July 2 at Traveler's Rest and anxious to begin his exploration of the Marias River, Lewis reported on a friendly bit of ceremony between him and one of his Nez Perce guides:

I gave the Cheif a medal of the small size; he insisted on exchanging names with me according to their custom which was accordingly done and I was called Yo-me-kol-lick which interpreted is *the white bearskin foalded.*

I have found no further mention of this name, or of its significance, in the journals of the expedition, though it could be that the name referred to Lewis's habit of collecting specimen bearskins, which the local people must surely have noticed and wondered about.

"a sertain fatality"

Among the remaining mysteries of western geography that most haunted the captains was the source of the Marias River, which had so puzzled the party on their way west.[1] It appeared without warning, and for a few days sorely tested the wisdom and intuition of the captains, who were more or less alone among the entire party in correctly believing that the Marias was not the Missouri. Now, in early July, it was Lewis's firm intent to solve the puzzle and seek out the source of this unheralded river.

While Clark returned to the Three Forks by way of their 1805 route, Lewis took nine of the men east, following Indian directions on a shortcut to the Missouri River. They crossed the site of present Missoula, Montana, then moved up the Clark Fork and Blackfoot River, crossed over to the Sun River (their "Medicine River") drainage, then down to the Missouri. They were back at the Great Falls area, "nearly opposite our old encampment" at the White Bear Islands, by July 11.

The day before, along the lower Sun River, Lewis's report described not only a bear encounter but also the familiar abundance of wildlife:

> a large brown bear swam the river near where we were and drewyer shot and killed it. by the time we butchered thes 2 elk and bar it was nearly dark. we loaded our horses with the best of the meat and pursud the party and found them encamped as they had been directed in the first timber. we did not reach them until 9 P. M. they informed us that they had seen a very large bear in the plains which had pursued Sergt. Gass and Thomson some distance but their horses enabled them to keep out of it's reach. they were afraid to

fire on the bear least their horses should throw them as they were unaccustomed to the gun. we killed five deer 3 Elk and a bear today.

On July 13, opening the cache from the previous year, Lewis discovered that their botanical specimens had been damaged, and found "my bearskins entirely destroyed by the water, the river having risen so high that the water had penitrated."

With the return to the Great Falls, Lewis's worries about bears resurfaced. Drouillard went off to recover some wandering horses, and after he had been gone three days Lewis was surprised when he returned unharmed:

> his safe return has releived me from great anxiety. I had already settled it in my mind that a white bear had killed him and should have set out tomorrow in surch of him, and if I could not find him to continue my rout to Maria's river. I knew that if he met with a bear in the plains even he would attack him. and that if any accedent should happen to seperate him from his horse in that situation the chances in favour of his being killed would be as 9 to 10.

Lewis had reason to worry, for the men were already having new close calls with the grizzly bears. The same day, July 15, Lewis reported that Private Hugh McNeal, a good hunter, barely escaped from one along the portage route:

> a little before dark McNeal returned with his musquet broken off at the breech, and informed me that on his arrival at willow run he had approached a white bear within ten feet without discover him the bear being in the thick brush, the horse took allarm and turning short threw him immediately under the bear; this animal raised himself on his hinder feet for battle, and gave him time to recover from his fall which he did in an instant and with his clubbed musquet he struck the bear over the head and cut him with the guard of the gun

and broke off the breech, the bear stunned with the stroke fell to the ground and began to scratch his head with his feet; this gave McNeal time to climb a willow tree which was near at hand and thus fortunately made his escape. the bear waited at the foot of the tree untill late in the evening before he left him, when McNeal ventured down and caught his horse which had by this time strayed off to the distance of 2 ms. and returned to camp. these bear are a most tremenduous animal; it seems that the hand of providence has been most wonderfully in our favor with rispect to them, or some of us would long since have fallen a sacrifice to their farosity. there seems to be a sertain fatality attatched to the neighbourhood of these falls, for there is always a chapter of accedents prepared for us during our residence at them.

Gass's account of the same episode is just different enough to deserve repeating:

> A white bear met him at Willow creek, that so frightened his horse, that he threw him off among the feet of the animal; but he fortunately (being too near to shoot) had sufficient presence of mind to hit the bear on the head with his gun; and the stroke so stunned it, that it gave him time to get up a tree close by before it could seize him. The blow, however, broke the gun and rendered it useless; and the bear watched him about three hours and went away; when he came down, caught his horse about two miles distant and returned to camp. These bears are very numerous in this part of the country and very dangerous, as they will attack a man every opportunity.

This was, no doubt, a harrowing and narrow escape, with some interesting elements. Lewis's (or McNeal's) assumption that a grizzly bear "raised himself on his hinder feet for battle" does not always jibe with typical bear behavior, which more often involves attacking on all fours. But individual bears do what they want. Gass gave us a more precise

An American having struck a Bear but not killed him, escapes into a Tree, *an engraving from the 1810 edition of the Gass journal, shows Private Hugh McNeal treed by the grizzly bear at Willow Creek, July 15, 1806. Gass scholar Carol Lynn MacGregor has rightly said that the bear looks "more like an English sheepdog" than a grizzly bear, but it got worse for this particular bear. In the 1812 edition, the bear very nearly became a pig. McNeal's clothing, which appears to be top hat and tails, is also an unaccountable bonus of additional misinformation.* COURTESY OF THE LEWIS AND CLARK TRAIL HERITAGE FOUNDATION LIBRARY, GREAT FALLS, MONTANA

reckoning of how long the bear lingered while McNeal waited in the tree. Modern hikers, treed by a bear but not sure if it has left the area or is just lurking somewhere nearby, would find the three-hour example helpful. Perhaps most interesting is McNeal's apparent success at stunning the bear by knocking it over the head with his "musquet." This would have taken a terrific blow, delivered from a position of some strength. As in so many cases in the journals, there is evidence of the toughness and strength of these men.

On July 16, just setting out with three of the men to explore the Marias drainage, Lewis was still along the Missouri when "on our way we saw two very large bear on the opposite side of the river. as we arrived in sight of the little wood below the falls we saw two other bear enter it; this being the only wood in the neighborhood we were compelled of course to contend with the bear for possession, and therefore left our horses in a place of security and entered the wood which we surched in vain for the bear, they had fled." He had no more to say about bears until his return from their unsuccessful attempt to reach the headwaters of the Marias— a side trip marred by their battle with a party of Piegan Indians, in which at least one and probably two Indians were killed.

On July 28, after Lewis and his men had completed their marathon ride from the site of the battle to the Lower Portage Camp downstream from the last of the Great Falls, his little party rejoined the rest of his men. He was disappointed to discover "that the cash had caved in and most of the articles burried therin were injured; I sustained the loss of two very large bear skins which I much regret; most of the fur and baggage belonging to the men were injured."

The party had no more geographical barriers to overcome in their quickening downstream run—just great stretches of river to be traveled as quickly as possible. On July 30, among the hunters' take was "a female brown bear with tallons 6 1/4 inches in length. I preserved the skin of this bear also with the tallons; it was not large and in but low order." Ordway reported that he and Private Alexander Willard had killed it.

On the morning of August 1, two hours before they passed the mouth of the Musselshell River, Lewis said that "at 9 A. M. we saw a large brown bear swiming from an island to the main shore we pursued him and as he landed Drewyer and myself shot and killed him; we took him on board the perogue and continued our rout." Later that day, when they made camp, another bear approached them:

> I halted at this place being about 15 ms. below Missel shell river, had fires built in the lodges and my skins exposed to dry. shortly after we landed the rain ceased tho' it still continued cloudy all this evening. a white bear came within 50 paces of our camp before we perceived it; it stood erect on it's hinder feet and looked at us with much apparent unconsern, we seized our guns which are always by us and several of us fired at it and killed it. it was a female in fine order, we fleesed it and extracted several gallons of oil. this speceis of bar are nearly as poor at this season of the year as the common black bear nor are they ever as fat as the black bear

is found in winter; as they feed principally on flesh, like the wolf, they are most fatt when they can procure a sufficiency of food without rispect to the season of the year. the oil of this bear is much harder than that of the black bear being nearly as much so as the lard of a hog. the flesh is by no means as agreeable as that of the black bear, or Yahkah or partycoloured bear of the West side of the rocky mountains.

From there to their reunion with Clark and his party, below the mouth of the Yellowstone, notes on bears were perfunctory. On August 3, among his recitation of the abundant wildlife Lewis reported "some bear." On August 4, the day the party passed the mouth of the Milk River, Ordway and Willard took a canoe and hunted, not catching up with the party until the middle of the night, but, according to Ordway, "we killed a large white or grizzly bear nearly of a Silver Grey." On August 5, two days upstream from the mouth of the Yellowstone, Lewis reported that "The Feildses killed 2 large bear this evening one of them measured nine feet from the extremity of the nose to that of his tail, this is the largest bear except one that I have seen. we saw several bear today as we passed but did not kill any of them." Apparently their haste, or a sufficient supply of oil, kept the men from shooting. On August 6, Lewis said "we saw several bear in the course of the day." On August 7, "we overtook the Feildses at noon. they had killed 2 bear and seen 6 others, we saw and fired on two from our perogue but killed neither of them. these bear resort to the river where they lie in wate at the crossing places of the game for the Elk and weak cattle; when they procure a subject of either they lie by the carcase and keep the wolves off until they devour it. the bear appear to be very abundant on this part of river." But he didn't mention them again until August 11, when "we had gone but little way before I saw a very large grizzly bear and put too in order to kill it, but it took wind of us and ran off." The next day Lewis and his party were reunited with Clark and the rest of the corps.

CHAPTER FOURTEEN

Yellowstone River Bears

lark and the majority of the party left Traveler's Rest on July 3, 1806. That day, traveling up the Bitterroot Valley, Clark reported that "We Saw great numbers of deer and 1 bear today." Passing through the Big Hole, they were back to Camp Fortunate and their canoes by July 8. On July 10, on their way down the Jefferson, Clark again noted that the bighorn sheep on nearby hills were able to elude predation: "those animals feed on the grass which grow on the Sides of the mountn. and in the narrow bottoms on the Water courses near the Steep Sides of the mountains on which they can make their escape from the pursute of wolves Bear &c." On July 13, when Nathaniel Pryor's party, returning from searching for lost horses, rejoined Clark at the Three Forks, Clark said that "his party had killed 6 deer & a white bear." By contrast, Ordway reported that the bear was only wounded.

Judging from the relative scarcity of mentions of bears, perhaps once again the grizzly bears of the Missouri headwater streams proved to be "shy." But as Clark's party crossed the upper Gallatin Valley, climbed over present Bozeman Pass, and dropped into the Yellowstone River drainage, they began to tell bear stories quite similar to those told on the Missouri River buffalo country.

They reached the Yellowstone somewhere in the vicinity of present Livingston on July 15. Here the Yellowstone has just issued from a steep canyon and is making a fairly abrupt turn to the northeast. Clark and his men were hoping to find cottonwoods large enough for canoes but were forced to travel downstream by horse for a few days more before they could find trees large enough for them to build usable watercraft.

On July 15, Clark reported seeing "two black bear on the side of the mountains this morning." From the context, it is possible he was referring to Sheep Mountain, a long, low ridge not far north of the river, just east of Livingston. On July 16, he saw "also two white or Grey Bear in the plains, one of them I Chased on horse back about 2 miles to the rugid part of the plain where I was compelled to give up the Chase."

On July 19, near present Park City, finally locating tolerable trees for their purposes, Clark said that John Shields "informed me that 2 white bear Chased him on horsback, each of which he Shot from his horse &c." The next day, with the party now engaged in canoe building, Lewis said that he "Saw a Bear on an Island opposit and Several Elk." Back among superabundant wildlife, the party also attempted to gather some bison meat, much of which scavenging animals ate while it was unattended on the night of the twenty-second. Clark mentioned no more bears until July 30, the day the party was downstream from present Miles City, Montana. That day, near or at Buffalo Shoals, they passed a rapid that Clark named "Bear rapid from the Circumstance of a bears being on a rock in the Middle of this rapid when I arrived at it."

On July 31, near present Glendive, Montana, Clark said, "as I was about landing this evening Saw a white bear and the largest I ever Saw eating a dead buffalow on a Sand bar. we fired two Shot into him, he Swam to the main Shore and walked down the bank. I landed and fired 2 more Shot into this tremendious animal without killing him. night comeing on we Could not pursue him he bled profusely."

On August 2, now in the neighborhood of Sidney, Montana, and finally approaching the junction of the Yellowstone and Missouri Rivers, Clark reported two bear encounters:

> about 8 A. M this morning a Bear of the large vicious
> Species being on a Sand bar raised himself up on his hind
> feet and looked at us as we passed down near the middle of
> the river. he plunged into the water and Swam towards us,
> either from a disposition to attack't or from the Cent of the
> meat which was in the Canoes. we Shot him with three
> balls and he returned to Shore badly wounded. in the
> evening I saw a very large Bear take the water above us. I
> ordered the boat to land on the opposit Side with a view to
> attack't him when the Came within Shot of the Shore.

when the bear was in a fiew paces of the Shore I Shot it in the head. the men hauled her on Shore and proved to be an old Shee which was so old that her tuskes had worn Smooth, and Much the largest feemale bear I ever Saw. after taking off her Skin, I proceeded on. . . .

Clark here seems almost to despair of using any of the prevailing terms for grizzly bear. He ignores "white," "grizzly," and even Lewis's "variagated," and simply settles for saying that the bear in the morning was of the large vicious species. But he returned to using "white" on subsequent days. On August 5, now back on the Missouri River in extreme western North Dakota, Clark ". . . Set out at 4 P. M and proceeded on but a fiew miles eeir I saw a Bear of the white Species walking on a Sand bear. I with one man went on the Sand bear and killed the Bear which proved to be a feemale very large and fat. much the fattest animale we have killed on the rout as this bear had got into the river before we killed her I had toed her across to the South Side under a high Bluff where formed a Camp, had the bear Skined and fleaced." On August 6, "This morning a very large Bear of white Species, discovered us floating in the water and takeing us, as I prosume to be Buffalow imediately plunged into the river and prosued us. I directed the men to be Still. this animal Came within about 40 yards of us, and tacked about. we all fired into him without killing him, and the wind So high that we could not pursue hi[m], by which means he made his escape to the Shore badly wounded." On August 7, somewhere upstream from the mouth of Tobacco Creek on a portion of the Missouri now drowned under the Garrison Reservoir, they ". . . Saw a Bear on the bank but Could not get a Shoot at it."

Five days later, the party was reunited with Lewis and his men, and the Corps of Discovery continued to pick up speed on their homeward run.

CHAPTER FIFTEEN

Big-Picture Bears

The remaining observations of and about bears by the captains and their men were perfunctory. Anyone familiar with their journey can well imagine the excitement and growing haste of the corps as they outran the Missouri's current, speeding through huge stretches of country each day, eagerly heading home. We can easily forgive them if their fast travel left them less time for detailed observations.

On August 22, while meeting with Indians at the Arikara villages, at the junction of the Grand River and the Missouri, Clark made some notes about the Cheyenne Indians who were there to trade, including that "they also ware Bear Claws about their necks," a modest additional anthropological tidbit that added yet another tribe to the bear-claw-necklace list. On September 16, east of Independence, Missouri, Ordway reported that he "Saw a black bear which run a thicket of bushes." On September 18, near Council Bluffs, Clark reported that "we saw very little appearance of deer, Saw one bear at a distance and 3 turkeys only to day. our party entirely out of provisions Subsisting on poppaws."

But before they left the upper Missouri, they gave us one more observation to consider—not just about bears, but about the reasons behind the incredible wildlife spectacle they were just then passing through. On August 29, near present Chamberlain, South Dakota, Clark estimated that from one vantage point he had "near 20,000" bison in sight at once. He then made a statement that has haunted historians and ecologists ever since:

> I have observed that in the country between the nations which are at war with each other the greatest number of wild animals are to be found.

This observation has added an engaging level of complexity to North American wildlife history. It proposes that not only did Native humans of the West practically eradicate certain species of wildlife from areas of dense human settlement—such as the Columbia River corridor—but they also enhanced other wildlife populations by conceding to them the no-man's-lands that occurred between warring tribes.

It is an intriguing notion for many reasons. First, the same effect has been documented, or at least effectively argued for, by historians in several other locations in North America. Harold Hickerson developed the concept of a "buffer zone" to characterize the growth of deer herds in central Minnesota, between warring Dakota and Chippewa tribes. Richard White provided evidence for a similar effect on the "borderlands" between tribes in eighteenth-century Mississippi. And both White and Dan Flores have demonstrated similar effects for the bison populations of portions of the Great Plains.[1]

Proposals for some of these zones are remarkably ambitious and take some getting used to. Recently, researchers Paul Martin and Christine Szuter have proposed that the entire region bounded by the Missouri and Yellowstone Rivers, clear from the present Montana–North Dakota border on the east almost to the Three Forks on the west, was in fact just such a war zone. They proposed a somewhat smaller but still enormous war zone west of the Missouri River in present southern Kansas, bounded on the north and south by the White and Niobrara Rivers. Martin and Szuter used Lewis and Clark's reports of where wildlife was abundant, and where it was scarce, to buttress their hypothesis.[2] Their theory was striking enough, and credible enough, that on March 30, 1999, *The New York Times* ran a lengthy feature article, "Unlikely Tool for Species Preservation: Warfare," which summarized their work and the reactions of other researchers who agreed or disagreed.[3]

These ideas are as controversial as they are intriguing, but the first thing to applaud about them is that they do assist us in overcoming what Dan Flores has called "one of the great fantasies of American history"— the persistent notion that North America generally, and the West specifically, was in some way a "pristine world, shaped solely by natural processes and untouched by the human hand."[4]

As we've already seen at many locations along their route, Lewis and Clark saw abundant proof that humans were having substantial effects on the ecological setting around them. Had we paid close attention to these "lessons" when Lewis and Clark presented them to us long ago, we might not have cherished so many less realistic ideas of the Wild West as a kind of rough-hewn mega-Eden from which human effects had been excluded. Many generations of Americans learned this simplistic view of pre-1492 North America—that it was a perfectly wild place in which the few Native people had no effect on the ecological setting—more or less by default, in high school and college history classes that made it clear that nothing significant happened on the continent before white people arrived to "conquer the wilderness."

Edenic terminology surfaces now and then in discussions of pre-Columbian America. Traditional portrayals of the Native people of the New World alternated between describing a barbaric, soulless land of sin (the view favored by many early missionaries) and a paradisical heaven-on-earth whose inhabitants lived in perfect harmony not only with each other but with all other creatures (a view attributed to many in the early stages of the environmental movement but now regularly debunked by anthropologists, environmental historians, and many others). *Eden* is a slippery, even treacherous, label to apply to any earthbound landscape.

On the other hand, the West of Lewis and Clark meets most of my personal definitions of Eden anyway. Many of us get an enormous vicarious thrill from following Lewis and Clark on their journey through this magnificent country with its incredible abundance of life and wonder. If there was an Eden on earth, for my money Lewis and Clark were describing it. But that's partly because I find the Biblical Eden a fairly boring place by comparison. A grizzly bear that contentedly lies down with the lambs and bunnies isn't really a grizzly bear.

Biblical overtones and implications aside, Lewis and Clark's description of "war zones" where wildlife thrived raises appealing questions, and the questions of how Native politics and warfare may have affected wildlife distribution and abundance are not even the most challenging we face. As usual, there are value judgments at play here that always have, and probably always will, affect the way we see this region and its animals.

I'm not the first, for example, to experience an involuntary eyebrow elevation at some of the remarks in the Martin-Szuter paper, remarks suggesting that much more is going on in this scientific dialogue than disagreements over anthropological theory or wildlife demographics. Most notably, in their concluding remarks, they said that "We find that neither historic scarcity of big game in the Columbia nor historic abundance in the Upper Missouri region is truly natural, that is, falling outside human influence or control."[5]

Here we suddenly leave science and—whether Martin and Szuter intended or even realized it—enter the stormy realm of human self-perception. Which is to say that we are talking more about religion than about empirical findings. The unmistakable implication of this statement is that humans are separate from nature—even Indians, whom most people today seem to regard as having been deeply integrated, both physically and spiritually, into the ecological setting, are apparently excluded from a "truly natural" scene by the Martin-Szuter definition. The idea of humans as separate from, or above, nature, has reigned in Western culture (but not in all others) for centuries. Such a bold assertion of this position smoked out some strong opposition, including Daniel Botkin, whose own study of the Lewis and Clark Expedition I have mentioned earlier. In that work, and in his previous book, *Discordant Harmonies: A New Ecology for the 21st Century* (1990), Botkin has taken a strongly integrative view of humans as an inextricable, if somewhat willful, part of the whole global ecological scene. For Botkin and many others, humans are a part of the complex weave of forces that drive natural processes and shape natural ecosystems.[6]

These debates, as deep, heated, and important as they are, reach well beyond the scope of this book. We each get to decide where we place humanity in our own personal scheme of the universe. It is worth pointing out, however, that the arguments are not merely academic. The stakes are high in the debates over whether or not we should view humans as part of nature or somehow separated from it.

For an example relating to the subject of this book, advocates of competing wildlife management approaches routinely employ Lewis and Clark's findings, interpreting them in whatever way serves them best. We have already seen that modern opponents of recovery of the grizzly bear in the Bitterroot Mountains of Montana and Idaho have attempted to enlist Lewis and Clark in their cause. But there are grander ways to invoke the captains. If you happen to be opposed to the concept of setting aside wilderness areas, or preserving rare or endangered species in general—let's say the grizzly bear, just to keep on track here—you will find it enormously convenient that Lewis and Clark's journals "prove" that humans have always influenced wildlife populations in the West. Therefore, you may assert, there is very little legitimacy in setting aside a large tract of land where human influences are largely excluded under the terms of legislation like the Wilderness Act. Therefore also, there is no harm in humans continuing to alter every western landscape, because nothing is "pristine" anyway. Therefore again, if humans cause the extinction of any particular species, they are just doing what humans have been in the process of doing for thousands of years. And therefore finally, anything goes, and why worry about it? What the hell—whatever we do, it's just *natural*.

Modern conservation biologists find this trend of thinking, which seems to be growing in popularity, very troubling. I do, too. Thanks to the entirely laudatory efforts of researchers in many fields, we have acquired a more realistic view of how Native people lived on and affected the North American landscape. But from that helpful and stimulating contribution, some people seem to have moved quickly on to less savory, more self-centered pursuits. The goal of these pursuits is to put Lewis and Clark to work on socioeconomic issues utterly foreign from their world. In other words, the goal is to clothe the old, selfish anthropocentric view—the one whose irresponsibility has already cost us many irreplaceable species whose worth to themselves and their fellow creatures was never even considered and will now never be known—in the bright new fabric of scientific inquiry. It would be a shame if Lewis and Clark's words were successfuly employed in such a small-minded enterprise.[7]

On the other hand, Botkin himself has undertaken a more constructive, and intellectually adventurous, effort. In *Our Natural History,* he used the sighting rate of grizzly bears that Lewis and Clark reported in an attempt to estimate the grizzly bear population throughout their range. Among the interesting conclusions he reached are: Such estimates are made only with full awareness of the many limitations of the information (a concern I have already expressed several times in this book); and the grizzly bear encounters of Lewis and Clark "tended to occur in clusters— Lewis and Clark reported seeing bears for a few days at a time, and then several weeks would pass without a sighting."[8] From this Botkin suggested that "There were not wall-to-wall grizzlies in the presettlement landscape of the American West."[9] This, he concluded, is especially important for modern wildlife managers to understand, because "a program to conserve these big, dangerous mammals has to take into account the habitats that are appropriate for them and the patchy distribution of them within that habitat, as well as their overall rarity."[10]

Botkin's calculations are offered with heavy, almost severe, caveats about the shortage of actual information provided by Lewis and Clark and its applicability to such an exercise as population estimation. I agree with his caution and perhaps even exceed him in my lack of faith in the information he is working with. But still, he has embarked on a very important project. Determining what the West was like before we began to change it is important to modern land managers for countless reasons. Even knowing that the West of Lewis and Clark was already experiencing tremendous changes because of Euro-Americans, we owe it to ourselves and the land to pursue such studies as Botkin made.

But the war zone hypothesis raises many other interesting questions. How, for example, does the reported wariness of bears along the Missouri above the Great Falls fit into the theory? If we were to accept Lewis and Clark's assessment of these bears as more shy than the bears farther downstream, was their shyness just because they lived on uneasy ground—kind of the zone between the zones—where there wasn't much warfare, but there weren't sufficiently high levels of human population to displace them entirely?

Or how scarce were the bears, even in the more heavily populated areas? It was while Lewis and Clark were in the Mandan villages and other areas of heavier Indian population that they gathered much of their information on how Indians dealt with bears. It was in these areas that they saw so many bear necklaces. Are we to believe that all these bear beliefs and bear claws were the result of Indians having traveled all the way to the war zones? How far back from the river and the Indian villages did you have to go in order to find abundant wildlife, including bears? Lewis and Clark observed a long, narrow corridor of land, not a broad ecoregion.

These are engaging questions, but I ask them with a certain restlessness, for the same reason that I withhold complete agreement with what

Martin and Szuter are proposing. It is the reason I mentioned earlier, having to do with overconfidence in the accuracy of Lewis and Clark's descriptions. We are relying quite heavily on the relatively limited observations of untrained observers, traveling through a land of enormous ecological, social, and political complexity. Martin and Szuter have been criticized, and I think justifiably, for grand generalizations based on fairly short facts about a landscape that was, even when Lewis and Clark got there, already in the throes of massive change. There was not a tribe they encountered on their entire journey whose lifeways hadn't undergone wrenching change in the previous century, for reasons I've mentioned before. The arrival of the horse, of trade firearms, of trade incentives to kill more animals, and of human and domestic animal disease epidemics had not simply changed the way these people lived. They had in almost every case changed *where* they lived, as tribes jostled each other back and forth across the map of North America. Lewis and Clark traveled through this land of incredibly fluid human population, and in their journals they opened a very long, very narrow window on the state of things over a two-year period in the middle of a dynamic situation in which change was if anything accelerating.

As Dan Flores and others have so ably demonstrated, modern Americans have long been conditioned to see the mounted Indian as somehow representing Native America at its best—as standing for the American Indian empire of the New World that was so brutally destroyed by European conquest. But even in the Southwest, where Spanish horses first made their way onto the Great Plains and into the mountains in numbers, the Indian horse culture was less than two hundred years old, and there are many indications that, far from allowing Indians to arrive at some new stable relationship with the land, it was leading them into precarious and perhaps even doomed conditions.[11] Horses changed the nature of the political relationships among tribes. Horses changed the society within the tribes. Horses greatly improved Indians' capacity for killing animals and transporting hides for trade. Horses, which multiplied from hundreds to thousands to millions, competed with native grazers for food.

So even if Martin and Szuter, in their provocative hypothesis about war zones and game sinks, have precisely nailed the situation surrounding wildlife abundance at the time of Lewis and Clark, the question remains—so what? What next? The conditions that Lewis and Clark observed may not have been the situation for very long, and in a very short time after they passed through, a matter of a few decades, the conditions would change beyond the imagination even of the most pessimisic observers of the time. Where does our gradually improving understanding of the West of Lewis and Clark lead us? And how might it affect our thinking about grizzly bears?

CHAPTER SIXTEEN

Legacies

The expert consensus has it that Lewis and Clark contributed hugely to our knowledge of the grizzly bear. This conviction was forcefully stated by the well-traveled naturalist Elliott Coues, editor of the classic 1893 edition of the journals:

> The grizzly bear is the most notable discovery made in zoology by Lewis and Clark. Their accounts are very full, as we have already seen [Coues cites many page numbers in the journals here], and shall see again in several places. This bear was found to be so numerous and so fierce, especially in the Upper Missouri region, as to more than once endanger the lives of the party, and form an impediment to the progress of the Expedition. Our authors carefully distinguish the grizzly, in all its color-variations, from the black bear *(Ursus americanus);* they are at pains to describe it minutely and repeatedly, laying special stress, for specific characters, upon its great size in all its dimensions, its general build and the form of the feet and claws, the peculiarity of the scrotum, together with the inability of this species to climb trees, its great ferocity, and its remarkable tenacity of life. Their remarks are for the most part judicious and pertinent, establishing the species as distinct from the black bear; and have been confirmed by subsequent investigators. The differences had long been known to the Indians, and are correctly set forth, as for example under dates of May 14th and 31st, which see beyond; the point being that the grizzly, in all its variety of color, is different from the black

bear, some color-varieties of which latter are nevertheless like some of those of the grizzly.[1]

If we set aside a few problems, such as Coues's apparent ignorance of earlier Euro-American "discoveries" of the grizzly bear and his confidence in the captains' erroneous report about bear testicles, we must enthusiastically agree with him, right down to his surprisingly enlightened admission that the Indians already knew all about grizzly bears.

In fact, Coues may have understated the depth of the information Lewis and Clark gave us. Lewis and Clark provided a sound outline of other aspects of grizzly bear natural history, including quite a few preferred foods and foraging behavior, mating season, and a surprising number of details about the relationship between grizzly bears and Indians. These last included obvious things as the popularity and importance of bear-claw necklaces and the beliefs attached to hunting grizzly bears (the cultural richness of the claw necklaces, other bear ornaments, and the hunting rituals appears to have been largely lost on the captains). But they also included various other Indian uses of bear skins and oils and methods for cooking bear meat.

Citizens of the United States knew essentially nothing about the grizzly bear. What Lewis and Clark brought back was more than enough to create a clear and reasonably careful portrait of the animal. Their insights were hardly improved upon over the course of the next century, and in some cases we even lost ground in our understanding and appreciation of the grizzly bear.

Of course, from the confident comfort of the early twenty-first century, we have the luxury of pointing out the errors they did make. Perhaps the most notable of these involves their statements about the aggressiveness of grizzly bears. A careful reading of the journals makes it clear that the grizzly bears they encountered were nowhere near as aggressive as Lewis and Clark seemed to believe they were.

It is not hard to sense a little Euro-American arrogance in their reports. Their shock at the "ferocity" of these animals comes across almost as indignation, that these wild animals were so unwilling to die when properly shot by civilized men. And of course the bears simply weren't as likely to attack as Lewis and Clark seemed to believe. Many of the bears were just minding their own business until they were shot, shot at, or otherwise disturbed or threatened. Only rarely in the journals do we find a human–bear encounter in which we can even wonder if *perhaps* the bear attacked the men on first sight. Besides that, quite a few bears tried to escape even after they were attacked by the men. On some level, the captains may have even understood this. They did wonder, for example, if bears that swam toward their canoes were mistaking them for swimming bison. Still, Paul Cutright was largely correct when he said that "Lewis and Clark gained most of their information about the disposition of the grizzly while looking down the barrels of their Kentucky rifles."[2]

Their misunderstanding of the temperament of grizzly bears is easy enough to sympathize with, though. Lewis, Clark, and their men had little to go on except what they'd heard from their Missouri River Indian and white informants. We cannot blame either their informants or the captains if they chose to fire on a bear that was coming fast toward them, rather than wait to see if the bear was just curious, or was bluffing aggression, or was actually attacking. Under those circumstances, knowing what little they knew, their actions seemed the only logical ones. They shot.

So we should admit that Lewis and Clark did contribute something to a national misunderstanding of grizzly bears that is still with us today. But far more of the misimpressions associated with Lewis and Clark's grizzly bears arose in the thinking and writing of later people—all those celebrators, commentators, sensationalizers, and others who tried to retell the stories of Lewis and Clark secondhand. Certainly William Wright was correct in his observation that later writers recklessly embellished the simple accounts left by Lewis and Clark. In fact, when it comes to the grizzly bear's legendary belligerence in those first meetings with white people, we owe most of what is attributed to Lewis and Clark to the people doing the attributing—the generations of careless, enthusiastic writers who built an ever more fearsome and monstrous grizzly bear upon the thin foundation of the captains' reports. Lewis, Clark, and their men used words like *ferocious* and *terrible* often enough to give later writers plenty to work with, but it is a long way from the bears that the Corps of Discovery described to the demoniacal beasts that inhabit the bear-hunting literature and the American consciousness of a century later, and that linger there all too frequently even today. Paul Cutright summed up this process:

> Lewis and Clark reported accurately their adventures with the grizzly. That these became exaggerated when retold, and the true character of the animal misrepresented, was no fault of theirs. Before long Old Ephraim (to use one of the various names applied by old-time hunters to the grizzly) had gained a reputation for strength and ferocity exceeding that of any other North American quadruped; it was a killer of unbridled passion.[3]

It has seemed to me, in my reading of the journals of the corps and then in my reading of so many who wrote about them, that as the decades passed the tradition of belief about grizzly bear aggressiveness that was launched upon the foundation of the journals grew ever more involved and muddled. It is soon impossible to know when a writer was influenced by actually having read the official "History" of Lewis and Clark published in 1814, or by having read any of the editions of Gass's journal, or by having read one of the many less authentic renditions of the story of the corps that appeared over the years, or, for that matter, just by having overheard something about Lewis and Clark in the local tavern. As I follow the grizzly bear stories of Lewis and Clark through the nineteenth-century literature they inspired, the trail of authority and authenticity quickly grows attenuated and murky.

If there is a lesson in that faded and convoluted trail, it may be that we are even yet working our way back to the reality of the grizzly bear that they actually encountered. We still have a lot of work to do if we would moderate the fearsome reputation Lewis and Clark's literary descendants so enthusiastically constructed around this animal.

And even though Wright's and Cutright's accusations against the careless and sensational writers of the nineteenth century are sound, I still wonder about some of the subtleties of how we got this so wrong. I wonder this especially when I read Lewis and Clark's relatively few comments on how the Indians dealt with bears. Consider again Lewis's comments on bears and Indians, made a few days after the corps set out on their way west from the Mandan villages in April 1805:

> the Indians give a very formidable account of the strength and ferocity of this anamal, which they never dare to attack but in parties of six eight or ten persons; and are even then frequently defeated with the loss of one or more of their party. the savages attack this anamal with their bows and arrows and the indifferent guns with which the traders furnish them, with these they shoot with such uncertainty and at so short a distance, that they frequently mis their aim & fall a sacrefice to the bear. two Minetaries were killed during the last winter in an attack on a white bear. this anamall is said more frequently to attack a man on meeting with him, than to flee from him. When the Indians are about to go in quest of the white bear, previous to their departure, they paint themselves and perform all those supersticious rights commonly observed when they are about to make war uppon a neighboring nation.

I propose that we continue to read this passage with more deference to the bear, and less to the Indians, than Lewis may have intended. Countless later writers have emphasized these remarks, usually to the implied effect that the Indians were scared to death of grizzly bears. This implication has invariably been employed to a certain effect—to further heighten the grizzly bear's reputation for belligerence and "ferocity." The line of reasoning implied in these secondhand accounts runs something like this: "Lewis and Clark said that even the Indian warriors were scared of the bears! What horrifying creatures the bears must have been! And thus, by implication, what brave guys the Corps of Discovery must have been!" Or, even more pointedly, "What brave, superior *white* guys the Corps of Discovery must have been!"

In fact, something other than that was going on. Indeed, Indians knew that grizzly bears were very dangerous. They knew that with the technology at hand it was foolish to take on an adult grizzly bear without a lot of help. But the point is that they *did* take on adult grizzly bears. They did it often, even routinely. How else could Lewis and Clark have reported so many Indians discussing the dangers of bear hunting? And perhaps more to the real point, how else could Lewis and Clark report, all along their route, Indians sporting bear-claw necklaces? How else could the hunting of the bear have generated such elaborate ceremonialism?

It might be helpful here to invite a comment from one of Lewis and Clark's few contemporary white travelers, the little-celebrated but extraordinary François-Antoine Larocque. Larocque, a Canadian trader, met Lewis and Clark during their winter at Fort Mandan and even offered to join them on their westward travels. They declined his offer (not wanting a Canadian observer along), so while Lewis and Clark worked their way up the Missouri in the summer of 1805, Laroque and two friends joined a group of Crow Indians and accompanied them on another historic journey, becoming among the first white men to travel to the Bighorn Mountain Range in north-central Wyoming. From there he traveled north to the Yellowstone River near the site of present Billings, Montana. He then followed the Yellowstone back to the Mandan villages, thus preceding Clark by a year in traveling that stretch of country. And, bless his heart, he kept a journal.[4]

Larocque's journal is fascinating for many reasons that must be passed over here, but listen to his observations on the hunting methods of his companions on August 15, 1805:

> The Indians killed Buffaloes and a few Bears, the latter they hunt for pleasure only as they do not eat the flesh but in case of absolute necessity. Perhaps the whole nation is employed about a bear, whom they have caused to take refuge in a thicket, there they plague him for a long while and then kill him, he is seldom stript of his Skin.[5]

Here is a slightly different and refreshing firsthand take on how at least one western tribe dealt with grizzly bears. They hunted them for "pleasure," by which Larocque seemed to mean sport. The Crow and, it appears, most of the other tribes Lewis and Clark met, didn't just kill the occasional bear, say, when it threatened them. Bears and bear hunting were integral parts of their culture. Each tribe no doubt developed its own unique approach to the animal as symbol, neighbor, rival, and target, and each tribe seems to have regarded hunting as an important part of that approach. Bear hunting was dangerous, but so were many other things they did. That they knew it was risky does not necessarily prove anything bad about their character—or about the bear's.

As well, it is worth wondering if Larocque's superficial impression of what the Indians were doing with the bears really did the event justice. It may have looked like sport to him (and sport itself is a far more complex institution than most people seem to realize) but, considering all we now know about the power of bears in human culture, it seems clear that killing a bear had levels of significance far beyond that for the hunters involved.[6] Larocque, like Lewis and Clark, was a product of his own culture, and his biases against native belief systems and his lack of interest in understanding them may have been just as strong. I assume that in the Crow bear hunt, things were going on that he simply didn't notice or know how to comprehend.

Similar perceptual challenges face us in our reading of the struggles of Lewis and Clark to name the grizzly bear. In his painstaking study of the words used and created by Lewis and Clark, Elijah Criswell suggested some of the reasons why the captains may have been somewhat ambivalent in their use of Indian names. Criswell's interest was in the naming of the grizzly bear, but his discussion applies more broadly than that:

> Without doubt the explorers could have made more use of Indian words, but they were difficult to manage and meant little to those in the East. . . . There may have been another reason why the Captains shied away from such names. They may have had little confidence in the scientific accuracy of the Indians, and, though this would not greatly damage the names, it might have created a suspicion in the minds of the explorers attaching to the names, too. The Indians had told them of the grizzly bear long before they ever encountered it, describing it as yellow or white and calling it the *white bear* or the *yellow bear*. Lo and behold, when they saw it, it was neither, but was predominantly brown, with grayish or "grizzly" tips to its long hair. And

yet, it should be said, in justice to the Indian, that he was the one who finally set the Captains right in their attempt to separate this species from the varieties of common black bear in that territory. And it is to be noted that they finally came around to a term denoting the whitish characteristics of the hair of this animal. But they scorned to use the outlandish Indian terms hoh-host (for the grizzly) and yack-kah (for the black). Their aversion to Indian terms, though not outwardly expressed, does not lack much of being as marked as that of the Indian for American words.[7]

It is true that Lewis and Clark regarded themselves as the civilized superiors of the Indians, and we have seen that they sometimes took Indian information with skepticism. Criswell did not explain why he personally found the Indian words for bears "outlandish." And though in the above passage Criswell seemed to state that Lewis and Clark were in the process of deciding that there were only two species of bears, elsewhere in his book he did seem to understand that "yack-kah" was not simply a name of the black bear, *Ursus americanus*. According to Lewis, in his May 31, 1806 entry, the "Yâck-kâh" of the Nez Perce was in fact a third species of bear, somewhere between the grizzly bear and the familiar eastern black bear. Lewis never corrected or revised this impression. His subsequent journal entries never overrode the observation of this day, that there were, in fact, three species of bears along their route: the black bear of the lower Missouri and the lower Columbia, the grizzly bear of the upper Missouri and Rocky Mountains, and the "Yâck-kâh" of the extreme western Rocky Mountains. If we were inclined to keep score of Lewis's accuracy in any rigidly formal way, this error on Lewis's part must be added to his mistaken impression of grizzly bear genitals and of the aggressive tendencies of the species. But again, compared to all the valuable information he provided about bears, these errors seem minor, if not trivial.

This all brings us to the naming of the grizzly bear, as muddled a story as might be found in all the bear chronicles of American history. Criswell stated that following Lewis's May 31 deliberations, the party tended to settle on the name *grizzly bear,* though they did fall back on other terms.[8] Here I find myself in complete disagreement with Criswell. My reading of the journal entries following May 31 does not reveal any special leaning toward the term *grizzly*. It is rarely used, in any variant spelling. Clark, particularly, continued to favor white when describing the animals, and Lewis seemed quickly to give up on his proposed *variagated* and returned to *brown* or *white* alternatively.

Here again, as on other occasions when I try to forget everything that everyone has *said* about what the corps's journalists wrote and concentrate solely on what the journals themselves said, I finally have to pay attention to something that we bear historians have long tended to slight. These men never stopped talking about white bears. Not tan, not cream, not pale, not blond—they said *white*. Sometimes they expressed puzzlement over the term, but they kept using it. I am finally persuaded by their persistence in this, which is to say that I am now inclined to accept that two hundred years ago, more of the grizzly bears of the upper Missouri River and the northern Rockies were a lot paler than we've been willing to imagine so far. I still can't bring myself to imagine that very many of these bears were polar bear white, or sheep white, much less snow white. But I do think that all of us who, all these years, have been busily interpreting "white bear" to simply be a carelessly applied label for a bear that was really gray or brown or grizzled have been paying more attention to our own knowledge of surviving grizzly bear populations than to the knowledge we were being given by the Corps of Discovery.

Who can say? Perhaps today's surviving bear populations, living as they have for so long in and near much more heavily forested environments than did the bears along the Missouri River in eastern and central Montana, tend to favor darker shades. After all, as we have already seen, black bears living in deciduous eastern forests are almost all black, while their western counterparts, living in mixed habitats, are often lighter shades. Just because we are used to seeing these dark bears does not mean that Lewis and Clark were seeing bears that looked the same. Perhaps the Great Plains grizzly bears of Lewis and Clark were lighter in response to their open environment. Perhaps other factors prevailed as well. But I am getting used to the idea that there were, indeed, some *fairly* white bears out there on the Montana prairies once—and maybe some *very* white ones.

Finally accepting that the Corps of Discovery knew what they were talking about when they described bears of different colors may simplify our approach to reading the journals, but it doesn't help us sort out the ongoing troubles over the naming of the species in the days of Lewis and Clark. The *Oxford English Dictionary* traces the origin of the variations on *grizzly,* including a host of variant spellings, back well before Lewis and Clark. For example, John Long, who traveled the nearer West in the years between 1768 and 1782, referred to the "grizzled bear" and the "grisley bear," which he also called the "white" bear.[9] Though George Ord's scientific description in 1815 named the animal the "grizzly bear," there continued to be confusion through much of the nineteenth century, especially over just what the term meant. Some later writers assumed that the bear was named exclusively or in part for its "character"—its "grisly" behavior. But we can see in the journals that in Lewis and Clark's time the name was applied in an attempt to describe the animal's appearance. If Lewis and Clark helped to clarify and settle this issue, their help is not especially noticeable in the literature.

With that, I would like to return to a more specific topic, one introduced in the previous chapter. I have already mentioned that biologist Daniel Botkin has tallied up the number of grizzly bear sightings made by Lewis and Clark and used that number in an instructive exercise to show how one might go about calculating the grizzly bear population of the entire West at the time. While he was at it, he introduced an abundance of variables that demonstrated just how difficult making such calculations is, even if you have good data, which he, admittedly, does not.

What interests me most especially about his discussion isn't the total number of bears he came up with (he considered only the northern United States, ignoring the Southwest and the Pacific Coast states, and still estimated a population of twelve thousand grizzly bears). It is where he started. Based on his reading of the journals of the Corps of Discovery, he said that "the expedition encountered 37 grizzlies described as individuals." From that start, that base number—and considering habitat variations across the region, wildly uneven viewing opportunities, and other factors—he made his very tentative calculations. I have already acknowledged my gratitude to Dan Botkin for so ably launching this little exercise, which I will now pursue, both because it is fun and to make a point.

Based on my reading of the journals of the Corps of Discovery I find an absolute minimum of sixty-two reliably identified grizzly bears that were sighted between the time the party left Fort Mandan in the spring of 1805 and the time they reached the present Idaho border late that summer.

I worked hard to make this a conservative, minimum estimate. I excluded from my total all nonsighting indications of grizzly bears, such as reports of tracks and mentions of bears being common, or around camp at night, or otherwise present but not specifically said to have been visually identified. I treated vague references to the reports of "several" or "plenty" grizzly bears being sighted as proof only of more than one, and tallied such reports as the minimum possible: two bears. I tried to err on the side of caution in any case where duplicate sightings of the same animal might be possible. In every way I know how, I minimized the total, but still I estimated that the Corps of Discovery did see substantially more bears than Botkins' thirty-seven. And after making this minimum estimate, I was left with the impression that in fact they probably saw or crossed paths with quite a few more than sixty-two grizzly bears. It seemed obvious to me.

Why are our numbers so different? There are probably several reasons, starting with my being a historian and his being a biologist, whatever those differences may do to our interpretations. Maybe I used some journals he did not, or perhaps he had reasons to discount some entries, reasons that I missed. Maybe I was too generous in assuming that some of the animals they described as "bears" could have been black bears, but I doubt it; once they were north of present Bismarck, North Dakota, they made it quite clear that black bears were not to be seen. Still, I'm not claiming my number is right or that his is wrong. I'm only offering our differences as further proof of what we are all up against in trying to learn the lessons of Lewis and Clark.

For me, the detective story continues. The harder we look at their journals, the more we find to wonder about. The Corps of Discovery, in all their encounters with grizzly bears, hardly ever reported seeing sows with young—whether cubs of the year, yearlings, or two-year-olds. Once in a while the nature of their journal entries made it impossible to know if perhaps they did see such a family group, as when they said only that they saw two, three, four, or five bears. Sometimes they didn't tell us if these bears were seen all at once, in smaller groups, or individually. But considering the interest that young bears attract among people (and considering the interest that *black bear* cubs sometimes attracted among the corps's men), I take their lack of reporting family groups to mean something—that they rarely saw sows with young.

What this means, I think, is that among the other biases in their observed "sample" of the grizzly bear population of western North America is a sexual one. The scientific and popular literature has made much of the secretiveness of mother bears, especially those with new cubs to defend. Certainly the corps were seeing a few females—at least two of grizzly bears they killed during this period were females. But at least five were specifically said to be males, and many others, because of their great size, almost certainly were males. As I've mentioned before, once they made their first couple of kills and reported the measurements of a couple of bears, they didn't bother to record details about the bears they killed (I also suspect that when they reported killing three bears at once, it was most likely a family group).

This all leads me to assume that Lewis and Clark were almost certainly not seeing a true cross section of the grizzly bear population. If this Great Plains grizzly bear was like modern populations, it was probably about half male and half female. If most of the grizzly bears that Lewis and Clark sighted—whether that number was thirty-seven, or sixty-two, or something else—were male, then they only represented some incomplete proportion of the population. Perhaps at this point, the highly conjectural population estimates we have been trying to make recede so far from reality that they become meaningless.

But I don't think so. The lessons of Lewis and Clark, as Botkin has introduced them, still hold. The members of the Corps of Discovery are still the teachers. The lessons are just getting more subtle and demanding. We are still feeling our way through their perceptions and their information, and we are still slowly approaching a better understanding of their world and ours.

—⊰◆⊱—

The image of the grizzly bear was of course bound up in the image of the Northwest, what John Logan Allen called the "Northwestern Mystery."[10] For more than two centuries, the Western nations had exercised their considerable imaginations on just what might be hidden in the vast North American interior. Any land with so many hoped-for or dreaded features—golden cities, volcanoes, mammoths, and descendants of Welsh colonists, among many others that were proposed in the two hundred years before Lewis and Clark—surely could have many other wonders and monsters.

We must remember that Lewis and Clark brought west with them their own idea of the bear. They were not absolute strangers to the idea of the bear or to the wealth of lore and legend surrounding the animal. It is popular in modern environmental writing to portray Euro-Americans as tragically divorced from nature—a portrayal usually heightened by comparison with the extent to which Native Americans were obviously tuned in, both intellectually and spiritually, to their native ecological scene. But something much more complicated was going on when white people encountered nature in the New World. They were, it is true, abjectly ignorant about their new surroundings, but they had an enduring acquaintance with the nature they had left behind. Without question, Euro-Americans included in their own diverse cultural baggage thousands of years of experience with the brown bear. Lewis's own inheritance as a British descendant included the folkloric sources of *Beowulf* and the Arthurian legends, among other bear-related elements in Britain's mythic and literary heritage.[11] That inheritance was not necessarily made less important to the Euro-Americans of Lewis's time just because the brown bear of England had been extinct for eight centuries.[12] Add to that ancient relationship of Lewis's culture with the brown bear his personal familiarity with the black bear, and he becomes a person whose experience may be weak in certain specifics but whose eyes and mind are as wide open as they could be, and as ready for new information as we could hope.

On the other hand, I will leave it to more adventurous souls to psychoanalyze Lewis and probe more deeply into his possible feelings about these bears. I would be hesitant to do this even if he had a healthier psyche than he apparently did. While it interests me that neither Lewis nor Clark makes allusions to Old World bears, either by way of comparison with the bears they met or as additional fortification of natural history information they gathered, it is difficult to define their position on wild, dangerous carnivores beyond vague generalizations that fit most people of their age. They were, indeed, the descendants of people who had, indeed, extirpated the brown bear (to say nothing of the wolf and other species) from England and many parts of Europe long before. Their inclinations were clear. At the same time that they were dutifully making their natural history notes, the Corps of Discovery's most pressing goals were oriented almost entirely toward commerce, agriculture, and the development of a young and violently ambitious nation.

Euro-Americans had, by Lewis and Clark's time, shown abundant evidence of what they would tolerate in wild nature. They might pause to admire the power or beauty of a bear or mountain lion or other predator, but we would be hard pressed to find anything in their makeup that resembled sympathy for competing carnivores. Their ancestors and descendants showed little sympathy for the Native humans of the East and the West; how could we expect them to have any fellow feeling for what they certainly felt were "lower forms" of animal species?

Even with all of that in mind, and knowing something of the attitudes that Lewis and Clark took into the West, I conducted this search of the journals with at least one other question in mind. Surely Lewis knew that his patron and president, Thomas Jefferson, had only a few decades earlier aggressively defended the quality and honor of North American wildlife in the face of attacks by European naturalists who maintained that the wild animals and humans native to the New World were diminished and inferior forms. In that defense, Jefferson listed bears among many other species whose North American representatives were as large and robust as their European counterparts.[13] I wondered if the findings of Lewis and Clark would, either in the minds of the explorers themselves or in the mind of Jefferson, reveal any patriotic attachments. Would the grizzly bear be enlisted in that old debate that had once meant so much to the younger Jefferson?

The answer to that question is somewhat uncertain. In short, it is no—the journalists did not specifically haul the grizzly bear into any argument on behalf of the superiority of North American animals. I would not necessarily have expected them to, because as Jefferson scholar Charles Miller pointed out, Jefferson did not intend to prove North American superiority, only that "the New World was not inferior. Equality was enough."[14]

But there is a longer answer that amounts to yes. The Corps of Discovery brought back news of a fabulous land that by its very size, variety, beauty, and potential, even in the most prosaic of their descriptions, announced the exceeding grandness—the raw, unbridled vitality—of the nation. I suppose in that respect the Lewis and Clark accounts of grizzly bears contributed something, perhaps something exciting, romantic, or even unique, to the portrait the captains provided of this huge new addition to the national domain. Perhaps in that way, the image of the grizzly bear that Lewis and Clark gave us had power beyond the practical matters of taxonomy and biology. The grizzly bear, like all the other dangers and obstacles inhabiting this new regime, might have served as a kind of challenge to the nation—a goad to the patriotism and ambition of people who wanted to make the West as civilized as the East and do so as quickly as possible.

⟫⟩◆⟨⟪

It is true about many things, but it is especially true about the grizzly bear, that Lewis and Clark perhaps served us best because they left us such a plainly true story. Unlike many of those who followed them, they had a charge to report everything accurately, and they honored it. It is ironic almost beyond expression that they are now seen as the vanguard of the "mountain men" whose cultural stock-in-trade was the fabulous lie or tall tale. Here were men, the entire Corps of Discovery, for whom the temptation to fantasize and embellish must at times have been acute, but, as Albert Furtwangler pointed out, they resisted the temptation to provide us with anything but the facts as they perceived them.

In the case of the grizzly bear, we could not have asked more of them than what they gave us. Their unadorned bear—weighted down with a minimum of romanticizing and glorification—was the best for our purposes. Not only was it best for all scientific purposes, it was also best for the sort of image making that such a creature inevitably inspires. If Lewis and Clark had overloaded the grizzly bear with their own visions of monstrosity or with their own personal mythic preferences, later generations perhaps couldn't have made as much of it as they did. We would have been constrained, channeled into their dream instead of being free to pursue our own.

And what a lot we have made of the grizzly bear, and what an incredible array of dreams have been borne on the businesslike descriptions of the Corps of Discovery. We have found so much to trust in the descriptions of bears left us by Lewis and Clark that modern scientists are applying ever more subtle and sophisticated thinking and analytical techniques to tease new information from the old—new wisdoms from the simple ones offered by the explorers. And we have found so much to wonder and marvel at in the bear they revealed that there seems no end to our capacity for finding new ways to imagine the animal.

But let's be fair to the other major participant in this performance. Lewis and Clark achieved heroic things in their accounts of the grizzly bear, but we probably owe that as much to the bear as to them. It is such an appealing, magnificent, inscrutable creature that we probably would have found our way to its magic even had Lewis and Clark not made their trip. If they had not gone, plenty of other people were poised to make the same trip; indeed, as the Corps of Discovery hurried homeward down the Missouri toward St. Louis, they met some of those ambitious souls coming upstream. Perhaps some of these other travelers would also have been able to bring back to us such a perfect combination of straightforward narrative and able conjecture about the grizzly bear. But I doubt it. I don't find much in the dozens of western narratives and journals that have survived from the decades following Lewis and Clark to indicate that those later adventurers could have matched the captains for clarity, accuracy, or attention to detail. Most could not have approached them.

We keep retelling the bear stories of Lewis and Clark. They're like favorite songs that we love to hear again and again. But we also retell them so we can rethink them. We pick at the details, we turn each statement this way and that, we look harder and harder, and sometimes we actually do get somewhere. We finally stare at the words long enough that some fresh insight emerges, and there is a bit of progress—even if it is only progress back to a clearer understanding of what Lewis and Clark saw, and thought, and said. If we're less wise and fortunate, we turn these great American bear stories to other purposes, in some social or political quarrel where they neither belong nor fit.

Our passion for these tales suggests to me that whatever other legacy we have found in the journals of the Corps of Discovery, we seem most

Close Quarters with Old Ephraim, *from Theodore Roosevelt's* Hunting Trips of a Ranchman *(1885). By the close of the nineteenth century, as the centennial of the Lewis and Clark expedition approached, the grizzly bear was taking on a new image. In much of the West, it was still widely regarded as vermin to be destroyed at any opportunity, but a growing number of forward-looking people, including sportsmen such as Roosevelt, recognized in the grizzly bear important symbolism of wild places and vanishing parts of America's natural heritage.*

devoted to their extraordinarily durable aura of authority. If Lewis and Clark said it, it must be true or, failing that, at least wise. If we need truth, or at least wisdom, surely we can find it in Lewis and Clark's journals. Their comments on the western landscape and its inhabitants have become part of our birthright, a documentary heritage almost on a plane with the Declaration of Independence and the Constitution. Whatever the issue or cause at hand, we always feel better if we can invoke Lewis and Clark on its behalf. Sometimes it even seems to me that by the lively descriptions and extended attention they gave to the grizzly bear, the Corps of Discovery helped make the bear so important to us today.

———⋙◆⋘———

There is a poignancy to our vicarious adventuring when we read the journals of the Corps of Discovery. Today's grizzly bears live in a tiny, pathetically restricted fragment of the habitat they occupied when Lewis and Clark met them. When we travel the Lewis and Clark trail we visit a former grizzly bear kingdom now lost under cities, ranches, and the very civilized landscapes that the captains and their president could only dream of. I suspect that if the three—Lewis, Clark, and Jefferson—could be transported to the upper Missouri today and could see what has become of the country they worked so hard to open up to settlement and society, they would be quite pleased. But I also like to imagine that Lewis, or perhaps more likely Clark, would feel a few twinges of regret at what was gone. Jefferson never saw it, but Lewis and Clark would remember.

It may be the final irony of the Lewis and Clark story that many of us are no longer as confident as they must have been that native humans, and grizzly bears, and bison herds, and all the rest of that earlier America should have to give way to industrial agriculture, to an urban order, and to such foreign ideas of proper human lifeways. We are, at least many of us, less confident about the righteous inevitability of all these changes. We aren't all that sure what we would prefer had happened instead, but when we read Lewis and Clark we pause to wonder if something has in some way gone wrong. We read books about returning the bison herds to the Great Plains, and even if we react with skepticism or complete disapproval we find the notion kind of satisfying. We stand along the Missouri River, and where there are now dams and roads and cities we feel a vague longing to see what Lewis and Clark saw. Sometimes we can still see much of what they saw, and we strain to imagine the rest.

Grizzly bears are gone from almost every mile of the routes traveled by Lewis and Clark. The bears survive only in isolated enclaves—a few mountain sanctuaries—places that at best the captains may have viewed from a hazy distance. The bears were gone long before we were born, but in some achingly vague, intergenerational way, we seem to recall them, and even miss them. In their absence these bears have become even more powerful symbols of the landscape than they were when they still roamed it so confidently. They are symbols not only of something lost, but of something we might decide to have again. Perhaps some day, we wonder, it might be possible to travel at least a few stretches of this immense, generous river and again have the chance Lewis and Clark had—to encounter this terrible, beautiful, unforgettable animal. What a discovery that would be.

I n this book I have followed literary tradition in not feeling obliged to provide an endnote citation every time I quote a passage from one of the Corps of Discovery's journals. Armed with the date of the journal entry (which I try always to provide), the reader can easily enough track down the quotation. Of course all other sources have been cited conventionally in the endnotes.

I have not seen, much less used, the original handwritten manuscript journals and notes of the Lewis and Clark Expedition. Very few scholars have, or have had any need to, because such thorough and hospitable published versions exist. I belong to the last generation of researchers and writers who, when they studied Lewis and Clark, relied almost entirely on the grand seven-volume edition of the journals edited by the great historical anthologist Reuben Gold Thwaites under the title of *Original Journals of the Lewis and Clark Expedition 1804–1806* (full citations for works mentioned in this discussion are given below). In this edition, Thwaites included his transcriptions not only of the manuscript journals of Lewis and Clark themselves but also of the manuscript journals of Charles Floyd and Joseph Whitehouse.

But even in 1905, the Thwaites edition was not all-inclusive. Thwaites did not include Patrick Gass's journal, which, as I mention in this book, had first appeared in print in 1807, in a form that had been revised and edited by David M'Keehan. The original manuscript journal written on the trip by Gass has disappeared, so all we have is this book, which has appeared in many editions. At least as much as the Moulton edition of the Gass journal (volume 10, 1996), I recommend the splendid new edition created by Carol Lynn MacGregor, which contains both a thoroughly annotated version of the original Gass book and Gass's account book from later in his life.

And Thwaites and Gass were not the end of it. As is so engagingly described in Paul Cutright's *A History of the Lewis and Clark Journals,* additional original material left by the Corps of Discovery continued to surface through much of the twentieth century. Among the most notable of these finds was the 1913 discovery of the journal of John Ordway, which was edited by Milo Milton Quaife and published, along with certain newly discovered journals of Meriwether Lewis, in 1916.

Exciting additional finds of Lewis and Clark material continued after 1916, with the happy result that half a century later, Gary Moulton undertook the creation of a new, inclusive edition of the journals. His thirteen volumes of *The Journals of the Lewis and Clark Expedition,* published beginning with the atlas in 1983, now comprise not only the definitive resource on the journals but also one of the great foundation documents in American history generally. (Add Donald Jackson's meticulously prepared *Letters of the Lewis and Clark Expedition with Related Documents, 1783–1854,* published in 1978, and you have essentially all of the original documentary material generated by the Corps of Discovery.)

With this background, I now turn to my own use of these materials. Bibliographical and editorial discussions of this sort are buried in the backs of books because they are of only marginal interest to most readers. But they are there at all because those few readers who do care about them care about them very much. What follows is offered in that spirit.

For the purposes of this book, I chose to think of myself as working from the Thwaites edition of the journals, that being the first comprehensive verbatim publication of the corps's authentic field accounts of the vast majority of the bear-related material that interested me. With only a few very brief exceptions, every passage I quote from the journals of Lewis, Clark, or Floyd was published in the Thwaites edition (Floyd's death early in the expedition makes his involvement in my work quite small, but I do quote him slightly, so I must mention him here).

But I paid considerable attention to the magnificent new edition of the journals prepared by Gary Moulton. In doing so, I found some intriguing challenges. In the process of making word-by-word comparisons of the bear-related journal entries of Lewis, Clark, and Floyd as they were transcribed by Thwaites and by Moulton, I noticed several things that might interest other readers or students of Lewis and Clark. Please understand that these are not observations that I in any way apply to the rest of the journal entries; they are only interesting editorial matters that arose in entries dealing with my specific topic. As well, they are not criticisms of either Thwaites or Moulton. I am too grateful to them both to find fault with either.

First, even a careful scholarly reader would find the passages virtually identical. The same words appear in the same order, spelled the same way, almost all the time. This should be no surprise; it would speak poorly of the high editorial standards we all expect from scholars across the generations if this were not true.

Second, there are in fact occasional differences between the Thwaites and Moulton editions. The differences are so minor and infrequent that, in less demanding publishing circles, a casual reader who noticed them would probably be inclined to write them off to typographical error and editorial inattentiveness.

I have to admit that I find this level of precise agreement—between two scholars operating eighty years apart—a little comforting. We naturally expect this kind of accuracy, but it is probably not as common as we might imagine. Over the years, as I have done historical research in various topics and have had occasion to cross-check the quotations of one writer against the original source, I have occasionally encountered supposed verbatim transcriptions—offered as exact quotes—that were nowhere near so faithful to the original as the transcriptions by Thwaites and Moulton are to one another. Of course it was not the intent of Moulton to transcribe Thwaites. The two of them just did equally good jobs of transcribing the same original.

With both parties exercising this level of care, the differences that I find between the Thwaites and Moulton transcriptions almost have to be the result of editorial intention (I did find a very few differences that do seem to be typographical errors). This meant that the differences sometimes demanded a decision of some sort from me—which version should I use?

I don't doubt that some scholars would say I should have adhered strictly to one or the other, but I disagree. I felt a greater responsibility to the reader than to the transcribers, and as trivial a matter as most of these editorial decisions were, I felt obliged to address them. Lacking the wherewithal to go examine the original manuscripts (even if I were allowed to paw through them for all these bear-related entries), I did what seemed the best I could. And as long as I explain my approach here, I don't see how any harm can come of it.

I will happily admit that my decisions seemed to waffle back and forth, perhaps because the choices open to me were largely subjective. I was further freed from a great deal of concern about the effects of my choosing between the two editorial interpretations because the differences were so minor that my choice would usually have little or no measurable effect on what the reader would "hear" from the journalists.

Here are the kinds of differences I found. Once in a great while the two spelled a word differently, usually, I assume, because they were interpreting a difficult-to-read letter (for instance was it an *a* or an *o*?) differently. But even this much disagreement was quite rare.

Moulton typically gave Clark credit for a good many more capitalized letters than did Thwaites, though on far fewer occasions it was Thwaites who capitalized while Moulton did not. Perhaps because Moulton is of my time and I somehow imagine scholarly attentiveness to be more finely tuned today, I almost always abandoned Thwaites's lowercase letters in favor of Moulton's uppercase letters (which is to say that I edited Thwaites to mimic Moulton). Or perhaps I did this just because, like many other modern readers, I find Clark's freewheeling writing style both quaint and refreshing. I think we all enjoy his little random acts of capitalization. Likewise, Moulton allowed Whitehouse a few more capitalized letters than did Thwaites, but apparently Whitehouse was easier to read, because Moulton and Thwaites disagree far less on his capitalization (Whitehouse seems to have had a special devotion to capitalizing the letter *S*). As with Clark, I almost always gave Whitehouse the capitalized version.

Moulton and Thwaites occasionally differed on punctuation. Moulton tended to include Clark's occasional long dashes between sentences or phrases, while Thwaites tended to ignore these. Though I favor these long dashes in my own writing, I usually chose to follow Thwaites here, mostly because Clark's long dashes had no impact on the strength or clarity of his statements (some seemed almost like the written equivalent of a speaker saying, "Uhhh").

Moulton and Thwaites also sometimes differed on whether a given punctuation mark was a period or a comma, and Thwaites also seemed to put in a few more periods than Moulton did, usually following abbreviations. Here I tended to revise Thwaites to resemble Moulton, but again tried to make the decision based primarily on which approach helped the reading of the sentence. (I should state that I never opted for any third course. I had no business adding yet another variant interpretation. In all my editorial decisions, the choice was always between the two competing existing editions.)

Only once did I find a significant difference between the two versions of those journals that were transcribed and published by both Thwaites and Moulton. According to Moulton, on August 21, 1805, Lewis, in discussing the bear-claw necklaces of the Shoshone Indians, said this:

> these claws are ornamented with beads about the thick end
> near which they are peirced through their sides and strung
> on a thong of dressed leather and tyed about the neck but
> sometimes are reversed.

According to Thwaites, the sentence should read like this (my italics signify the additional words):

> these claws are ornamented with beads about the thick end
> near which they are peirced through their sides and strung
> on a thong of dressed leather and tyed about the neck *com-*
> *monly with the upper edge of the tallon next to the breast or*
> *neck* but sometimes are reversed.

Both Thwaites and Moulton seemed to be quite careful about noting any variants, editorial emendations, erasures, or other departures from the main text, but neither noted a complication or problem here. Perhaps the Moulton version just missed this passage in transcription. In any event, it is an intriguing tidbit of information that I wanted to discuss in the text, so I chose the more full Thwaites version.

I have made one other departure from both Thwaites and Moulton. Several editors of the journals routinely placed very brief bracketed comments and explanations in the text, to help clarify confusing points or language; Thwaites and Moulton carried on this tradition, each in his own way. There were quite a few of these in the bear-related material, and though they were of course helpful in some greater context, none seemed essential, so I have removed them. On the other hand, I have added one or two of my own that seemed useful in this book's context.

A most delightful complication arose in the growing volume of Lewis and Clark Expedition materials in 1966, when a second version of Joseph Whitehouse's journal was discovered. Not only did it cover a greater period of time than the surviving portion of the original Whitehouse journal (that is, the one published by Thwaites), but also its entries were sometimes more fulsome, and it was much more professionally written. Historians judge this new version to be a "paraphrase," almost certainly rewritten by a professional editor in preparation for a publication that apparently never happened. The existence of this alternative version of the Whitehouse journal gave me two choices for each Whitehouse entry about bears.

As I explain in the text, editor Moulton included both versions in his new edition of the journals (volume 11), an act of editorial generosity I appreciate. Especially early in the expedition, Whitehouse offered some important, and sometimes even unique, observations on bears. In fact I would say that in this confined little area of study—bears—Whitehouse's journal is proportionately much more important than it is in the greater picture of the expedition's overall history. But because his original diary, though terse, almost always contained the same information as the longer, paraphrased version, I almost always quote the original. Not only does it have a more authentic flavor, but also I suspect that it is slightly more trustworthy for my needs. On a couple occasions when I quote both versions, I point out why I prefer the original.

The journals of Gass and Ordway, both of considerable importance in this business of bear history, likewise have existed in print for many years, and my use of them is straightforward. In the Gass quotations I have used, which are all based on precise transcriptions of the original published Gass journal of 1807, Moulton and MacGregor differ only by one comma in their transcriptions. In the Ordway quotations I have used, Quaife's 1916 transcription of the Ordway journal is also almost identical to Moulton's more recent edition, though Moulton tends to find just a few more capital letters in Ordway's script than Quaife did. I have tended to edit Quaife to favor Moulton's interpretations of the capital letters, but otherwise I confess that Quaife's interpretations were sometimes more appealing to me.

That more or less covers my approach, except to say that for all my efforts to sort out past interpretations of the journals, I suppose that I too will add some complications here and there, typographical, editorial, or other. For those I apologize in advance.

Publications Mentioned

Paul Russell Cutright. *A History of the Lewis and Clark Journals.* Norman: University of Oklahoma Press, 1976.

Patrick Gass. *A Journal of the Voyages and Travels of a Corps of Discovery,* ... edited by David M'Keehan. Pittsburgh: David M'Keehan, 1807.

Donald Jackson, editor, *Letters of the Lewis and Clark Expedition with Related Documents, 1783–1854.* Urbana: University of Illinois Press, 1978.

Carol Lynn MacGregor, editor. *The Journals of Patrick Gass, Member of the Lewis and Clark Expedition.* Missoula: Mountain Press Publishing Company, 1997.

Gary Moulton, editor. *The Journals of the Lewis and Clark Expedition.* 13 volumes. Lincoln: University of Nebraska Press, 1983–2001.

Milo Milton Quaife, editor. *The Journals of Captain Meriwether Lewis and Sergeant John Ordway.* Madison: State Historical Society of Wisconsin, 1916.

Reuben Gold Thwaites, editor. *Original Journals of the Lewis and Clark Expedition 1804–1806.* 7 volumes. New York: Dodd, Mead & Company, 1904–1905.

Introduction

1. The premier source on Cruzatte, as well as on the other men under the command of Lewis and Clark, is Charles G. Clarke, *The Men of the Lewis and Clark Expedition: A Biographical Roster of the Fifty-one Members and a Composite Diary of Their Activities from All Known Sources* (Glendale, California: The Arthur H. Clark Company, 1970).

2. Daniel Slosberg, "Pierre Cruzatte: Fiddling Around with Lewis and Clark," *Folkworks* 1, no. 1 (January–February 2001), p. 5. It is worth noting that a grizzly bear had actually been seen by many people in the eastern United States before Lewis and Clark began their expedition. In the summer of 1803, Charles Wilson Peale had put on exhibit in his Philadelphia museum a young "Grisley-bear," apparently a yearling that had been brought from the West (though exactly where is unknown). The bear was destroyed after it escaped captivity in March 1804. I have not yet determined whether or not Lewis might have seen this bear, or at least its skin, skull, or claws, during his extended visit in Philadelphia prior to leaving for the West. But Peale did send a hindquarter of the bear to Jefferson in March 1804, along with a careful description of the whole animal. For this and other instances of early grizzly bear knowledge and artifacts in the East, see Donald Jackson, *Thomas Jefferson & the Stony Mountains: Exploring the West from Monticello* (Urbana: University of Illinois Press, 1981), pp. 188–89. Jackson, pp. 259–60, also chronicles the misadventures of a pair of young grizzly bears that Zebulon Pike brought back from his western trip of 1806–1807, which also were sent to Peale. Some later writers have confused the source of these bears, saying that Lewis and Clark brought them.

3. Albert Furtwangler, *Acts of Discovery: Visions of America in the Lewis and Clark Journals* (Urbana: University of Illinois Press, 1993), p. 240.

4. Of course if Cruzatte did indeed manage to wound the bear, the odds are

best that it fled immediately. See Stephen Herrero, *Bear Attacks: Their Causes and Avoidance* (New York: Nick Lyons Books, 1985), p. 41.

5. My article appeared as "Bear Myths," *Field & Stream* 89, no. 8 (August 1984), pp. 64–65, 87–88. For background on other very early Euro-American encounters with grizzly bears, such as Henry Kelsey's first-known Canadian encounter (at the extremely early date of 1691), see Bessie Doak Haynes and Edgar Haynes, editors, *The Grizzly Bear: Portraits from Life* (Norman: University of Oklahoma Press, 1966). Herrero's *Bear Attacks* (*the* bear book to buy if you're buying only one), p. 10, quotes the key passage from Kelsey's journal. For an even earlier Euro-American encounter with North American grizzly bears, see Tracy I. Storer and Lloyd P. Tevis, *California Grizzly* (Berkeley: University of California Press, 1955). On pp. 105–6, Storer and Tevis described the experience of Father Antonio de la Ascensión, who visited Monterey Bay in December 1602 and reported seeing grizzly bears come to the beach to feed on a dead whale. These and other early grizzly bear encounters are of course noteworthy, but compared to the Lewis and Clark stories these earlier episodes seem to have value only as historical curiosities.

6. Paul Shepard and Barry Sanders, *The Sacred Paw: The Bear in Nature, Myth, and Literature* (New York: Viking, 1985), p. 1. The great pioneering work on bear beliefs is Irving A. Hallowell, "Bear Ceremonialism in the Northern Hemisphere," *American Anthropologist* 28 (1926), pp. 1–175.

7. According to Furtwangler, *Acts of Discovery*, p. 3, the term *Corps of Discovery* originated, in print at least, when expedition member Patrick Gass used the term in the title of his published journal, which appeared in 1807 (see footnote 6, chapter 2). In this book I use the terms *expedition*, *Corps of Discovery*, and the less formal *corps* interchangeably.

8. Daniel Botkin, *Our Natural History: The Lessons of Lewis and Clark* (New York: G. P. Putnam's Sons, 1995).

9. John Logan Allen, *Passage through the Garden: Lewis and Clark and the Image of the American Northwest* (Urbana: University of Illinois Press, 1975), p. 398. I used the 1991 Dover reprint of this book.

Chapter One: First Bears, and Other Matters

1. Clarke, *The Men of Lewis and Clark,* p. 45.

2. Ken Walcheck, "Wapiti, The Ubiquitous American Elk Was a Staple in Both the Diet and the Journals of Lewis and Clark," *We Proceeded On* 26, no. 3 (August 2000), pp. 26–32, and Ken Walcheck, "Pronghorn, As Documented by the 1804–1806 Lewis and Clark Expedition," *We Proceeded On* 24, no. 3 (August 1998), pp. 4–9.

3. Raymond Burroughs, in his compilation of journal excerpts and commentary, *The Natural History of the Lewis and Clark Expedition* (East Lansing: Michigan State University Press, 1995), p. 283, listed total kills for seventeen categories of animals, including the major ungulates (he grouped all deer together for the largest single total, 1,001 animals killed), several types of birds, and Indian dogs and horses. He listed forty-three grizzly bears and twenty-three black bears. He also cited Clark's statement that the party needed four deer, or an elk and a deer, or one bison, to provide the party with sufficient meat for a twenty-four-hour period (p. 282).

4. Peter Kalm, *Peter Kalm's Travels in North America, the English Version of 1770,* revised from the original Swedish and edited by Adolph B. Benson (New York: Dover Publications), vol. 2, p. 566.

5. Two outstanding sources on the creation and history of the journals themselves are Gary Moulton's "Introduction" to volume 2 of the *Journals,* especially pp. 8–48, and Paul Russell Cutright's bibliographical masterpiece, *A History of the Lewis and Clark Journals* (Norman, Oklahoma: University of Oklahoma Press, 1976). The Cutright book is probably my personal favorite among the Lewis-and-Clark-related books I have read—except, of course, for the journals themselves.

6. Patrick Gass, *The Journals of Patrick Gass, Member of the Lewis and Clark Expedition,* edited by Carol Lynn MacGregor (Missoula: Mountain Press Publishing Company, 1997), pp. 268–73.

7. Cutright, *A History of the Lewis and Clark Journals,* pp. 242–64.

Chapter Two: "tracks of white bear, verry large"

1. Many studies have been done of denning and hibernation in grizzly bears and black bears. A good popularly written summary of the findings is in Gary Brown, *The Great Bear Almanac* (New York: Lyons & Burford, 1993), pp. 146–55.

2. J. Knox Jones Jr., David M. Armstrong, Robert S. Hoffmann, and Clyde Jones, *Mammals of the Northern Great Plains* (Lincoln: University of Nebraska Press, 1983), p. 267. Perhaps the most concise overview of scientific information on the grizzly bear in North America is the Interagency Grizzly Bear Committee and the National Wildlife Federation, *Grizzly Bear Compendium* (Washington, D.C.: National Wildlife Federation, 1987). The historic range of the grizzly bear in the lower forty-eight states is covered in pp. 3–12. One of the early authoritative works on the distribution of grizzly bears was Ernest Thompson Seton, Lives of Game Animals (Boston: Charles T. Branford, 1953), the last edition of a work previously published in 1926. "Ancient Range" of the species is covered on pp. 16–24, with a range map on p. 9 (see further discussion of this map later in the book). Ecological histories of the states and regions along the edge of historic grizzly bear range are helping refine our understanding of exactly where the grizzly bear appeared in the past few centuries. One student of wildlife history along the historic eastern boundary of grizzly bear range, James J. Dinsmore, in *A Country So Full of Game: The Story of Wildlife in Iowa* (Iowa City: University of Iowa Press, 1994), p. 53, said that "It is possible that grizzlies may have occasionally wandered into Iowa, but I know of no documented records of such an occurrence." For an overview of the distribution of fossil remains of past and present North American bear species, see Russell W. Graham and Ernest L. Lundelius, *Faunmap: A Database Documenting Late Quaternary Distributions of Mammal Species in the United States,* Illinois State Museum Scientific Papers, vol. XXV, no. 2 (Springfield: Illinois State Museum, 1994), pp. 410–17.

3. E. Stirling, "The Grizzly Bear in Labrador," *Forest and Stream* 22, no. 17(May 22, 1884), p. 324; Anonymous, "Grizzly Bears in Labrador," *Forest and Stream* 46, no. 10 (March 7, 1896), p. 195. I assume that most of the unsigned notes and news items in *Forest and Stream* in this period were probably written by George Bird Grinnell, the longtime editor. Grinnell was himself a scientist, sportsman, and traveler who was quite familiar with grizzly bears in the West. David Rockwell, author of the excellent book *Giving Voice to Bear* (see chapter 3, footnote 5), provided me with material from anthropologist Frank G. Speck's

book *Naskapi: The Savage Hunters of the Labrador Peninsula* (Norman: University of Oklahoma Press, 1935), in which Speck makes the following statements about a band of Labrador Natives and their belief in a "great bear":

> They believe it to be a different race several times as large as the ordinary bear. This may refer to the so-called Barren Ground bear of Labrador. I have, however, no more information upon this reputed form than the following statements by Chief Kurtness of the Lake St. John band, and corroborated without expansion by several others with whom I discussed it. This bear does not hibernate in a den but "sits upright in the snow with his head uncovered above the drift." He has a very savage humor and his flesh is more tender than that of the common bear. His claws are so long that he can scarcely climb a tree. But the most puzzling thing about this legend is that something like it is related by the Penobscot of Maine as what they believe to be a second species of bear, known as a "ranger bear," inhabiting their own forests far south of the St. Lawrence. The story, one might imagine, could possibly be of a legendary nature. (p. 109)

See also Frank G. Speck, "Discussion and Correspondence, Mammoth or 'Stiff-legged Bear,'" *American Anthropologist* n.s. 37 (1935), pp. 159–63, and C. S. Elton, "Further Evidence about the Barren-Ground Grizzly Bear in Northeast Labrador and Quebec," *Journal of Mammalogy* 35, no. 3 (August 1954), pp. 345–57. I have not attempted a thorough review of the archaeological, paleontological, or anthropological literatures for more clues to the known or suspected presence of grizzly bears in eastern North America. It is clear from the sources cited in this and subsequent footnotes, however, that such a search would be very interesting.

4. Arthur Spiess and Steven Cox, "Discovery of the Skull of a Grizzly Bear in Labrador," *Arctic* 29, no. 4 (1976), pp. 194–200.

5. John E. Guilday, "Grizzly Bears from Eastern North America," *The American Midland Naturalist* 79, no. 1 (1968), p. 247. Guilday's article (pp. 247–50) is a serviceable overview of previous work on the question and provides citations to numerous earlier papers and reports on eastern fossil bears.

As I was finishing up this manuscript, I received a review copy of a new book by John Pezzenti Jr., *Shooting Bears: The Adventures of a Wildlife Photographer*

(New York: Rizzoli International Publications, 2001), in which Mr. Pezzenti states (p. 51) that grizzly bears inhabited New England well into historical times. He says that he has seen old photographs of New England hunters with both black and grizzly bears they had killed but that "all the grizzlies had been killed off one to two hundred years ago." I have so far been unsuccessful in my efforts to follow up on these very interesting statements.

6. For an overview of the history of changing attitudes and values among anthropologists dealing with Native American belief systems, see David Hurst Thomas, *Skull Wars, Kennewick Man, Archaeology, and the Battle for Native American Identity* (New York: Basic Books, 2000). For a spirited critique of the biases of anthropology in studying Native Americans, written by an outspoken Native American, see Vine Deloria Jr., *Red Earth, White Lies: Native Americans and the Myth of Scientific Fact* (New York: Scribner, 1995).

7. Anonymous, "Bears and Bear-Hunting," *Harper's New Monthly Magazine* 11, no. 65 (October 1855), p. 592. As mentioned in note 4, the lore and scholarship of the distribution of grizzly bears in eastern North America, as well as allegations that grizzly bears survived into relatively recent times in that part of the continent, deserve further exploration. See also Reuben Gold Thwaites, editor, *Early Western Travels 1748–1846,* vol. 16, *Part III of James's Account of S. H. Long's Expedition* (Cleveland: The Arthur H. Clark Company, 1905), pp. 47–48, which, in discussing the grizzly bear, said, "That they formerly inhabited the Atlantic states, and that they were then equally formidable to the Indians, we have some foundation for belief in the tradition of the Delaware Indians, respecting the big naked bear; the last one of which they believe formerly existed east of the Hudson River, and which Mr. Heckewelder assures us, is often arraigned by the Indians before the minds of their crying children to frighten them to quietness." According to James, De Witt Clinton, "An Introductory Discourse Delivered before the Literary and Philosophical Society of New York," May 4, 1814, stated that his sources maintained that the Delaware and Mohican Indians of New York had traditions of grizzly bears living in the region. James was correct: This is what Clinton said, but Clinton, like Thwaites, relied on Heckewelder. It does seem possible that the Clinton paper, which was very well known, might have been a source of the *Harper's* story quoted here. Clinton's work, which is full of fascinating asides on North American natural history, including an extended discussion of mammoths, is rarely given a full citation: De Witt Clinton, *Introductory Discourse Delivered before the Literary and Philosophical Society of New York on the Fourth of May, 1814, by De Witt Clinton,*

LL.D., *President of the Literary and Philosophical Society of New York, &c.* (New York: David Longworth, at the Shakespeare-Gallery, N. Van Riper, Print., 1815). See especially pp. 27, 74–76.

See William Wright, *The Grizzly Bear* (New York: Scribner's, 1913), pp. 26–29, and Harold McCracken, *The Beast That Walks Like Man: The Story of the Grizzly Bear* (Garden City, New York: Hanover House, 1955), pp. 38–40, 89–90, for two very similar secondary discussions of this subject.

8. Stephen Herrero, personal communication with the author, October 3, 2001, reminded me that "in heavily forested environments black bears can outcompete grizzly bears." Black bears can produce more young and exist at higher densities.

Chapter Three: Red and Yellow, Black and White

1. James P. Ronda, *Lewis and Clark among the Indians* (Lincoln: University of Nebraska Press, 1984), p. 114.

2. Ibid.

3. Ibid.

4. Ibid., p. 123.

5. Shepard and Sanders, *The Sacred Paw,* p. 1. The most thorough modern work on bear–Indian relationships and beliefs is David Rockwell's *Giving Voice to Bear: North American Indian Rituals, Myths, and Images of the Bear* (Niwot, Colorado: Roberts Rinehart, 1991).

6. Besides Shepard and Sanders, *The Sacred Paw,* Hallowell, "Bear Ceremonialism," and Rockwell, *Giving Voice,* see also "Circumpolar Cults of the Master Bear," in Joseph Campbell, *Historical Atlas of World Mythology,* vol. 1, "The Way of the Animal Powers, Pt. 2, Mythologies of the Great Hunt" (New York: Harper & Row, 1988), pp. 147–55.

7. Allen, *Passage through the Garden,* pp. 206–51, describes their various white informants during the winter at Fort Mandan.

Chapter Four: "a turrible looking animal"

1. Paul Russell Cutright, *Lewis and Clark: Pioneering Naturalists* (Lincoln: University of Nebraska Press, 1969), p. 143.

2. Adolph Murie, *A Naturalist in Alaska* (Old Greenwich, Connecticut: Devin Adair, 1961), p. 29.

3. Brown, *Great Bear Almanac,* p. 56.

4. Moulton, *Journals,* vol. 4, p. 88.

5. I checked with a number of bear managers and biologists who, in the process of trapping, studying, and otherwise handling grizzly bears, have had ample opportunity to examine the genitals of hundreds of individuals. These authorities have studied bears from Alaska to the lower forty-eight states, and have never seen even one case of a bear whose testicles were carried in separate pouches as described by Lewis. Thanks especially to Gary Brown, Bozeman, Montana; Mark Johnson, Bozeman, Montana; Chuck Schwartz, Interagency Grizzly Bear Study Team, Bozeman, Montana; Stephen Herrero, University of Calgary, Calgary, Alberta; and Marc Cattet, University of Saskatchewan, Saskatchewan, Canada, for their comments on this question.

6. For a study of the remarkable amount of "abnormal sexual differentiation" among black and brown bears, see Marc Cattet, "Abnormal Sexual Differentiation in Black Bears (*Ursus americanus*) and Brown Bears *(Ursus arctos)*," *Journal of Mammalogy* 69, no. 4 (1988), pp. 849–52. These variations involved females, which apparently are more subject to such noticeable differentiation than are males. Cattet provided me with the following comment on at least one possible answer to the puzzle of what Lewis was describing:

A possibility is that Lewis was looking at the caudal most mammae on the abdomen of a female brown bear. Older females occasionally develop mammary tumors that become apparent as palpable masses in some or all of their six mammae. In this situation, the mammae could appear superficially as testes. I'm aware, however, that Lewis and Clark are considered to have been careful observers of nature, so I don't think this speculation will be of much help to you. (personal communication from Marc Cattet, University of Saskatchewan, to the author, December 27, 2000)

This speculation on Cattet's part may not be as far off the mark as he suggests. His studies of female bears, cited above, included a female brown bear with a "short (30 mm) penis-like structure that lacked a urethra" (p. 849). If by chance the grizzly bear that Lewis described was an older female with such an abnormal structure, she also might have had the enlarged mammae. That combination would more or less meet the criteria of Lewis's description, especially if the hunters were not inclined to examine the genitals very closely.

For additional examples of genital abnormalities among bears, see Oystein Wiig, Andrew E. Derocher, Matthew M. Cronin, and Janneche U. Skaare, "Female Pseudohermaphrodite Polar Bears at Svalbard," *Journal of Wildlife Diseases* 34, no. 4 (1998), pp. 792–96.

7. Brown, *Great Bear Almanac*, p. 79.

8. For reviews of fishing behavior by brown and grizzly bears, see Tom Walker, *The Way of the Grizzly* (Stillwater, Minnesota: Voyageur Press, 1993); Tamara Olson and Ronald Squibb, *Brown Bears of Brooks River* (Kodiak, Alaska: Squibb, 1993); and Daniel Reinhart and David Mattson, "Bear Use of Cutthroat Trout Spawning Streams in Yellowstone National Park," in L. Darling and W. Archibald, editors, *Bears—Their Biology and Management,* Proceedings of the Eighth International Conference on Bear Research and Management (no location given: International Association for Bear Research and Management, 1990).

9. Interagency Grizzly Bear Committee, *Grizzly Bear Compendium,* pp. 42–45.

10. George Ord, *A Reprint of the North American Zoology, by George Ord, Being an Exact Reproduction of the Part Originally Compiled by Mr. Ord for Johnson & Warner, and First Published by Them in Their Second American Edition of Guthrie's Geography, in 1815,* edited by Samuel N. Rhoads (Haddonfield, New Jersey: Samuel N. Rhoads, 1894).

11. Cutright, *A History of the Lewis and Clark Journals,* pp. 53–72, reviews the process of producing this first edition. Of course Biddle had access to other material besides the captains' journals, including the journal of John Ordway. See Kerry Oman, "Serendipity: A Newly Discovered Letter Reveals That John Ordway Planned to Publish His Expedition Journal," *We Proceeded On* 27, no. 4 (November 2001), pp. 7–10, for the latest information on the early history of the Ordway journal.

12. Gass's journal first appeared as *A Journal of the Voyages and Travels of a Corps of Discovery under the Command of Capt. Lewis and Capt. Clarke of the Army of the United States. . . .* [etc.] (Pittsburgh: David M'Keehan, 1807).

13. Cutright, *A History of the Lewis and Clark Journals,* p. 64, says that the edition did not sell well, though of course over the next century there were subsequent printings and editions that did eventually accumulate a large audience. James Ronda, personal communication to the author, August 27, 2001, explained to me that there were only "1,417 perfect sets" of the Biddle edition.

14. Harold McCracken, *The Beast That Walks Like Man,* pp. 89–90, 286–90, reviews the bibliographical history of the Ord description. It is important to understand that Brackenridge's account of the grizzly bear was not entirely derivative of the writings of Lewis and Clark. Henry Marie Brackenridge, a geographer, traveled up the Missouri River in 1811 with Manuel Lisa, so he would have had his own additional insights and informal sources of information on grizzly bears to add to his account. See William H. Geotzmann, *Exploration and Empire: The Explorer and the Scientist in the Winning of the American West* (Austin: Texas State Historical Association, 1993), p. 29.

15. Ord, *A Reprint,* pp. 299–300.

16. McCracken, *The Beast That Walks Like Man,* p. 89. The most complete list of early alternative scientific and popular names that I have seen appears in John James Audubon and John Bachman, *The Quadrupeds of North America,* vol. 3 (New York: V. G. Audubon, 1854; Arno Press facsimile reprint, 1974), p. 141, which lists fourteen previous published names, some informal and some formal, that had appeared by 1854. Audubon and Bachman preferred *Ursus Ferox.*

17. C. Hart Merriam, *Review of the Grizzly and Big Brown Bears of North America (Genus Ursus) with Description of a New Genus, Vetularctos,* U.S. Department of Agriculture, Bureau of Biological Survey, North American Fauna No. 41 (Washington, D.C.: U.S. Government Printing Office, 1918).

18. Theodore Roosevelt, *The Letters of Theodore Roosevelt,* Elting Morison, editor (Cambridge, Massachusetts: Harvard University Press, 1951), vol. 1, p. 612.

19. Merriam, *Review of the Grizzly and Brown Bears,* p. 18.

20. My thanks to Steve Herrero for alerting me to this revision and to Curtis Strobeck of the University of Edmonton, Alberta, and Lisette Waits of the University of Idaho, Moscow, for acquainting me with recent brown bear genetics literature. Though scientists have not yet formally proposed a new species terminology for grizzly or brown bears, their studies have built quite a case for eliminating the last subspecific designations in North America. For background, see D. Paetkau, L. P. Waits, P. L. Clarkson, L. Craighead, E. Vyse, R. Ward, and

C. Strobek, "Variation in Genetic Diversity across the Range of North American Brown Bears," *Conservation Biology* 12, no. 2 (April 1998), pp. 418–29, and L. Waits, S. Talbot, R. Ward, and G. Shields, "Phylogeography of the North American Brown Bear and Implications for Conservation," *Conservation Biology* 12, no. 2 (April 1998), pp. 408–17. The one possible exception to this simplification of North American brown bear designation is the population of bears on Kodiak Island, which have apparently been isolated longer and with more genetic effects, than have other Alaskan island populations. See D. Paetkau, G. F. Shields, and C. Strobeck, "Gene Flow between Insular, Coastal and Interior Populations of Brown Bears in Alaska," *Molecular Ecology* 7 (1998), 1283–92.

Chapter Five: "I do not like the gentleman"

1. Furtwangler, *Acts of Discovery*.

2. Herrrero, *Bear Attacks*, p. 157.

3. Meriwether Lewis and William Clark, *The Journals of Lewis and Clark*, John Bakeless, editor (New York: The New American Library, 1964), p. 144.

4. Editor Moulton, *Journals*, vol. 11, p. 158, says that they named a creek just before their encounter with the bear on May 14 "Brown Bear Defeated Creek," and that the name was changed later to Snow Creek, Garfield County, Montana.

5. Herrero, *Bear Attacks*, p. 186.

6. The discussion of firearms is based primarily on Carl P. Russell, *Firearms, Traps, & Tools of the Mountain Men* (Albuquerque: University of New Mexico Press, 1977), especially pp. 34–96.

7. Ibid., p. 38.

8. Ibid., p. 39.

9. McCracken, *The Beast That Walks Like Man*, p. 100.

10. Russell, *Firearms, Traps, & Tools*, p. 96.

Chapter Six: Seeking and Sorting Bears

1. Among the dozens of books that have been published about bears, there are a few essential classics on the history of the species' demise. Among these are the books by Wright and McCracken, already mentioned, and Andy Russell, *Grizzly Country* (New York: Knopf, 1967). There are many other worthy titles, but these three all do a fine job of summarizing the decline of grizzly bear populations to the time of their publication.

2. Paul Schullery, *The Bears of Yellowstone,* third edition (Worland, Wyoming: High Plains Publishing Company, 1992), and Paul Schullery, "Yogi Lives: The Evolving Image of the Bears of Yellowstone," in A. Peyton Curlee, Anne-Marie Gillesberg, and Denise Casey, *Greater Yellowstone Predators: Ecology and Conservation in a Changing Landscape,* Proceedings from the Third Biennial Scientific Conference on the Greater Yellowstone Ecosystem (Jackson, Wyoming: Northern Rockies Conservation Cooperative and the Yellowstone Center for Resources, 2000), pp. 3-15.

3. Hans Huth, *Nature and the American* (Berkeley: University of California Press, 1957); Roderick Nash, *Wilderness and the American Mind* (New Haven: Yale University Press, revised third edition, 1982); Max Oelschlaeger, *The Idea of Wilderness* (New Haven: Yale University Press, 1991).

4. An especially readable result of such intensive studies is Terry DeBruyn, *Walking with Bears* (New York: The Lyons Press, 1999).

5. Paul Schullery, *The Bear Hunter's Century: Profiles from the Golden Age of Bear Hunting* (New York: Dodd, Mead & Company, 1988), pp. 1–7.

6. Thomas McNamee, *The Grizzly Bear* (New York: Knopf, 1985), and Schullery, *The Bears of Yellowstone,* review the controversy surrounding the closing of the dumps.

7. John J. Craighead, Jay S. Sumner, and John A. Mitchell, *The Grizzly Bears of Yellowstone, Their Ecology in the Yellowstone Ecosystem, 1959–1992* (Washington, D.C.: Island Press, 1995), pp. 322–28.

8. Paul Schullery, review of *The Grizzly Bears of Yellowstone* by Craighead, Sumner, and Mitchell, *Journal of Wildlife Management,* 61, no. 4 (1997), pp. 1451–52.

Chapter Seven: Courage

1. Furtwangler, *Acts of Discovery,* p. 53.

2. Ibid., p. vii.

3. Ibid.

4. Ibid., p. 60.

5. Ibid., p. 68.

6. Herrero, *Bear Attacks,* pp. 207–28. I also review some of the older literature on charges in my book, *Real Alaska: Finding Our Way in the Wild Country* (Mechanicsburg, Pennsylvania: Stackpole Books, 2001).

7. All authoritative advice on what to do when encountering a bear in wild country agrees that you should not run, which might trigger a chasing response in the bear. One highly recommended expert opinion is provided by Gary Brown, *Safe Travel in Bear Country: Safe Camping, Hiking, Fishing, and More* (New York: Lyons & Burford, 1996), pp. 128–30.

8. The Old Cattleman, "Why the Grizzly Is Discreet," *Recreation* 17, no. 3 (September 1902), p. 238.

9. Fred R. Gowans, *Mountain Man and Grizzly* (Orem, Utah: Mountain Grizzly Publications, 1986).

10. Short of half a mile or more, there is no surefire "magic" distance that will always guarantee your safety, so it is difficult to give one number for all occasions. It is far more important to be alert and stay attentive to the advice offered in official bear-safety pamphlets, and in such books as Herrero's *Bear Attacks* and Brown's *Safe Travel in Bear Country.* There are a number of other respected guides to bear–human safety in print. If possible, find a copy of Charles Jonkel, *How to Live in Bear Country* (Missoula, Montana: Ursid Research Center, P.O. Box 9383, Missoula, Montana, 59807, no publication date given).

11. John K. Townsend, "Narrative of a Journey across the Rocky Mountains, to the Columbia River," in *Early Western Travels, 1748–1846,* vol. 21, Reuben Gold Thwaites, editor (Cleveland: The Arthur H. Clark Company, 1905), p. 218.

12. Osborne Russell, *Journal of a Trapper,* Aubrey Haines, editor (Lincoln: University of Nebraska Press, 1955), p. 47.

13. Wright, *The Grizzly Bear,* pp. 34–35. Audubon's role in portraying the "ferocity" of the grizzly bear may not have been as simple as Wright said. Though his various writings no doubt did inflame the casual reader's perception of the grizzly bear, he also was one of the first writers to gather an assortment of accounts of the bear that suggested how complex an animal it was. In *The Quadrupeds of North America,* vol. 3 (New York: V. G. Audubon, 1854; Arno Press facsimile reprint, 1974), by John James Audubon and John Bachman, there appeared, mixed in with many other accounts of the bear from many other sources, this summary of the experiences of one early adventurer who did not find the bear all that aggressive:

> Mr. DRUMMOND, in his excursions over the Rocky Mountains, had frequent opportunities of observing the manners of the Grizzly Bear, and it often happened that in turning the point of a rock or sharp angle of a valley, he came suddenly upon one or more of them. On such occasions they reared on their hind legs and made a loud noise like a person breathing quick, but much harsher. He kept his ground without attempting to molest them, and they, on their part, after attentively regarding him for some time, generally wheeled round and galloped off, though, from their disposition, there is little doubt but he would have been torn in pieces had he lost his presence of mind and attempted to fly. When he discovered them from a distance, he generally frightened them away by beating on a large tin box, in which he carried his specimens of plants. He never saw more than four together, and two of these he supposes to have been cubs; he more often met them singly or in pairs. He was only once attacked, and then by a female, for the purpose of allowing her cubs time to escape. His gun on this occasion missed fire, but he kept her at bay with the stock of it, until some gentlemen of the Hudson's Bay Company, with whom he was travelling at the time, came up and drove her off. (p. 148)

"Mr. Drummond" must be the botanist Thomas Drummond, who visited the West in the mid-1820s. Perhaps his scientific background made him a somewhat more cautious observer. It appears from this summary of Drummond's observations that Audubon and Bachman understood that fleeing from a bear might trigger its urge to chase, though their expressed conviction that such flight will always result in being "torn in pieces" is the sort of hyperbole that Wright rightly disapproved of. But they also revealed that sows with cubs are most likely to hurt people out of defensive reaction.

On the other hand, to get back to Wright's criticism of Audubon, Wright (pp. 34–35) believed that Audubon did not adequately acknowledge what Drummond was saying about the true nature of grizzly bears, and that Audubon overemphasized the dangers of being in grizzly bear country. I agree, but compared to some other early writings, the overall effect of Audubon's account is at least a little better balanced. As for Drummond, Wright concluded that "One wishes, by the way, that Drummond had been a student of animals instead of plants. He had the right kind of stuff in him" (p. 35).

14. Ibid., pp. 35–36.

15. For Roosevelt's bear-related writings, see *Theodore Roosevelt, American Bears: Selections from the Writings of Theodore Roosevelt,* Paul Schullery, editor (Boulder: Colorado Associated University Press, 1983).

16. Associated Press, "Some Question Effectiveness of Pepper Spray," *Bozeman (Montana) Chronicle,* August 7, 2001, pp. 1, 12.

Chapter Eight: The Great Falls Bear Crisis

1. Interagency Grizzly Bear Study Team, *Grizzly Bear Compendium,* pp. 42–45.

2. Botkin, *Our Natural History.* Botkin has also written a splendid guide to the Missouri River portion of the Lewis and Clark trip route, *Passage of Discovery: The American Rivers Guide to the Missouri River of Lewis and Clark* (New York: Perigee, 1999).

3. The historiography of early travel and exploration accounts as a source of information on ecological conditions is dealt with in some detail in several publications by Lee Whittlesey and me. These include Paul Schullery and Lee Whittlesey, "Summary of the Documentary Record of Wolves and Other Wildlife Species in the Yellowstone National Park Area Prior to 1882," in L. N. Carbyn, S. H. Fritts, and D. R. Seip, editors, *Ecology and Conservation of Wolves in a Changing World,* Canadian Circumpolar Institute, occasional publication no. 35 (1995), pp. 63–76; Paul Schullery and Lee Whittlesey, "Greater Yellowstone Carnivores: a History of Changing Attitudes," in T. W. Clark, A. Peyton Curlee, S. C. Minta, and P. M. Kareiva, editors, *Carnivores in Ecosystems: The Yellowstone*

Experience (New Haven: Yale University Press, New Haven, 1999), pp. 63–76; and Paul Schullery and Lee Whittlesey, "Mountain Goats in the Greater Yellowstone Ecosystem: A Prehistoric and Historical Context," *Western North American Naturalist* 61, no. 3 (2001), pp. 289–307.

Chapter Nine: Shy Bears

1. Cutright, *A History of the Lewis and Clark Journals,* pp. 242–64.

2. Ibid., p. 252.

3. Moulton, *Journals,* vol. 5, page 17.

4. Dan Flores, *The Natural West: Environmental History in the Great Plains and Rocky Mountains* (Norman: University of Oklahoma Press, 2001), p. 80. In their important scientific synthesis paper, "Grizzly Bear, *Ursus arctos,*" in Joseph A. Chapman and George A. Feldhamer, editors, *Wild Mammals of North America: Biology, Management, and Economics* (Baltimore: The Johns Hopkins University Press, 1982), p. 517, John J. Craighead and John A. Mitchell, in discussing the grizzly bears killed by the Corps of Discovery, say that they killed "a number that journals of the expedition do not correlate clearly with a need for food." It is true that there is not a perfect correlation, in that not every bear killed was directly described by expedition journalists as being needed for food. But there is a perhaps inappropriate value judgment implicit in the Craighead-Mitchell statement, which certainly intends to suggest that there was wasteful killing going on. The first inappropriate element of this statement may be simply that these were not men of the late twentieth century, and we should not expect them to be attuned to our sense of urgency about predator conservation. More to the point of the "need" for food, it does seem clear to me that grizzly bears were prized meat for the corps and were even more prized as a source of the grease that made so much of their other food more palatable, even edible. I do not have the impression that many of the bears killed by the party, for whatever reason, were not also put to use at least for their grease, unless circumstances of their travel made it impractical for the men to acquire the grease and butcher the meat, or the animal was in such poor condition that it's meat and grease were not useful to them.

5. Schullery, *The Bear Hunter's Century,* pp. 145–49.

6. Theodore Roosevelt, *Hunting Trips of a Ranchman* (New York: G. P. Putnam's Sons, 1885), p. 299.

7. A compilation of tales of such bear-legend characters appears in W. P. Hubbard Seale Harris, *Notorious Grizzly Bears* (Chicago: The Swallow Press, 1960).

8. Herrero, *Bear Attacks,* p. 184.

9. Russell, *Grizzly Country,* p. 118.

10. Francis Parkman, *The Oregon Trail,* E. N. Feltskog, editor (Madison: University of Wisconsin Press, 1969), p. viii.

Chapter Ten: Rare Bears

1. Allen, *Passage through the Garden,* is devoted to the work of Lewis and Clark in attempting to sort fact from fiction in centuries of accumulated beliefs about the crossing of the continent.

2. Allen, *Passage through the Garden,* p. 305.

3. Apparently the tribe in question was the Nez Perce.

4. Patricia Robins Flint, "The Probable Location of a Medicine Tree," *Proceedings of the Montana Academy of Science* 38 (1979), p. 161.

5. Personal communication from James Ronda, December 27, 2000. Other sources on medicine trees in the region include George F. Weisel Jr., "The Ram's Horn Tree and Other Medicine Trees of the Flathead Indians," *The Montana Magazine of History* 1, no. 3 (July 1951), pp. 5–13, and Caleb Irvine, "Medicine Tree Hill," *Contributions to the Montana Historical Society* 6 (1907), 482–83.

6. Stephen E. Ambrose, *Undaunted Courage: Meriwether Lewis, Thomas Jefferson, and the Opening of the American West* (New York: Simon & Schuster, 1996), p. 294.

7. Arthur W. Adams, "Migration," in Jack Ward Thomas and Dale E. Toweill, editors, *Elk of North America: Ecology and Management* (Harrisburg, Pennsylvania: Stackpole Books, 1982), pp. 317–18.

8. Leonard Lee Rue III, *The Deer of North America* (Danbury, Connecticut: Grolier Book Clubs, Inc., 1989), pp. 303–8.

9. Ronda, *Lewis and Clark among the Indians,* at several points summarizes the extent to which the Indians—and their location and political reach—whom Lewis and Clark saw had been affected by the epidemics. There are many books and

articles on the spectacular effects of European diseases on North American Natives. The study of pre-Columbian human population size has been a going concern among anthropologists and archaeologists for much of the past century. A few of the most important and representative works include David E. Stannard, *American Holocaust: the Conquest of the New World* (New York: Oxord University Press, 1992); Ann F. Ramenofsky, *Vectors of Death: The Archaeology of European Contact* (Albuquerque: University of New Mexico Press, 1987); and William M. Denevan, *The Native Population of the Americas in 1492,* revised edition (Madison: University of Wisconsin Press, 1992). For a provocative scholarly reaction against the tendency of each generation of scholars to further increase pre-Columbian population estimates, see David Henige, *Numbers from Nowhere: The American Indian Contact Population Debate* (Norman: University of Oklahoma Press, 1998). An excellent and fascinating summary of how the epidemics affected wildlife, specifically bison, is Andrew C. Isenberg, *The Destruction of the Bison: An Environmental History, 1750–1920* (New York: Cambridge University Press, 2000), pp. 113–22.

10. Elers Koch, "Big Game in Montana from Early Historical Records," *Journal of Wildlife Management* 5, no. 4 (October 1941), pp. 366–68.

11. National Park Service, *Yellowstone's Northern Range: Complexity & Change in a Wildland Ecosystem* (Yellowstone National Park: Yellowstone Center for Resources, National Park Service, 1997), pp. 1–29. For an overview of how these issues fit in the larger scene of evolving management of Yellowstone, see Paul Schullery, *Searching for Yellowstone: Ecology and Wonder in the Last Wilderness* (Boston: Houghton Mifflin, 1997).

12. National Park Service, *Yellowstone's Northern Range,* pp. 1–29; Paul Schullery, *The Yellowstone Wolf: A Guide and Sourcebook* (Worland, Wyoming: High Plains Publishing Company, 1996).

13. U.S. Fish and Wildlife Service, *Draft Environmental Impact Statement: Grizzly Bear Recovery in the Bitterroot Ecosystem* (Missoula: Region 6, U.S. Fish and Wildlife Service, 1997), pp. 6–207. James Ronda, personal communication to the author, August 27, 2001, captured the authority and magic that Lewis and Clark hold for the American public in this way:

> Have you noticed how John C. Fremont—the great 19th century pathfinder—has completely vanished from our national memory, along with so many other government and private explorers? How many Pike and Fremont interpretive centers are there?!

Chapter Eleven: Pacific Slope Bears

1. Ernest Thompson Seton, *Lives of Game Animals,* vol. 2 (Boston: Charles T. Branford, 1953), p. 9.

2. Two recent accounts of the changes in the Columbia River, including the decline of its salmon, over the past two hundred years are Richard White, *The Organic Machine* (New York: Hill and Wang, 1995), and William Dietrich, *Northwest Passage: The Great Columbia River* (New York: Simon & Schuster, 1995).

3. Paul Schullery, "A History of Native Elk in Mount Rainier National Park," Final Report to the National Park Service, Mount Rainier National Park, January 1, 1984. Copy on file in Mount Rainier park library.

4. Ibid., pp. 16–25.

5. Paul Sullivan, "A Preliminary Study of Historic and Recent Reports of Grizzly Bears, *Ursus arctos,* in the North Cascades Area of Washington," unpublished research report, Washington Department of Game, 1983, pp. 2–3.

6. Storer and Tevis, *California Grizzly.*

7. Allen, *Passage through the Garden,* p. 316, note 25, suggests that the population of that region may have been higher than Lewis and Clark estimated. See also Douglas H. Uebelaker, "North American Indian Population Size, A.D. 1500 to 1985," *American Journal of Physical Anthropology* 77 (1988), pp. 289–94. Uebelaker (p. 292) estimated that the first-contact population of the Northwest Coast (not the same as the Columbia River Basin) was 175,330, and that in 1800, roughly the time of the Lewis and Clark visit, it was 98,333. The decline was presumably because of diseases brought to the coast by European traders.

8. Ted Birkedal, "Ancient Hunters in the Alaskan Wilderness: Human Predators and Their Role and Effect on Wildlife Populations and the Implications for Resource Management," *Seventh Conference on Research & Resource Management in Parks and on Public Lands:* Partners in Stewardship, November 16–20, 1992, Jacksonville, Florida. The George Wright Society, 1993, pp. 228–34. The question could be asked: The bears seem willing to share with human fishermen now; why wouldn't they have been willing to share back then? The answer probably has to do with relative willingness to share at all. Today's human users are not allowed to build small villages right along the river, in which they construct large drying

racks upon which they hang hundreds of pounds of freshly caught salmon. When the human fishermen needed to do such things, it seems likely that there would be conflicts with the bears—conflicts that the humans very quickly would find intolerable and would kill or drive off the bears.

9. Though I have not found a comprehensive study of grizzly bears or their remains in the lower Columbia River area, my communications with a variety of specialists on this topic yielded several thoughtful responses. My comments in this book are based in good part on the consensus of regional expert opinion in these responses, so I might share some of them here. I asked knowledgable people if humans were probably the reason grizzly bears were scarce in the lower Columbia area. Greg Burtchard of the National Park Service, Mount Rainier National Park, said this:

> Your most probable answer essentially is the one you suppose. Humans are a vigorously competitive species against which, to my knowledge, no mammal has been successful over the long term. For the last 4,000 years or so, humans have relied on Columbia River salmon as a dietary staple. Assuming increasing population density, salmon use intensity almost certainly increased, perhaps exponentially, through time. There is no reason to expect that these populations would have tolerated competition from bears. (personal communication with the author, January 5, 2001)

Bob Miernedorf of the National Park Service in North Cascades National Park emphasized also the variability of such human use of salmon over time:

> Overall, I believe that the last 1,000 years in the Northwest was characterized by several significant shifts in climate (the Little Ice Age) and culture (population decline and cultural stress), and that these were in progress well before contact [with Euro-Americans], after which a whole new set of stressors were laid on the existing ones. Because of these and other factors, whatever the interaction of griz and humans that characterized the contact period historic record, this is not likely to be an accurate characterization of the situation over the last 10,000 or so years of human co-habitation

with bears in the landscape. (personal communication with the author, January 12, 2001)

Becky Saleeby, also of the National Park Service, provided additional information on lower Columbia River bears, based on her archaeology work:

> As I did my dissertation (many years ago) on several sites in the Portland Basin of the Lower Columbia River, I decided to pull it out and dust it off. According to my faunal ID tables, I identified black bear bones *(Ursus americanus)* at four of the six sites studied, but did not find any evidence of brown bear. The strata from which these faunal remains were collected range from A.D. 1690 at the Pumphouse site to 900 B.C. at the Merrybell site. (personal communication with the author, January 5, 2001)

In a review of archaeological finds somewhat farther upstream, in eastern Washington, R. Lee Lyman, "On the Holocene History of *Ursus* in Eastern Washington," *Northwest Science* 60 (1986), pp. 67–72, said that humans in the eastern part of the state made a significant shift about 4,000 to 4,500 years ago, and began to shift "from following a relatively opportunistic nomadic hunting and gathering lifeway prior to 4500 yr B.P. to a semi-sedentary fishing, plant-gathering, and hunting lifeway wherein people depended more heavily on stored fish and plant resources during winter by about 4000 yr B.P." Lyman's article contains several interesting ideas about the reasons that bear distribution and abundance might vary over time, including climate and changing human activities and numbers.

On this matter of the length of human use of Columbia River salmon, we do have evidence of some use for perhaps more than eight thousand years. According to R. E. Taylor, Donna L. Kirner, John R. Southon, and James C. Chatters, "Radiocarbon Dates of Kennewick Man," *Science* 280 (May 22, 1998), pp. 1171–72, the remains of a man whose bones were discovered along the Columbia River were analyzed not only for age but also for chemical constituents that reveal information about diet. Though their scientific conclusions are expressed with even more caution than is customary in such studies, it is clear that the majority of this man's diet was "marine," presumably salmon.

All of this is not to imply that bears and humans have identical needs in fishing sites. Bears fish with their teeth and feet, while humans use a great variety of other tools. Some of the fishing sites favored by humans along the Columbia would have not been of use to bears, who could not have successfully captured very many fish in the open water of the main river. But the bears would have been attracted to such sites by the fish that the humans caught and would have wanted to frequent nearby tributary streams whose smaller channels were more suitable to the fishing techniques bears used.

10. Paul S. Martin and Christine R. Szuter, "War Zones and Game Sinks in Lewis and Clark's West," *Conservation Biology* 13, no. 1 (February 1999), p. 41.

Chapter Twelve: Variagated Bears

1. Herrero, *Bear Attacks,* pp. 210–16. Herrero, in a widely accepted consideration of the divergent evolution of black and grizzly bears, suggested that black bear mothers have good reasons for being less aggressive. They tend to spend much of their time in or near forests and are aware that they can send their cubs up a tree to safety if a threat appears. Grizzly bears evolved to be adapted to more open, treeless environments, so mother grizzly bears do not have the option of trees for security. Under those conditions, evolution favored mothers that were more aggressive in defending their young, which of course would then favor the young of those mothers. Herrero, personal communication with the author, October 3, 2001, stated that "black bear females very, very seldom attack in defense of young—or otherwise."

2. For an early example of interfering with cubs in the den, see Dorr Yeager, "Bringing Up Barney," *Nature Magazine* (January 1933), pp. 27–30, which is the story of a cub that began life in a "den" under one of the buildings at Old Faithful, Yellowstone National Park. Yeager, a park naturalist, reached through the floor of the building into the den area, lifted the cubs out for measurement, and then decided to keep one, which he raised to adulthood in the park. Cubs are routinely handled by biologists in live-trapping operations.

3. Moulton, *Journals,* vol. 7, p. 241.

4. G. V. Hilderbrand, S. D. Farley, C. T. Robbins, R. A. Hanley, K. Titus, and C. Servheen, "Use of Stable Isotopes to Determine Diets of Living and Extinct bears," *Canadian Journal of Zoology* 74 (1996), p. 2085.

5. Burroughs, *The Natural History of the Lewis and Clark Expedition,* p. 56.

6. Herrero, *Bear Attacks,* p. 146.

7. Richard J. Poelker and Harry D. Hartwell, *Black Bear of Washington,* Biological Bulletin 14 (Olympia: Washington State Game Department, 1973), pp. 107–8. See also Herrero, *Bear Attacks,* pp. 145–47. In the 1920s, naturalist Milton Skinner, after ten years of observing the bears of Yellowstone National Park (Montana/Wyoming/Idaho), reported that "I have seen 228 black bears to 241 of lighter shade." Milton Skinner, *Bears in the Yellowstone* (Chicago: A. C. McClurg, 1925), p. 133.

8. Moulton, *Journals,* vol. 7, p. 331.

9. Ibid., vol. 8, p. 21.

Chapter Thirteen: "a sertain fatality"

1. Ambrose, *Undaunted Courage,* pp. 230–34.

Chapter Fifteen: Big-Picture Bears

1. Howard Hickerson, "The Virginia Deer and Intertribal Buffer Zones in the Upper Mississippi Valley," in Anthony Leeds and Andrew Vayda, editors, *Man, Culture, and Animals* (Washington, D.C.: American Association for the Advancement of Science, 1965), pp. 43–66; Richard White, *The Roots of Dependency: Subsistence, Environment, and Social Change among the Choctaws, Pawnees, and Navajos* (Lincoln: University of Nebraska Press, 1983), pp. 8–12; Richard White, "The Winning of the West: The Expansion of the Western Sioux in the Eighteenth and Nineteenth Centuries," *Journal of American History* 65 (September 1978), pp. 319–43; Dan Flores, "Bison Ecology and Bison Diplomacy: The Southern Plains from 1800 to 1850," *Journal of American History* 78 (September 1991), pp. 465–85. I am grateful to historian Thomas Haynes for his guidance with this literature and for his thoughts on Native American hunting practices generally.

2. Martin and Szuter, "War Zones and Game Sinks."

3. William K. Stevens, "Unlikely Tool for Species Preservation," *The New York Times,* March 30, 1999.

4. Flores, *The Natural West,* p. 46.

5. Martin and Szuter, "War Zones and Game Sinks," p. 10.

6. Daniel Botkin, *Discordant Harmonies: A New Ecology for the Twenty-First Century* (New York: Oxford University Press, 1990). Ironically, Botkin himself has been criticized for not adequately considering the effects of Native Americans on the North American scene prior to 1492. See Gary Paul Nabhan, "Cultural Parallax in Viewing North American Habitats," in Michael E. Soule and Gary Lease, editors, *Reinventing Nature? Responses to Postmodern Deconstruction* (Washington, D.C.: Island Press, 1995), p. 92.

7. Soule and Lease, editors, *Reinventing Nature,* is a stimulating collection of essays on the future of our perception of nature and the risks attendant to different directions we might take.

8. Botkin, *Our Natural History,* p. 68.

9. Ibid.

10. Ibid., pp. 68-69.

11. Flores, "Bison Ecology and Bison Diplomacy."

Chapter Sixteen: Legacies

1. Meriwether Lewis and William Clark, *The History of the Lewis and Clark Expedition,* Elliott Coues, editor (New York: Dover Publications, no date), vol. 3, pp. 841–42. It seems odd that Coues, who had traveled more than once for field research in the West, at a time when grizzly bears were still widespread, should not have questioned the captains' description of a bear scrotum.

2. Cutright, Lewis and Clark, *Pioneering Naturalists,* p. 142. Except, of course, that we're not absolutely sure they were using Kentucky rifles.

3. Ibid., p. 141.

4. W. Raymond Wood and Thomas D. Thiessen, *Early Fur Trade on the Northern Plains, Canadian Traders among the Mandan and Hidatsa Indians, 1738–1818, The Narratives of John Macdonell, David Thompson, François-Antoine Larocque, and Charles McKenzie* (Norman: University of Oklahoma Press, 1985), pp. 129–220.

5. Ibid., p. 183.

6. The significance and prevalence of bear-claw necklaces seems clear from the number of Indians whom early artists depicted wearing them. See Rockwell, *Giving Voice to Bear,* for numerous examples. Almost all tribes developed complex ceremonials and protocols by which bears were hunted and killed. See Rockwell, *Giving Voice to Bear,* pp. 25–61, for an overview of the beliefs related to the hunting of bears, which concludes with this:

> For whatever reason Indians hunted bears—whether to obtain food, to acquire power, or to protect one's camp or family—the hunt was steeped in reverent, sometimes fearful ceremony. The people endeavored always to please the animal's spirit, to preserve a harmony between humans and animals, a harmony as fragile as autumn ice. (p. 61)

7. Elijah H. Criswell, "Lewis and Clark: Linguistic Pioneers," *The University of Missouri Studies, a Quarterly of Research* 15, no. 2 (April 1, 1940), p. cxxiv.

8. Ibid., p. cxliv.

9. John Long, "John Long's Journal," 1768–1782, Reuben Gold Thwaites, editor, *Early Western Travels, 1748–1846,* vol. 2 (Cleveland: The Arthur H. Clark Company, 1904), pp. 78, 133. McCracken, *The Beast That Walks Like Man,* pp. 71–74 and 292–93, summarized other equally early and subsequent mentions of "grizzly" and "grizzled" bears in the literature of North American exploration.

10. Allen, *Passage through the Garden,* p. 49. I understand that Allen was indebted to Bernard DeVoto for this term.

11. Shepard and Sanders, *The Sacred Paw,* pp. 128–29, discussed British adoption and adaptations of the Beowulf story ("the first great work of English literature") and Arthur's connections with bears, among many other early bear-related traditions of Europe.

12. Christopher Servheen, *The Status and Conservation of the Bears of the World,* Eighth International Conference on Bear Research and Management, Monograph Series No. 2 (1990), p. 1.

13. Thomas Jefferson, *Notes on the State of Virginia* (New York: Harper Torchbooks, 1964), pp. 36–55.

14. Charles A. Miller, *Jefferson and Nature: An Interpretation* (Baltimore: The Johns Hopkins University Press, 1988), p. 62. There is little doubt that the issue of the alleged superiority of European forms of life (all the way down to germs!) was still under discussion, at least among some North Americans, at the time of the Lewis and Clark Expedition. Clinton, *An Introductory Discourse,* pp. 3–4, reminds his readers of "the accusations which are brought against our country by the literati of Europe" (p. 3).

ACKNOWLEDGMENTS

Writing about Lewis and Clark's experiences with grizzly bears put me at the juncture of two great and highly specialized literatures—that devoted to the Corps of Discovery and that to bears. I must first express a general debt of gratitude to the many previous investigators who have built such magnificent scholarly libraries for today's students in these fields. In my text and my endnotes I attempt to acknowledge my debts to these authorities, but here I will also recommend to you their combined works as worthy of your attention.

My entry into the world of Lewis and Clark research and lore was greatly eased by the hospitable reception I received from many longtime Corps of Discovery enthusiasts. I don't think I've ever dealt with a research topic in which my fellow students were so consistently cordial and eager to take time to help an absolute stranger. The "Lewis and Clark crowd" are indeed a special bunch.

I must especially thank Jeremy Skinner, former librarian at the library of the Lewis and Clark Trail Heritage Foundation, at the Lewis & Clark National Historic Trail Interpretive Center, in Great Falls, Montana, for his assistance during and after a research visit there. If you are interested in Lewis and Clark, you should consider joining the Foundation. For information, contact them at the Lewis and Clark Trail Heritage Foundation, Inc., P.O. Box 3434, Great Falls, MT 59403. Their journal, *We Proceeded On,* is a uniquely valuable informational resource on Lewis and Clark, and a lot of fun to read.

As always, the staffs of the Renne Library at Montana State University, Bozeman, Montana, and the Yellowstone Park Research Library, Yellowstone National Park, Wyoming, were consistently and repeatedly helpful. In Yellowstone, I must also especially thank my longtime research partner, park archivist Lee Whittlesey, with whom I have spent years studying the early documentary record of western wildlife; as my citations suggest, that work was essential preparation for this project.

This project is an outgrowth of at least half a dozen previous books I have done on bears. Since the late 1970s, I have had the immense good fortune to meet, communicate with, and learn from many biologists, managers, writers, and others involved in the world of bears, and I have tried to thank them in each of those previous books. I have had the even more amazing good fortune to live for many years in grizzly bear country, for which I must thank various supervisors with the National Park Service, especially John Varley and Bob Barbee.

As for the present book, those who assisted me by providing information and publications, answering questions, or just having conversations about Lewis and Clark, bears, and other related topics, include the following: Doug Backlund, Nathan Bender, Ted Benzon, Bob Bigart, Ted Birkedal, Daniel Botkin, Anne Braaten, Gary Brown, Greg Burtchard, Holly Calkins, Kenneth Cannon, Mike Carrick, Marc Cattet, Brian Dippie, Dan Flores, Valerius Geist, Tom Haynes, Steve Herrero, Richard Hoffmann, Douglas Houston, Ann Johnson, Mark Johnson, Ken Karsmizki, Carol Lynn Mac-Gregor, Mike Madel, J. I. Merritt, Bob Mierendorf, David Ode, Charles Robbins, David Rockwell, Becky Saleeby, Jeremy Schmidt, Tom Schmidt, Chuck Schwartz, Dan Slosberg, Curtis Strobeck, Lisette Waits, and Lee Whittlesey.

The manuscript benefited enormously from readings by Richard Balkin, Steve Herrero, Marsha Karle, J. I. Merritt, James Ronda, Tom Schmidt, Jeremy Schmidt, and Lee Whittlesey. To these readers, who pointed out to me any number of matters that needed further attention, or revision, or rethinking on my part, I would say this: I am equally grateful for the affirmative elements of your readings. Encouragement of that sort, especially toward the end of the long haul of writing a book, is priceless.

At Falcon Publishing, Inc., Bill Schneider and Megan Hiller's enthusiasm for the project made it possible.

My agent and friend Rick Balkin as often protected me from myself as from the world and offered his customary terrific advice on all aspects of the project.

Marsha Karle, to whom I am married, shared several wonderful trips along the Lewis and Clark route with me, encouraged me constantly, and never once lost patience as she listened to me drone on and on about this or that obscure historical matter. Our life together is the greatest source of wonder I know.

INDEX

Numbers in italics refer to illustrations.

Abruzzo National Park, Italy, 119–20
Acts of Discovery (Furtwangler), 61, 87
Adams, W. H. Davenport, 154
Admiralty Island, 55
Alaska, 39, 55, 57, 120, 139, 154
Allen, John Logan, 9, 127, 194
Ambrose, Stephen, 133
antelope (*see* pronghorn)
Appalachian Mountains, 127
Appenine Mountains, Italy, 119
Arikara villages, 175
Atlantic Coast, 158
Audubon, John James, 100

Bakeless, John, 64
bear, black, 1, 11–21, 38–41, 41–43, 49,
    77, 82, 114, 115, 116, 120, 142, 143,
    146, 147, 149–62, 169–70, 171, 175,
    183, 190, 193, 194. *See also* Yâck-kâh
bear, grizzly
    abundance, 107–12, 116, 121–24,
        179–81, 192–93, 200
    changing Euro-American attitudes
        toward, 63, 71–76, 87–91, 93–94,
        97, 115–25, 176–78, 182–201
    claw necklaces, 1, 23, 24, 25–26, 128,
        147, 175, 188, 207
    daybed, 62
    denning habits, 25
    distinguishing and identifying species,
        34, 35, 38–40, 50–57, 77–78, 82–83,
        114, 146–47, 152–53, 155–60,
        183–84, 189–92
    first Euro-American sightings of, 4
    food habits, 25, 35, 38, 46–49, 78–80,
        92–93, 98, 105, 107, 113, 115,
        120, 153
    genitalia, 41, 43–44, 47–49, 183,
        190

historical distribution in North America,
    25–29, 34, 82, 115, 121–24, 139–46,
    175–82, 192–93, 200
mating habits, 49–50, 105
physical appearance, size, and weight,
    41–49, 53–54, 62, 66–67, 77–78, 82,
    108, 114, 146–47, 152–53, 155–60,
    169, 173, 183–201
speed and agility, 36, 62–64, 86, 91–92,
    102
strength and durability, 42, 45–46, 49,
    52, 62, 64, 66–67, 69, 77, 80, 81
temperament and aggression, 36, 45–46,
    52–53, 66, 72, 77, 85–102, 106–12,
    116–25, 150, 155, 156, 166–168,
    172, 173, 183–186
tracks and other sign, 4, 19, 35, 36, 37,
    82, 108, 115, 129, 162
tree climbing, 16, 108–9, 168
value to corps as food, grease, and hide,
    12–13, 18, 46–47, 63, 67, 77, 116,
    142, 151–52, 154, 162, 169–70, 173
See also Hoh-host; Native Americans;
    Toklat grizzly bear
bear, short-faced, 134
bear, unspecified
    in human culture, 6–8
    meat, 12–13, 15, 128, 129
    myths, 5–6, 32–33
Bear Attacks: Their Causes and Avoidance
    (Herrero), 67
Bear Hunter's Century, The (Schullery), 116
Bear-Hunters of the Rocky Mountains, The
    (Bowman), 16, 118
Bear Pursueing His Assailant, The (Gass),
    88
Beard, J. C., 161
Bears On All Sides (Bowman), *118*
beaver, 13, 25, 37, 81, 106, 129

Beaverhead River, 2
Beowulf, 195
Bewick, Thomas, 28
Biddle, Nicholas, 50–52, 99
Big Hole, 171
Bighorn Mountains, 188
bighorn sheep, 78, 171
Big Muddy Creek, Montana, 41
Billings, Montana, 3, 188
birds of prey (unspecified), 105
Bismarck, North Dakota, 3, 4, 23, 25, 193
bison (referred to by corps as buffalo or
    cattle), 5, 35, 36, 37, 78, 79, 80,
    86 88, 89, 90, 105, 106, 107, 120–24,
    134, 136, 137, 170, 172, 173, 175,
    176, 188, 200
Bitterroot Ecosystem, 138
Bitterroot Mountains, 131, 136, 137, 178
Bitterroot River, 2, 129, 130, 131, 171
Blackfoot River, 2, 165
Black Hills, South Dakota, 25, 34
Botkin, Daniel, 8, 111–12, 178–80,
    192–93
Bowman, Anne, 16, 118
Bozeman, Montana, 2
Bozeman Pass, 171
Brackenridge, H. M., 52, 97, 99, 101
Bridger, Jim, 100
Brooks River, 145
Brown, Gary, 43, 44
Brown Bear Defeated Creek, 66
Buffalo Shoals, Montana, 172
Burroughs, Raymond, 158–59

California Grizzly (Storer and Tevis), 144
Cameron, E. S., 56
Cameron, Mrs. E. S., 56
Camp DuBois, 11
Camp Fortunate, 127, 129, 131, 171
Canada, 139
Captain Clark and His Men Shooting Bears
    (Gass), *37*
Carson, Kit, 100
Cascade Mountain Range, 140, 143–44,
    159

catfish, 47, 48
Catlin, George, 24, 33
Chamberlain, South Dakota, 175
Charbonneau, Toussaint, 67, 80
Cheyenne Indians, 175
Cheyenne River, 25
Chippewa Indians, 176
Civil War, 76, 97, 144
Clark, William
    approach to reporting wildlife abun-
        dance, 111
    correlates intertribal war with wildlife
        abundance, 175
    discovers Giant Spring, 105–6
    explores lower Yellowstone River,
        171–73
    first kills a grizzly bear, 45
    first sees grizzly bear tracks, 4, 25
    journal-writing style, 206
    notes theft of bear meat by his men, 11
    reports bear tracks near Fort Clatsop,
        142
    sees largest grizzly bear, 172
Clarke, Charles, 11
Clark Fork, 137, 165
Clearwater River, 2, 156
Close Quarters with Old Ephraim (Roo-
    sevelt), *199*
Coleridge, Samuel, 89
Collins, John, 11, 149, 150, 152, 155,
    156, 162
Collins Creek (*see* Lolo Creek)
Colter, John, 18, 106, 150, 156, 160, 162
Columbia River, 115, 140–47, 149,
    176, 190
Columbus, Christopher, 87
Constitution of the United States, 200
Continental Divide, 127
Coues, Elliott, 104, 183–84
cougar, 88, 116, 129
Council Bluffs, Iowa, 175
coyote, 116
Craighead, Frank, 79–80
Craighead, John, 79–80
Criswell, Elijah, 189–91

Crow Indians, 188–89
Cruzatte, Pierre, 1, 4–5, 8, 23
Culbertson, Montana, 38, 42
Cumberland Gap, 60
Cutright, Paul, 42, 111, 114, 185, 186,
    204
cutthroat trout, 61

Dakota Indians, 176
Dalles, The, 151
Dalles Dam, The, 142
Dearborn River, 113
Declaration of Independence, 200
deer, 5, 13, 18, 19, 20, 21, 36, 78, 80, 81,
    105, 115, 128, 129, 135, 142, 146,
    149, 150, 162, 166, 171, 176
Denali National Park, 39, 73
Discordant Harmonies (Botkin), 178
diseases, effects of Euro-American on
    Native Americans, 135, 229n. 7
dog, 107, 109
Drouillard, George, 11, 15, 18, 19, 45,
    46, 57, 80, 107, 115, 146, 150, 155,
    166, 169

ecocenter, 80
Edenic terminology, 177
elk, 5, 12, 17, 20, 25, 36, 47, 48, 78, 80,
    81, 90, 106, 108, 114, 115, 128, 129,
    133, 134, 136, 137, 142, 146, 149,
    150, 162, 166, 170, 172
Eskimo, 26
espontoon, 64, 106

Falls and Portage, The (Coues), 104
Fields, Joseph, 80, 107, 156–57, 160, 170
Fields, Reuben, 152, 156–57, 160, 162,
    170
firearms, 37, 45, 64, 66–69, 80, 86–87,
    91, 94–96, 117–19, 125, 166–68,
    181, 185
Firearms, Traps, and Tools of the Mountain
    Men (Russell), 68
Flint, Patricia Robins, 130

Flores, Dan, 115–16, 176, 181
Floyd, Charles, 13, 18, 203, 204
Forest and Stream, 26
Fort Clatsop, Oregon, 142, 146, 149
Fort Colville, Washington, 144
Fort Mandan, North Dakota, 3, 12, 25,
    36, 59, 85, 127, 188
Fort Miles, Montana, 56
Fort Nez Perce, Washington, 144
Fort Nisqually, Washington, 144
Fort Peck Lake, 61, 66
Fort St. Jean, 13
Fort Vancouver, Washington, 159
Forty Years on the Frontier (Stuart), 130
Furtwangler, Albert, 4, 61, 87–91

Gallatin River, 121, 171
Garrison Reservoir, 173
Gass, Patrick, 8, 17, 20, 37, 42, 63, 78,
    81, 88, 107, 110, 149–50, 162, 165,
    167, 186, 203, 208
General History of Quadrupeds, A
    (Bewick), 28
Geographical, Historical and Commercial
    Grammar; and present state of the Several
    Kingdoms of the World (Gutherie), 50
Giant Spring, 105–6
Gibson, George, 65, 157, 161
Glacier National Park, 73
Glendive, Montana, 3, 172
Gowans, Fred, 97–98
Grand River, 18, 175
Great Bear Almanac, The (Brown), 42–43
Great Falls, Montana, 2
Great Falls of the Missouri River, 59, 76,
    81, 85, 90, 93, 103–12, 113, 115, 116,
    120, 121, 123, 124, 143, 147, 165,
    166, 169
Great Plains, 97, 131, 181, 191, 194, 200
Great Smoky Mountains National Park, 43
Grizzly, The (Marcy), 96
Grizzly Bear, The (Wright), 100–101
Grizzly Bears of the Yellowstone Ecosystem,
    The (Craighead et al.), 80

Grizzly Bears overhauling us (Catlin), *110*
Grizzly Country (Russell), 121
Gutherie, William, 50

Harper's New Monthly Magazine, 27
Hartwell, Harry, 159
Head of Grizzly Bear, Shot September 13, 1884 (Roosevelt), *161*
Helena, Montana, 2
Hell Creek State Park, 66
Herrero, Steve, 67, 119, 121
Hickerson, Harold, 176
Hidatsa Indians, 32, 85
History of Four-Footed Beasts, The (Topsell), 7
History of the Expedition under the Command of Captains Lewis and Clark, The (Biddle, ed.), 50, 52
History of the Expedition Under the Command of Lewis and Clark (Coues, ed.), 104
History of the Lewis and Clark Journals, A (Cutright), 204
Hoh-host, Nez Perce name for grizzly bear, 157, 190
Hohots Ilpplip, Chief, 151, 152, 154–55
Hood River, 142
horse, 96, 128, 131, 146, 152, 162, 171, 172, 181
Hudson Bay, 26
Hudson's Bay Company, 144
Hunter and Trapper in North America, The (Davenport), 154
Hunting Trips of a Ranchman (Roosevelt), 117, 161, 199
Huth, Hans, 72

ibex (*see* sheep, bighorn)
Idea of Wilderness, The (Oelschager), 72
Independence, Missouri, 175

Jefferson, Thomas, 31, 75, 127, 196, 200
Jefferson River, 2, 114, 121, 123, 171
Jenkins, 100

Journal of Wildlife Management, The, 136
Journals of Lewis and Clark, The (Bakeless, ed.), 64
Journals of the Lewis and Clark Expedition, The (Moulton), 204
Judith River, 2, 79

Kalm, Peter, 13
Katmai National Park, 73, 145
Kentucky, 27
Knife River, 3
Koch, Elers, 136–37
Kooskooske (*see* Clearwater River)

LaBiche, Francis, 160, 161
Labrador, 26–27, 140
La Croix, Madame, 13
Lake Oahe, 25
Lake Sakakawea, 35
Larocque, François-Antoine, 188–89
Lawrence, 100
Lemhi Pass, 2, 127
Leopold, Aldo, 72
Letters of the Lewis and Clark Expedition with Related Documents, 1783–1854 (Jackson), 204
Lewis, Meriwether
    accidentally shot, 1
    attitudes toward Indian religion, 36
    decides there are three species of bear on their route, 158, 190
    differences from Clark in journal keeping, 45, 46
    explores Marias River, 168–69
    expresses greater caution about grizzly bears, 49, 62
    given bear-related name, 163
    kills the first grizzly, 41–42
    mysterious and symbolic aspects of encounter with wildlife, 87–91
    on Indian bravery in hunting grizzly bears, 187
    proposes name "variagated bear" for grizzly bear, 153

reports bear claws among Pacific Coastal Indians, 147

stands off grizzly bear, 86–87

Lewis and Clark among the Indians (Ronda), 31, 130

Lewis and Clark Expedition (Corps of Discovery)

anticipation of grizzly bears, 1, 23–25, 36–37, 42, 49

assessment of contributions to natural history and image of grizzly bear, 183–201

candid reporting of touchy subjects, 19

controversy over North American animals as inferior to European counterparts, 196–97

editing and publication of journals, 203–9

exploited in modern wildlife-management controversies, 178–79

information-gathering techniques, 25, 31–35

inspiration to historians, 8

journal keeping habits and accuracy, 13–18, 19, 20–21, 45, 46, 76, 197–98

legendary status in American History, 5–7, 9, 183–201

sense of cultural superiority, 31–32

size of party, 12

studies of Native Americans, 31–34, 52, 129, 184–90

Lewis and Clark: Pioneering Naturalists (Cutright), 42, 111

Lewis & Clark National Historic Trail Interpretive Center, Great Falls, Montana, 103

Lewis & Clark Trail Heritage Foundation, 130

Lewiston, Idaho, 2

Life Amongst the Indians (Catlin), 33, 110

Little Missouri River, 3, 53, 60

Little Wolf, a Famous Warrior (Catlin), *24*

Lives of Game Animals (Seton), 139

Livingston, Montana, 2, 171

Lochsa River, 2

Lolo, Montana, 2, 129

Lolo Creek, 2, 129, 156

Lolo Pass, 2

Long, John, 192

Lookout Mountain, 60

Lower Portage Camp, 169

MacGregor, Carol Lynn, 17, 168, 203

Madison River, 121

magpie, 6

Man and the Natural World (Thomas), 72

Mandan Indians, 32, 34

Mandan villages, 53, 188

Marcy, Colonel Randolph B., 96

Marias River, 81, 162, 165, 166, 168, 169

Marsh, Montana, 56

Martin, Paul, 176

mastodons, 134

McCracken, Harold, 69

McNeal, Hugh, 104, 166–68, *168*

Medicine River (*see* Sun River)

medicine tree, 129–31, *132*

Medicine Tree Creek, 130

Men of the Lewis and Clark Expedition, The (Clarke), 11

Merriam, Clinton Hart, 54–57

Middle Fork Selway River, 2

Miles City, Montana, 3, 172

Milk River, 2, 3, 59, 60, 61, 170

"Minataree" Indians, 34, 35

Mississippi River, 26

Missoula, Montana, 2

Missouri, 13, 14

Missouri Breaks, 56, 136

Missouri River, 1, 12, 14, 35, 59, 60, 61, 80, 81, 85, 103, 105, 106, 110, 113, 114, 121, 122, 128, 136, 153, 155, 165, 171, 172, 173, 175–76, 188, 190, 198

M'Keehan, David, 203

Montana Department of Fish, Wildlife and Parks, 106

Moreau River, 25
mosquitoes, 103
Moulton, Gary, 44, 66, 79, 106, 114, 130, 151, 160, 161, 203–9
Mound City, Missouri, 20
Mount Rainier, 143
Mountain Man and Grizzly (Gowans), 97–98
Muir, John, 72
Murie, Adolph, 42
Musselshell River, 2, 169

Nash, Roderick, 72
Native Americans
    bear ceremonialism and cultural significance, 31–34, 52, 129, 147, 184, 186–90
    effects of Euro-American diseases on, 135
    stories of eastern grizzly bears, 27–29
    use of bear meat, 13, 151–52
    See also individual tribes
Natural West, The (Flores), 115–16
Nature and the American (Huth), 72
New Caledonia, Idaho, 159
New Fork, North Dakota, 36
New York Times, The, 176
Nez Perce Indians, 131, 150, 151–52, 154–55, 162, 190
Niobrara River, 176
North Cascades National Park, 140, 144

Oakak Bay, 26
Oelschager, Max, 72
Ohio, 27
Old Cattleman, The, 94–97, 99, 116–17
Omaha Indians, 1
Ontario, 27
Ord, George, 50–57, *51*, 97, 99, 192
Ordway, John, 8, 14, 17, 23, 35, 38, 42, 47, 49, 77, 78, 105, 110, 114, 115, 161, 162, 169, 170, 204, 208, 209
Oregon Trail, The (Parkman), 125

Original Journals of the Lewis and Clark Expedition 1804–1806 (Thwaites, ed.), 20, 203–9
Osage River, 13
Our Natural History (Botkin), 111, 179
Oxford English Dictionary, 192

Pacific Coast, 97, 158, 159
Pacific Ocean, 76, 147
Pacific Slope, 127, 139–47
panther (*see* cougar)
Park City, Montana, 172
Parkman, Francis, 124
Passage Through the Garden (Allen), 127
Pat's Encounter With The Bear (Bowman), *16*
pheasant, 152
Piegan Indians, 169
Platte River, 34
Pleistocene extinctions, 133–34
Poelker, Richard, 159
Poplar, Montana, 45
Poplar River, 60
Portland, Oregon, 149
Potts, John, 156
predators (unspecified), 137–38
pronghorn, 12, 36, 78, 81, 115
Pryor, Nathaniel, 155, 171

Quaife, Milo Milton, 204, 209
Quicksand River (*see* Sandy River)

Ranges of the Grizzly-Bears and of the Barren-Ground Bear (Seton), *141*
rattlesnakes, 6, 64, 103
Recreation, 94
Reid, Captain Mayne, 100
Review of the Grizzly and Big Brown Bears of North America (Genus Ursus) with a Description of a New Genus, Vetularcos (Merriam), 54, 56
Rime of the Ancient Mariner (Coleridge), 89
Rocky Mountains, 97, 98, 118, 127, 131, 133, 134, 138, 142, 144, 147, 150, 151, 159, 160, 190

Ronda, James, 31, 130, 132
Roosevelt, Theodore, 55, 72, 100, 117, 161, 199
Russell, Andy, 121–22
Russell, Carl P., 68, 69
Russell, Osborne, 98

Sacagawea, 121
Salish Indians, 129
salmon, 80, 120–21, 140–42, 145, 153, 154
Salmon River, 129
Sand Coulee Creek, 106
Sanders, Barry, 7, 32
Sandy River, 149
Sacred Paw, The (Shepard and Sanders), 7–8, 32
Selkirk, Alexander, 95
Seton, Ernest Thompson, 139–41, 143
Shannon, George, 20, 150, 156, 160
sheep, bighorn, 129, 136, 171
Shepard, Paul, 7, 32
Shields, John, 68, 157, 172
Short Narrows, Columbia River, 142
Shoshone Indians, 115, 127–29, 207
Sidney, Montana, 172
Silver Star, Montana, 121
Sioux Indians, 23, 35
Skull of Ursus Horribilis Horribilis (Merriam), 56, 56
Slosberg, Daniel, 4
Snow Creek, 66
St. Joseph, Missouri, 20
St. Louis, 35
Stevens, Wallace, 89
Storer, Tracy, 144
Stuart, Granville, 130
Sullivan, Paul, 144
Sun River, 2, 85, 88, 91, 104, 165
swift fox, 61
Szuter, Christine, 176

Tevis, Lloyd, 144
Thirty Years of Army Life on the Border (Marcy), 96
Three Forks, Montana, 2, 113, 114, 165, 171, 176
Thomas, Keith, 72
Thompson, John, 165
Thompson's River, British Columbia, 144
Thoreau, Henry David, 72
Thwaites, Reuben Gold, 20, 203–9
Tobacco Creek, 173
Toklat grizzly bear, 39
Topsell, Edward, 7
Tosten Dam, 114
Townsend, John, 98
Traveler's Rest, Montana, 129, 130, 149, 162, 171
Twain, Mark, 89

United States Biological Survey, 141
Upper Portage Camp, 104, 106, 109
Ursus americanus (see bear, black)
Ursus arctos (see bear, grizzly)
Ursus arctos middendorffi, 57

Views of Louisiana (Brackenridge), 52
Vinson, Edrie, 130

Walcheck, Ken, 12, 17
Walden Pond, 60
Walla Walla, Washington, 144
"war zone" effects on wildlife abundance, 175–82
Weippe, Idaho, 2, 160
West Bank Park, Great Falls, Montana, 85
White, Richard, 176
White Bear Islands, 104, 106, 165
White River, 176
Whitehouse, Joseph, 14, 18, 19, 20–21, 45, 48, 62, 67, 77, 79, 81, 109, 112, 113–4, 130, 131, 142, 156, 203, 206, 208

Wilderness Act, 179
Wilderness and the American Mind
    (Nash), 72
wildlife
    Clark's attitude in reporting abundance,
    111
    controversy over historical abundance
    in the West, 131–38
Willamette River, 149
Willard, Alexander, 106–7, 157, 160, 169,
    170
Williston, North Dakota, 3, 38
Willow Run, *104*
Windsor, Richard, 149
Winnie-the-Pooh, 100, 101
Wishram-Wasco Indians, 142
wolf, 36, 79, 81, 105, 119, 120, 129
wolf, dire, 134

Wolf Creek, 60
Wolf Point, Montana, 3
wolverine, 88
Wordsworth, William, 89
Wright, William, 100, 185, 186
Writing-On-Stone Provincial Park, Alberta,
    Canada, 59

Yâck-kâh, Nez Perce name for black bear-
    like animal, 157–58, 162, 170, 190
Yankton, South Dakota, 23, 26
Yellowstone National Park, 65, 73, 79–80,
    92, 136, 137
Yellowstone River, 3, 37, 53, 60, 170, 171,
    172, 176, 188
Yogi Bear, 100, 101
Yo-me-kol-lick, Nez Perce name given to
    Lewis, 163

P AUL SCHULLERY is the author, coauthor, or editor of more than thirty books on conservation, natural history, and outdoor sport, and has contributed chapters to twenty others. In recognition of his work as a historian and science writer, he has received an honorary doctorate of letters from Montana State University and the Wallace Stegner Award from the University of Colorado Center of the American West.